Bolshevik and Stalinist Russia 1918–56 THIRD EDITION

access to history

Bolshevik and Stalinist Russia 1918–56 THIRD EDITION

Michael Lynch

Hodder Murray

A MEMBER OF THE HODDER HEADLINE GROUP

The publishers would like to thank the following individuals, institutions and companies for permission to reproduce copyright illustrations in this book: © Bettman/Corbis, page 71; David King Collection, pages 98, 102 (bottom); Getty Images, page 21; © Hulton-Deutsch Collection/Corbis, pages 48, 55; Russian State Archives of Film and Photo Documents (Krasnogorsk), page 37; Solo Syndication, page 118.

The Publishers would also like to thank the following for permission to reproduce copyright material: The publishers would also like to thank the following for permission to reproduce material in this book: AQA material is reproduced by permission of the Assessment and Qualification Alliance, used on page 90, 109; Edexcel Limited for extracts used on pages 66, 88, 178, 180; Harper Collins for an extract from *The Rise and Fall of the Soviet Empire* by D. Volkogonov (1998), used on page 43–4; Houghton Mifflin for an extract from *Triumph and Tragedy* by W. Churchill (1954), used on page 150–1; Little Brown & Company for an extract from *Cold War* by J. Isaacs and T. Downing (1996), used on page 152; Longman for an extract from *The Origins of the Cold War* by M. McCauley (1995), used on page 151; Oxford, Cambridge and RSA (OCR) examinations for extracts used on pages 43, 65, 89, 129, 150; Oxford University Press for an extract from *Bukharin and the Bolshevik Revolution* by S. Cohen (1971), used on pages 43, 67; Pathfinder Press (New York) for an extract from *On the Suppressed Testament of Lenin* by L. Trotsky (1932), used on page 66–7; Pimlico for an extract from *A People's Tragedy: Russian Revolution, 1891–1924* by O. Figes, used on page 43; Thames & Hudson for an extract from *The Soviet Achievement* by J. Nettl (1967), used on page 42.

Every effort has been made to trace and acknowledge ownership of copyright. The publishers will be glad to make suitable arrangements with any copyright holders whom it has not been possible to contact.

Although every effort has been made to ensure that website addresses are correct at time of going to press, Hodder Murray cannot be held responsible for the content of any website mentioned in this book. It is sometimes possible to find a relocated web page by typing in the address of the home page for a website in the URL window of your browser.

Orders: please contact Bookpoint Ltd, 130 Milton Park, Abingdon, Oxon OX14 4SB. Telephone: (44) 01235 827720. Fax: (44) 01235 400454. Lines are open 9.00–5.00, Monday to Saturday, with a 24-hour message answering service. Visit our website at www.hoddereducation.co.uk

© Michael Lynch 2005
First published in 2005 by
Hodder Murray, an imprint of Hodder Education,
a member of the Hodder Headline Group
338 Euston Road
London NW1 3BH

Impression number	10 9 8 7 6 5 4 3
Year	2010 2009 2008 2007 2006

Cover photo Propaganda portrait of Stalin 1938 © TopFoto.co.uk
Typeset in Baskerville 10/12pt and produced by Gray Publishing, Tunbridge Wells.
Printed in Malta

A catalogue record for this title is available from the British Library

ISBN-10: 0340 88590 4
ISBN-13: 978 0340 885 901

Contents

Dedication

Keith Randell (1943–2002)

The *Access to History* series was conceived and developed by Keith, who created a series to 'cater for students as they are, not as we might wish them to be'. He leaves a living legacy of a series that for over 20 years has provided a trusted, stimulating and well-loved accompaniment to post-16 study. Our aim with these new editions is to continue to offer students the best possible support for their studies.

1

Revolutionary Russia 1918–24

POINTS TO CONSIDER

In October 1917 the Bolshevik Party, led by Lenin, took power in Russia. It faced an enormous task. The Bolsheviks were a minority party trying to impose their will on Russia and facing fierce opposition within the nation and from outside. The great test was whether the Bolsheviks could retain their power and build upon it. Their efforts to do so are studied in this chapter under the following themes:

- The Bolshevik consolidation of power under Lenin
- The Civil War
- The foreign interventions
- The Red Terror
- War Communism
- The Kronstadt rising
- The New Economic Policy (NEP)
- Soviet society under Lenin
- Lenin's legacy

Key dates

1917	November	Bolsheviks issued the Decrees on Land, on Peace, and on Workers' Control
		Elections for Constituent Assembly
	December	Armistice signed at Brest-Litovsk
		Cheka created
1918–20		Russian Civil War and foreign interventions
		War Communism
1918	January	Bolsheviks forcibly dissolved the Constituent Assembly
		Red Army established
	March	Treaty of Brest-Litovsk
	June	Decree on Nationalisation
	July	Formation of Russian Socialist Federal Soviet Republic
		Forced grain requisitions begun
		Murder of tsar and his family
	September	Red Terror officially introduced

1919	March	Comintern established
		Bolshevik Party renamed the
		Communist Party
1920	April	Invading Red Army driven from
		Poland
1921	March	Kronstadt Rising
		Introduction of the New Economic
		Policy (NEP)
		Decree against factionalism
1922–3		Lenin suffered a number of
		increasingly severe strokes
1922	December	Soviet state became the USSR
		Lenin completed his 'testament',
		critical of all the leading Bolsheviks
1924	21 January	Lenin's death

1 | The Bolshevik Consolidation of Power Under Lenin

The Bolsheviks were a **Marxist** revolutionary party, founded in 1903 and led by Vladimir Ulyanov (Lenin). In the October Revolution of 1917, they had cleverly exploited the troubled situation in Russia that followed the fall of tsardom in February to outmanoeuvre their opponents and seize power. But once in government, the Bolsheviks faced huge difficulties in trying to consolidate their hold over the Russian nation. These can be identified as four basic questions:

- Could the Bolsheviks survive at all?
- If so, could they extend their control over the whole of Russia?
- Could they negotiate a swift end to Russia's war with Germany?
- Could they bring economic stability to Russia?

The traditional Soviet view was that after the Bolsheviks had taken power they transformed old Russia into a socialist society by following a set of measured, pre-planned reforms. Few historians now accept that was what happened. Lenin's policy is now seen as having been a pragmatic adjustment to the harsh realities of the situation.

In their government of Russia, the Bolsheviks had few plans to help them. Before 1917 they had spent their time in preparing for revolution and had, therefore, given little thought to the details of how affairs would be organised once this had been achieved. It had always been a Marxist belief that after the triumph of the **proletariat** the State would 'wither away'. Leon Trotsky, who had played a central role in the Bolshevik seizure of power, had expressed this simple faith at the time of his appointment in October 1917 as **Commissar for Foreign Affairs** when he said 'all we need to do is issue a few decrees, then shut up shop and go home'. But circumstances were not to allow such a relaxed approach to government.

Key question
How did the Bolsheviks plan to tackle the problems confronting them in governing Russia?

Marxist
Relates to the ideas of Karl Marx (1818–83), a German revolutionary, who believed that the whole of history was a story of class struggle between those who possessed economic and political power and those who did not.

Proletariat
The exploited industrial working class.

Commissar for Foreign Affairs
Equivalent to the Foreign Secretary in Britain.

Key terms

Key question
How was power distributed in revolutionary Russia?

The structure of power under the Bolsheviks

Lenin claimed that the October Revolution had been a taking of power by the **soviets**. In fact, it had been a seizure of power by the Bolshevik Party. Nevertheless, Lenin persisted with the notion that *Sovnarkom* had been appointed to govern by the Congress of Soviets. According to this view, the distribution of power in revolutionary Russia took the form of a pyramid, with *Sovnarkom* at the top, drawing its authority from the Russian people who expressed their will through the soviets at the base (see Figure 1.1).

The reality was altogether different. With the fall of tsardom in 1917, traditional forms of government had broken down. This left the Bolsheviks in a position to make up their own rules. The notion that it was the soviets who had taken over was a fiction. From the beginning, it was in fact the Bolsheviks who held power. The key body here was the Central Committee of the Bolshevik Party. It was this organisation, under Lenin's direction, that provided the members of the government. In a sense, *Sovnarkom* was a wing of the Bolshevik Party.

In theory, the Central Committee derived its authority from the All-Russian Congress of the Bolshevik Party whose locally elected representatives voted on policy. In practice, the Congress and the local parties did as they were told. This was in keeping with Lenin's insistence that the Bolshevik Party operate according to the principle of **democratic centralism**, a formula that guaranteed that power was exercised from the top down, rather than the bottom up.

Key terms

Soviets
The soviets began as organisations to represent the workers and soldiers. However, by October 1917 they had been infiltrated by the Bolsheviks, who then made them a cover for their actions.

Sovnarkom
The government that Lenin set up after coming to power. It was composed of commissars (ministers) under his direction.

Democratic centralism
The notion that true democracy in the Bolshevik party lay in the obedience of the members to the instructions of the leaders.

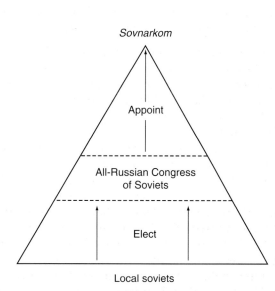

Figure 1.1: The pyramid of the distribution of power in revolutionary Russia

The Bolsheviks' early measures

In Bolshevik theory, the October Revolution had marked the victory of the proletariat over the **bourgeoisie**, of socialism over capitalism. But theory was of little immediate assistance in the circumstances of late 1917. A hard slog lay ahead if the Bolsheviks were truly going to transform the Russian economy.

Before the October Revolution, Lenin had written powerfully against oppressive landlords and capitalists, but he had produced little by way of a coherent plan for their replacement. It is understandable, therefore, that his policy after taking power in 1917 was based on the facts of the situation rather than theory. He argued that the change from a bourgeois to a proletarian state could not be achieved overnight. The Bolshevik government would continue to use the existing structures until the transition had been completed and a fully socialist system could be adopted. This transitional stage was referred to as **state capitalism**.

Lenin was aware that there were many Bolsheviks who wanted the immediate introduction of a sweeping revolutionary policy, but he pointed out that the new regime simply did not possess the power to impose this. Its authority did not run much beyond Petrograd and Moscow. Until the Bolsheviks could exercise a much wider political and military control, their policies would have to fit the prevailing circumstances. The war against Germany and Austria had brought Russia to the point of economic collapse:

- The shortage of raw materials and investment capital had reduced industrial production to two-thirds of its 1914 level.
- Inflation had rocketed.
- The transport system had been crippled.
- Hunger gripped large areas of Russia – grain supplies were over 13 million tons short of the nation's needs.
- Within a few months of the October Revolution, the food crisis had been further deepened by the ceding to Germany of the Ukraine, Russia's richest grain-producing region.

All Lenin's economic policies after he took power can be seen as attempts to deal with these problems, the most pressing being whether Russia could produce enough to feed itself. Lenin was a realist on this question. Although he considered that the future lay with the industrial workers, he was very conscious that the peasantry, who made up the mass of the population, were the food producers. The primary consideration, therefore, was how best the peasants could be persuaded or forced to provide adequate food supplies for the nation.

The Decree on Land and the Decree on Workers' Control

Immediately after coming to power, the new government introduced two measures, which are usually regarded as having initiated Bolshevik economic policy. These were the 'Decree on Land' and the 'Decree on Workers' Control', both issued in November 1917. However, these were not so much new departures as formal recognitions of what had already taken place.

Key question
What problems confronted the Bolsheviks after they had taken power in 1917?

Key terms

Bourgeoisie
The owners of capital, the boss class, who exploited the workers.

State capitalism
The pre-revolutionary economic system, which the Bolsheviks left in place during their first year of rule, 1917–18.

> ## Principal changes introduced by the Bolsheviks, October 1917–July 1918
> - Decrees on Peace, Land and Workers' Control
> - The old class system declared to be abolished
> - Moscow brought under Red (Bolshevik) control
> - All titles abolished – 'comrade' became the standard greeting
> - Old legal system replaced with 'people's courts'
> - Creation of the *Cheka* (see page 18)
> - Armistice, followed by a peace treaty, with Germany
> - *Vesenkha* set up to plan the economy
> - Red Army founded
> - Russia formally became the Russian Socialist Federal Soviet Republic (RSFSR)
> - Bolshevik Party retitled the Communist Party
> - Russian calendar modernised in line with system used in the advanced world (though old dating kept when referring to the 1917 Revolution)
> - Marriage Code gave married women equal rights with husbands
> - Schools brought under State control

The key article of the Decree on Land stated:

> Private ownership of land shall be abolished forever. All land, whether state, crown, monastery, church, factory, private, public, peasant, etc., shall be confiscated without compensation and pass into the use of all those who cultivate it.

February Revolution
The collapse of the tsarist system in February 1917.

Vesenkha
The Supreme Council of the National Economy.

In fact, the decree simply gave Bolshevik approval to what had happened in the countryside since the **February Revolution**: in many areas the peasants had overthrown their landlords and occupied their property.

The Decree on Workers' Control was also largely concerned with authorising what had already occurred. During 1917 a large number of factories had been taken over by the workers. However, the workers' committees that were then formed seldom ran the factories efficiently. The result was a serious fall in industrial output. The decree accepted the workers' takeover, but at the same time it instructed the workers' committees to maintain 'the strictest order and discipline' in the workplace.

Passing decrees was one thing, enforcing them another. A particular problem for the government was that not all the workers' committees were dominated by Bolsheviks. Until the party gained greater control at shopfloor level, it would be difficult for the central government to impose itself on the factories. Nevertheless, the government pressed on with its plans for establishing the framework of State direction of the economy, even if effective central control was some way off. In December, **Vesenkha** was set up 'to take charge of all existing institutions for the regulation of economic life'.

Initially, *Vesenkha* was unable to exercise the full authority granted to it. However, it did preside over a number of important developments:

- The banks and the railways were nationalised.
- Foreign debts were cancelled.
- The transport system was made less chaotic.

These were important practical achievements, which suggested how effective centralised control might become should the Bolshevik regime be able to gain real power.

The dissolution of the Constituent Assembly

As a revolutionary, Lenin had never worried much about how many people supported the Bolsheviks. Mere numbers did not concern him. He had no faith in democratic elections, which he dismissed as tricks by which the bourgeoisie kept itself in power. His primary objective was not to win mass support, but to create a party capable of seizing power when the opportune moment came.

After the successful October *coup* in 1917, Lenin was determined not to allow elections to undermine the Bolsheviks' newly won power. However, there was an immediate problem. The October Revolution had come too late to prevent the elections to the **All-Russian Constituent Assembly** being held in November. When the results came through by the end of the year they did not make pleasant reading for the Bolsheviks (see Table 1.1):

- They had been outvoted by nearly two to one by their major rival the **Social Revolutionaries** (SRs).
- They had won only 24 per cent of the total vote.
- They had gained barely a quarter of the seats in the Assembly.

Table 1.1: Results of the election for the Constituent Assembly, November 1917

	Votes	Seats
Social Revolutionaries (SRs)	17,490,000	370
Bolsheviks	9,844,000	175
National minority groups	8,257,000	99
Left SRs (pro-Bolshevik)	2,861,000	40
Kadets	1,986,000	17
Mensheviks	1,248,000	16
Total	41,686,000	717

Lenin had originally supported the idea of a Constituent Assembly, not out of idealism but because it offered a way of further weakening the Provisional Government that had replaced the tsar after February 1917. Now, however, with his party in power, Lenin had no need of an Assembly. Furthermore, since it was overwhelmingly non-Bolshevik it would almost certainly make life difficult for his government. One possibility was that he could have tried to work with the new Assembly. But that was not how Lenin operated. He was not a democrat; he did not deal in

Key question
Why did Lenin dissolve the Assembly?

Key terms

All-Russian Constituent Assembly
A parliament representing the whole of Russia.

Social Revolutionaries
The largest of the revolutionary parties in Russia, particularly popular among the peasants.

Kadets (The Constitutional Democrats)
The major liberal reforming party in Russia.

Mensheviks
A Marxist party that had broken with the Bolsheviks in 1903.

compromise. He was a revolutionary who believed that the only way to govern was by totally crushing all opposition.

Hence his response to the Constituent Assembly, when it gathered in January 1918, was simple and ruthless. After only one day's session, it was dissolved at gun-point by the **Red Guards**. A few members tried to protest, but, with rifles trained on their heads, their resistance soon evaporated.

Reasons for dissolution

Lenin's act of violence in January 1918 has to be viewed in context. The Bolsheviks' hold on power was precarious. Indeed, the prospects of Bolshevik survival seemed slim. There was strong and widespread opposition inside the country. Moreover, Russia was still at war with Germany, and the Allies, France and Britain, were all set to interfere should the new Russian government make a separate peace. In such an atmosphere, the Bolsheviks were not prepared to consider power sharing.

Lenin justified the Bolshevik action by arguing that the original reason for electing an Assembly, the establishing of an all-Russian representative body, had already been achieved by the creation of a soviet government in the October Revolution of 1917. The Constituent Assembly was, therefore, superfluous. More than that, Lenin claimed, it was corrupt. The elections had been rigged by the SRs and the Kadets; consequently, the results did not truly reflect the wishes of the Russian people. In such circumstances, he argued:

> To hand over power to the Constituent Assembly would again be to compromise with the malignant bourgeoisie. Nothing in the world will induce us to surrender the soviet power. The Soviet Revolutionary Republic will triumph no matter what the cost.

Commenting on Lenin's attitude at this stage, Trotsky approvingly and revealingly recorded a remark Lenin had made to him in private: 'The dissolution of the Constituent Assembly by the Soviet Government means a complete and frank liquidation of the idea of democracy by the idea of dictatorship.'

Lenin's ruthlessness caused unease among some of his own supporters. Maxim Gorky, one of the Bolshevik Party's leading intellectuals, wrote at the time:

> The best Russians have lived for almost 100 years with the idea of a Constituent Assembly as a political organ which could provide Russian democracy as a whole with the possibility of freely exercising its will. On the altar of this sacred idea rivers of blood have been spilled – and now the 'people's commissars' have ordered the shooting of this democracy.

Such criticism left Lenin unmoved. As he saw it, the desperately vulnerable position the Bolsheviks were in, surrounded by enemies on all sides, demanded the sternest of measures.

Summary diagram: The Bolshevik consolidation of power

Problems confronting them

- Bolsheviks controlled only Petrograd and Moscow
- Low industrial production
- High inflation
- Severe food shortages
- Occupation by Germany

Measures to tackle problems

Economic	Political
Adoption of state capitalism – a compromise measure to achieve the transition to a socialist economy	Bolshevik Party retained control in name of the soviets
Decree on Land – abolished private property – recognised peasant takeovers	Forcible dissolution of the Constituent Assembly
Decree on Workers' Control – an attempt to assert government authority over the factories which had been seized by workers	
Vesenkha – body to oversee economic development	

2 | The Russian Civil War 1918–20

Key question
How far was Lenin personally responsible for the Civil War?

The crushing of the Constituent Assembly by the Bolsheviks was immediately followed by their banning of all other parties. Clearly, they were not willing to share power. This bid for absolute authority made civil war highly likely. The Bolsheviks were bound to face military opposition from their wide range of opponents, who were not prepared to accept subjection to the absolute rule of a minority party.

Modern research strongly suggests that Lenin truly wanted a destructive civil war. Although it involved obvious dangers to the Bolsheviks, Lenin was convinced that his forces could win and that in winning they would wipe out all their opponents, military and political. Better to have a short, brutal struggle than face many years of being harassed and challenged by the anti-Bolsheviks who were a large majority in Russia, as the Constituent Assembly election results had shown all too clearly (see page 6).

Lenin knew that had he chosen to co-operate in a coalition of all the revolutionary parties in 1918, the Bolsheviks would have been unable to dominate government since they were very much a minority compared with the Mensheviks and Social Revolutionaries. It was something he refused to contemplate. As Dominic Lieven, an outstanding modern scholar, observes:

Some Bolsheviks would have accepted a socialist coalition but Lenin was not one of them. The Bolshevik leader rejected this course and pursued policies, which, as he well knew, made civil war inevitable.

A class war?

Key question
Who were the opposing sides in the war?

The conflict that began in the summer of 1918 was principally a military struggle between the Bolsheviks (the Reds) and their political enemies (the Whites). These included all those parties who had been outlawed or suppressed by the new regime, and monarchists looking for a tsarist restoration.

The Bolsheviks presented the struggle as a class war, but it was never simply this. The sheer size of Russia often meant that local or regional considerations predominated over larger issues. As in all civil wars, the disruption provided a cover for settling old scores and pursuing personal vendettas, and it was not uncommon for villages or families to be divided against each other.

It was ironic that, although most of the leading Bolsheviks were non-Russian, their rule was seen by many as yet another attempt to re-assert Russian authority over the rest of the country – the very situation that had prevailed under the tsars. Significantly, a number of Russia's national minorities, such as the Ukrainians and the Georgians, fought in the war primarily to establish their independence from Russia. These national forces became known as the Greens. The best known of the Green leaders was Makhno, a one-time Bolshevik, who organised a guerrilla resistance to the Reds in the Ukraine.

A war over food?

On occasion, the fighting was simply a desperate struggle for food. Famine provided the backdrop to the Civil War. The breakdown in food supplies that had occurred during the war against Germany resulted in whole areas of Russia remaining hungry. The failure of the new regime to remedy this was an important factor in creating the initial military opposition to the Bolsheviks in 1918.

In addition to the problems of a fractured transport system, Lenin's government was faced with the loss to Germany of Russia's main wheat-supply area, the Ukraine. In March 1918, the month in which the **Brest-Litovsk Treaty** was signed, the bread ration in Petrograd reached its lowest ever allocation of 50 grams per day. Hunger forced many workers out of the major industrial cities. By June 1918 the workforce in Petrograd had shrunk by 60 per cent and the overall population had declined from three to two million. A visitor to the city at this time spoke of 'entering a metropolis of cold, of hunger, of hatred, of endurance'. The Bolshevik boast that October 1917 had established worker-control of Russian industry meant little now that the workers were deserting the factories in droves.

Key term

Brest-Litovsk Treaty
Ended the war with Germany. Russia had to give up a third of its European territory, including the Ukraine, and pay three million roubles to Germany for the cost of the war.

The role of the SRs

These dire circumstances encouraged open challenges to the Bolsheviks from both left and right. The SRs, who had been driven from the government for their refusal to accept the Brest-Litovsk settlement, organised an anti-Bolshevik *coup* in **Moscow**. The Civil War could be said, therefore, to have begun not as a counter-revolution but as an effort by one set of revolutionaries to take power from another. In that sense it was an attempted revenge by a majority party, the SRs, against a minority party, the Bolsheviks, for having usurped the authority that they claimed was properly theirs.

The SRs' military rising in Moscow failed, but their terrorism came closer to success. Lenin narrowly survived two attempts on his life, in July and August. The second attempt, by Dora Kaplan, an SR fanatic, left him with a bullet lodged in his neck, an injury that contributed to his death four years later. In their desperation at being denied any say in government, the SRs joined the Whites in their struggle against Lenin's Reds.

Key question
Why did the SRs join the Whites?

Moscow
In 1918, for security reasons, Moscow replaced Petrograd as the capital of Soviet Russia.

Key term

The Czech Legion

Armed resistance to the Bolsheviks had occurred sporadically in various parts of Russia since October 1917. What gave focus to this struggle was the behaviour in the summer of 1918 of one of the foreign armies still in Russia. The 40,000 Czechoslovak troops, who had volunteered to fight on the Russian side in the First World War as a means of gaining independence from Austria-Hungary, found themselves isolated after the Treaty of Brest-Litovsk. They formed themselves into the Czech Legion and decided to make the long journey eastwards to Vladivostok.

Their aim was eventually to rejoin the Allies on the western front in the hope of winning international support for the formation of an independent Czechoslovak state. The presence of this well-equipped foreign army making its way arrogantly across Russia was resented by the Bolsheviks. Local Soviets began to challenge the Czech Legion and fierce fighting accompanied its progress along the trans-Siberian railway.

All this encouraged the Whites, and all the revolutionary and liberal groups who had been outlawed by the Bolsheviks, to come out openly against Lenin's regime.

Key question
What was the importance of the Czech Legion?

- The SRs organised a number of uprisings in central Russia and established an anti-Bolshevik Volga 'Republic' at Samara.
- A White 'Volunteer Army', led by General Denikin, had already been formed in the Caucasus region of southern Russia from tsarist loyalists and outlawed Kadets.
- In Siberia, the presence of the Czech Legion encouraged the formation of a White army under Admiral Kolchak, the self-proclaimed 'Supreme Ruler of Russia'.
- In Estonia, another ex-tsarist general, Yudenich, began to form a White army of resistance.
- White units appeared in many regions elsewhere. The speed with which they arose indicated just how limited Bolshevik control was outside the cities of western Russia.

Key question
Was the Bolshevik
victory a result of Red
strength or White
weakness?

Red victory

The patchwork of political, regional and national loyalties inside
Russia made the Civil War a confused affair. It is best understood
as a story of the Bolsheviks' resisting attacks on four main fronts,
and then taking the initiative and driving back their attackers
until they eventually withdrew or surrendered. Unlike the First
World War, the Civil War was a war of movement, largely dictated
by the layout of Russia's railway system. It was because the
Bolsheviks were largely successful in their desperate fight to
maintain control of the railways that they were able to keep
themselves supplied, while denying this to the Whites.

The reasons for the final victory of the Reds in the Civil War
are not difficult to determine:

- The various White armies fought as separate detachments.
  They were never more than an uncoordinated group of forces,
  whose morale was seldom high.
- They were unwilling to sacrifice their individual interests in
  order to form a united anti-Bolshevik front. This allowed the
  Reds to pick off the White armies separately.
- In the rare cases in which the Whites did consider combining,
  they were too widely scattered geographically to be able to
  mount a sustained attack on the Reds.
- The Whites were a collection of dispossessed socialists, liberals
  and moderates, whose political differences often led them into
  bitter disputes among themselves.
- Save for their hatred of Bolshevism, the Whites lacked a
  common purpose.
- They became too reliant on supplies from abroad, which
  seldom arrived in sufficient quantity, in the right places, at the
  right time.
- Although the Reds imposed a reign of terror, the Whites' own
  record in ill-treating local populations was equally notorious.
- The Whites lacked leaders of the quality of Trotsky.

The Reds, in contrast, had a number of overwhelming advantages:

- They remained in control of a concentrated central area of
  western Russia, which they were able to defend by maintaining
  their inner communication and supply lines (see Figure 1.2).
- The two major cities, Petrograd and Moscow, the administrative
  centres of Russia, remained in their hands throughout the war.
- The Reds kept control of the railway network.
- The Reds' strongest hold was over the industrial centres of
  Russia. This was a key advantage since it gave them access to
  munitions and resources unavailable to the Whites.
- The dependence of the Whites on supplies from abroad
  appeared to prove the Red accusation that they were in league
  with the foreign interventionists (see page 17). The Civil War
  had produced a paradoxical situation in which the Reds were
  able to stand as champions of the Russian nation as well as
  proletarian revolutionaries.

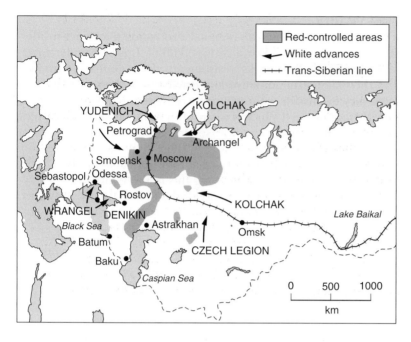

Figure 1.2: The Russian Civil War, 1918–20

- Waging war is not just a matter of resources and firepower. Morale and dedication play vital roles. Throughout the struggle the Reds were sustained by a driving sense of purpose.
- The Red Army was brilliantly organised and led by Trotsky as the Bolshevik war commissar. He created an army with an unshakable belief in its own eventual victory (see page 20).

Impact of the war on the Bolsheviks

On the domestic front, the Civil War proved to be one of the great formative influences on the Bolshevik Party (renamed the Communist Party in 1919). Their attempts at government took place during a period of conflict in which their very survival was at stake. The development of the party and the government has to be set against this background.

Key question
What marks did the Civil War leave on the character of the Bolshevik Party?

Toughness

The revolution had been born in war, and the government had been formed in war. Of all the members of the Communist Party in 1927, a third had joined in the years 1917–20 and had fought in the Red Army. This created a tradition of military obedience and loyalty. The Bolsheviks of this generation were hard men, forged in the fires of war.

Authoritarianism

A number of modern analysts have emphasised the central place that the Civil War had in shaping the character of Communist rule in Soviet Russia. Robert Tucker stresses that it was the military aspect of early Bolshevik government that left it with a 'readiness to resort to coercion, rule by administrative fiat [command], centralised administration [and] summary justice'. No regime

Key terms

Politburo
Short for the Political Bureau, responsible for major policy decisions.

Orgburo
Short for Organisation Bureau, which turned the policies into practice.

Secretariat
A form of civil service that carried out the administration of policies.

placed in the Bolshevik predicament between 1917 and 1921 could have survived without resort to authoritarian measures.

Centralisation

The move towards centralism in government increased as the Civil War dragged on. The emergencies of war required immediate day-to-day decisions to be made. This led to effective power moving away from the Central Committee of the Communist (Bolshevik) Party, which was too cumbersome, into the hands of the two key sub-committees, the **Politburo** and the **Orgburo**, set up in 1919, which could act with the necessary speed. In practice, the authority of *Sovnarkom*, the official government of Soviet Russia, became indistinguishable from the rule of these party committees, which was served by the **Secretariat**.

The centralising of authority was also evident in the official renaming in 1922 of the Soviet state as the Union of Soviet Socialist Republics (USSR), which replaced the looser Russian Socialist Federal Soviet Republic (RSFSR) created in 1918.

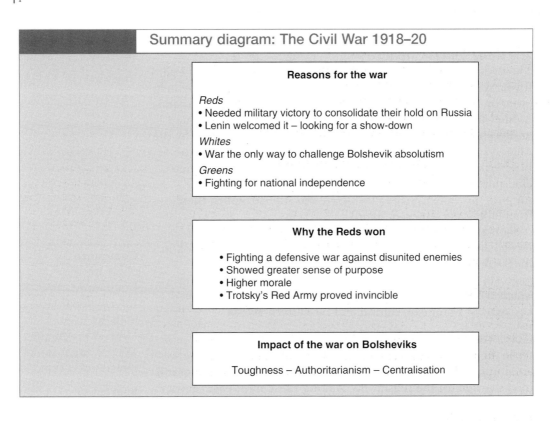

Summary diagram: The Civil War 1918–20

Reasons for the war

Reds
• Needed military victory to consolidate their hold on Russia
• Lenin welcomed it – looking for a show-down

Whites
• War the only way to challenge Bolshevik absolutism

Greens
• Fighting for national independence

Why the Reds won

• Fighting a defensive war against disunited enemies
• Showed greater sense of purpose
• Higher morale
• Trotsky's Red Army proved invincible

Impact of the war on Bolsheviks

Toughness – Authoritarianism – Centralisation

Key question
What led the foreign powers to intervene in Russia?

3 | The Foreign Interventions 1918–20

When tsardom collapsed in 1917 the immediate worry for the Western Allies was whether the new Russian regime would continue the war against Germany. If Russia made a separate peace, the Germans would be free to divert huge military resources from the eastern to the western front. To prevent this, the Allies offered large amounts of capital and military supplies to Russia to keep her in the war. The new Russian government eagerly accepted the offer.

This produced an extraordinary balance. On one side stood Lenin and his anti-war Bolsheviks financed by Germany; on the other was the pro-war Provisional Government funded by the Allies. However, the balance was destroyed by the October Revolution. The seizure of power by the Bolsheviks had precisely the effect hoped for by Germany and feared by the Allies. Within weeks, an armistice had been agreed between Germany and the new government, and fighting on the eastern front stopped in December 1917.

The initial response of France and Britain was cautious. In the faint hope that the Bolsheviks might still be persuaded to carry on the fight against Germany, the same support was offered to them as to their predecessors. David Lloyd George, the British prime minister, declared that he was neither for nor against Bolshevism, but simply anti-German. He was willing to side with any group in Russia that would continue the war against Germany.

The Brest-Litovsk Treaty

The Brest-Litovsk Treaty in March 1918 ended all hope of Lenin's Russia renewing the war against Germany. From now on, any help given by Britain to anti-German Russians went necessarily to anti-Bolshevik forces. It appeared to the Bolsheviks that Britain and its allies were intent on destroying them. This was matched by the Allies' view that in making a separate peace with Germany the Bolsheviks had betrayed the Allied cause. The result was a fierce determination among the Allies to prevent their vital war supplies, previously loaned to Russia and still stockpiled there, from falling into German hands

Soon after the signing of the Brest-Litovsk Treaty, British, French and American troops occupied the ports of Murmansk in the Arctic and Archangel in the White Sea (see Figure 1.3, page 16). This was the beginning of a two-year period during which armed forces from a large number of countries occupied key areas of European, central and far-eastern Russia.

Comintern

Once the First World War had ended in November 1918, the attention of the major powers turned to the possibility of a grand offensive against the Bolsheviks. Among those most eager for an attack were Winston Churchill, the British cabinet minister, and Marshal Foch, the French military leader. They were alarmed by the creation of the **Comintern** and by the spread of revolution in Germany and central Europe:

- In January 1918, the **'Spartacists'** tried unsuccessfully to mount a *coup* in Berlin.
- During 1918–19, a short-lived Communist republic was established in Bavaria.

- In March 1919 in Hungary, a Marxist government was set up under Bela Kun, only to fall five months later.

Foreign debts

There was also a key financial aspect to anti-Bolshevism in western Europe. One of the first acts of the Bolshevik regime had been to declare that the new government had no intention of honouring the foreign debts of its predecessors. In addition, it nationalised a large number of foreign companies and froze all foreign assets in Russia. The bitter reaction to what was regarded as international theft was particularly strong in France where many small and middle-scale financiers had invested in tsarist Russia. It was the French who now took the lead in proposing an international campaign against the Reds.

- In 1918 British land forces entered Transcaucasia in southern Russia and also occupied part of central Asia.
- British warships entered Russian Baltic waters and the Black Sea, where they were joined by French naval vessels.
- The French also established a major land base around the Black Sea port of Odessa.
- In April 1918, Japanese troops occupied Russia's far-eastern port of Vladivostok.
- Four months later, they were joined by units from France, Britain, the USA and Italy.
- Czech, Finnish, Lithuanian, Polish and Romanian forces crossed into Russia.
- In 1919 Japanese and United States troops occupied parts of Siberia.

Key question
Why did the interventions fail?

Failure of the interventions

An important point to stress is that the interventions were not co-ordinated attacks. There was little co-operation between the occupiers. The declared motive of Britain, France, Germany, Italy, Japan and the USA was the legitimate protection of their individual interests. The objective of Czechoslovakia, Finland, Lithuania, Poland and Romania, all of whom directly bordered western Russia, was to achieve their separatist aim, which went back to tsarist times, of gaining independence from Russia.

Despite the preaching of an anti-Bolshevik crusade by influential voices in western Europe, no concerted attempt was ever made to unseat the Bolshevik regime. This was shown by the relative ease with which the interventions were resisted. The truth was that, after four long years of struggle against Germany between 1914 and 1918, the European interventionists had no stomach for a prolonged campaign. There were serious threats of mutiny in some British and French regiments ordered to embark for Russia. Trade unionists who were sympathetic towards the new 'workers' state' refused to transport military supplies bound for Russia.

After the separate national forces had arrived in Russia, there was seldom effective liaison between them. Furthermore, such efforts as the foreign forces made to co-operate with the White

Figure 1.3: The foreign interventions 1918–21

Principal armies attempting to destroy Bolshevism in bold italic font

— Under Bolshevik rule November 1918

– – Maximum advance of the anti-Bolshevik forces 1918–19

▓ Remnant of anti-Bolshevik forces, defeated 1920–1

--- Established Russian frontiers, March 1921–October 1939

armies were half-hearted and came to little. The one major exception to this was in the Baltic states where the national forces, backed by British warships and troops, crushed a Bolshevik invasion and obliged Lenin's government to recognise the independence of Estonia, Latvia and Lithuania, a freedom which they maintained until taken over by Stalin in 1940 (see page 119).

Such interventionist success was not repeated elsewhere. After a token display of aggression, the foreign troops began to withdraw. By the end of 1919, all French and American troops had been recalled, and, by the end of 1920, all other western forces had left. It was only the Japanese who remained in Russia for the duration of the Civil War, not finally leaving until 1922.

Consequences of the interventions

Key question
What propaganda value did the failed interventions have for Lenin and the Bolsheviks?

In no real sense were these withdrawals a military victory for the Bolsheviks, but that was exactly how they were portrayed in Soviet propaganda. Lenin's government presented itself as the saviour of the nation from foreign conquest; all the interventions had been imperialist invasions of Russia intent on overthrowing the revolution. This apparent success over Russia's enemies helped the Bolshevik regime recover the esteem it had lost over its 1918 capitulation to Germany. It helped to put resolve into the doubters in the party and it lent credibility to the Bolshevik depiction of the Whites as agents of foreign powers, intent on restoring **reactionary** tsardom.

Key term

Reactionary
Resistant to any form of progressive change.

The failure of the foreign interventions encouraged the Bolsheviks to undertake what proved to be a disastrous attempt to expand their authority outside Russia. In 1920, the Red Army marched into neighbouring Poland expecting the Polish workers to rise in rebellion against their own government. However, the Poles saw the invasion as traditional Russian aggression and drove the Red Army back across the border. Soviet morale was seriously damaged. It brought home to Lenin that the revolution could not easily be exported.

Summary diagram: The foreign interventions 1918–20

Why the interventions?

- Resentment at Russian withdrawal from war
- To recover war supplies
- Fear of Bolshevism
- Anger at writing off of Russian debts by Bolsheviks

Who were the interventionists?

Britain – France – Japan – USA – Italy – Finland – Lithuania – Poland – Romania

Where were the interventions?

The Black Sea – Murmansk – Vladivostok – Siberia – the Caspian Sea

Why did the interventions fail?

- Lack of co-ordination and liaison
- Interventionists had no real stomach for a fight
- Very limited objectives
- Not a concerted effort to bring down the Bolsheviks

Consequences

- The Bolsheviks overextended themselves by invading Poland – only for the Red Army to be beaten back by the Poles
- Lenin realised revolution not easily exported

4 | The Red Terror

So severe was the suppression by the Bolsheviks of their internal enemies that it gained the title the Red Terror. The chief instruments by which it was imposed were the ***Cheka*** and the Red Army, both of which played a critical role during the Civil War.

The *Cheka*

In essentials, the *Cheka* was a better-organised and more efficient form of the tsarist secret police, at whose hands nearly every Bolshevik activist had suffered. Its express purpose was to destroy '**counter-revolution** and sabotage', terms that were so elastic they could be stretched to cover anything of which the Bolsheviks disapproved.

This state police force, often likened historically to the Gestapo in Nazi Germany, had been created in December 1917 under the direction of Felix Dzerzhinsky, an intellectual of Polish aristocratic background who sought to atone for his privileged origins by absolute dedication to the Bolshevik cause. Lenin found him the ideal choice to lead the fight against the enemies of the revolution. Dzerzhinsky never allowed finer feelings or compassion to deter him from the task of destroying the enemies of Bolshevism. His remorseless attitude was shown in the various directives that issued from the *Cheka* headquarters in Moscow.

> Our Revolution is in danger. Do not concern yourselves with the forms of revolutionary justice. We have no need for justice now. Now we have need of a battle to the death! I propose, I demand the use of the revolutionary sword which will put an end to all counter-revolutionaries.

The *Cheka*, which was to change its title several times over the years, but never its essential character, remains the outstanding expression of Bolshevik ruthlessness. Operating as a law unto itself, and answerable only to Lenin, it was granted unlimited powers of arrest, detention and torture, which it used in the most arbitrary and brutal way. It was the main instrument by which Lenin and his successors terrorised the Russian people into subservience and conformity.

The murder of the Romanovs

In July 1918, a group of SRs assassinated the German ambassador as a protest against the Brest-Litovsk Treaty. A month later an attempt was made on Lenin's life (see page 10), followed by the murder of the Petrograd chairman of the *Cheka*. These incidents were made the pretext for a Bolshevik reign of terror. It was in this atmosphere that a local *Cheka* detachment, on Lenin's personal order, executed the ex-tsar and his family in Ekaterinburg in July 1918.

The summary shooting of the Romanovs without trial was typical of the manner in which the *Cheka* went about its business.

Key question
What were the distinctive features of the *Cheka* as an instrument of terror?

Key terms

Cheka
'The All-Russian Extraordinary Commission for Fighting Counter-Revolution, Sabotage and Speculation'.

Counter-revolution
A term used by the Bolsheviks to cover any action of which they disapproved by branding it as reactionary.

Key date

Ex-tsar and his family assassinated:
16–17 July 1918

Key date

Announcement of Red Terror as official Bolshevik policy: 5 September 1918

In accordance with Dzerzhinsky's instructions, all pretence of legality was abandoned; the basic rules relating to evidence and proof of guilt no longer applied. Persecution was directed not simply against individuals, but against whole classes. This was class war of the most direct kind. One instruction began:

> Do not demand incriminating evidence to prove that the prisoner has opposed the Soviet government by force or words. Your first duty is to ask him to which class he belongs, what are his origins, his education, his occupation. These questions should decide the fate of the prisoner.

Some Bolsheviks were uneasy about the relentless savagery of the *Cheka* but there were no attempts to restrict its powers. The majority of party members accepted that the hazardous situation they were in justified the severity of the repression. The foreign interventions and the Civil War, fought out against the background of famine and social disorder, threatened the existence of the Communist Party and the government. This had the effect of stifling criticism of the *Cheka*'s methods. Dzerzhinsky declared that the proletarian revolution could not be saved except by 'exterminating the enemies of the working class'.

Key steps in the Terror programme

1918	21–22 February	'The Socialist Fatherland in Danger!' decree authorises execution of Bolsheviks' opponents
	1 May	Right of inheritance of property and money ended
	13 May	Declaration of war on 'peasant bourgeoisie'
	20 May	'Food supply detachments' created grain requisition squads
	16 June	Death penalty introduced
	16–17 July	Ex-tsar and his family murdered in Ekaterinburg
	29 July	Military conscription imposed
	10 August	Lenin appeals to workers to exterminate Kulaks
	5 September	Formal introduction of Red Terror as state policy
	10 December	'Labour Code' imposed rigid discipline on industrial workers
1919	17 February	Dzerzhinsky announced creation of forced labour camps
	27 December	Trotsky announced militarisation of labour

The Red Army

Dzerzhinsky's work as head of the *Cheka* was complemented by Trotsky, who became Commissar for War after the signing of the Brest-Litovsk Treaty. Trotsky used his powers to end the independence of the trade unions, which had first been legalised in 1905. Early in 1920, the workers were brought under military discipline on the same terms as soldiers. They were forbidden to question orders, could not negotiate their rates of pay or conditions, and could be severely punished for poor workmanship or not meeting production targets. Trotsky dismissed the unions as 'unnecessary chatterboxes' and told them: 'The working classes cannot be nomads. They must be commanded just like soldiers. Without this there can be no serious talk of industrialising on new foundations'.

Key question
What role did Trotsky and the Red Army play in the Terror?

Trotsky's role

Trotsky's outstanding achievement as Commissar for War was his creation of the Red Army, which more than any other factor explains the survival of the Bolshevik government. This has obvious reference to the Reds' triumph in the Civil War, but the Red Army also became the means by which the Bolsheviks imposed their authority on the population at large.

Lenin showed his complete trust in Trotsky by giving him a completely free hand in military matters. From his heavily armed special train, which served as his military headquarters and travelled vast distances, Trotsky supervised the development of a new fighting force in Russia. He had inherited 'The Workers' and Peasants' Red Army', formed early in 1918. Within two years he had turned an unpromising collection of tired Red Guard veterans and raw recruits into a formidable army of three million men. Ignoring the objections of many fellow Bolsheviks, he enlisted large numbers of ex-tsarist officers to train the rank and file into efficient soldiers. As a precaution, Trotsky attached **political commissars** to the army. These became an integral part of the Red Army structure. No military order carried final authority unless a commissar countersigned it.

Trotsky tolerated no opposition within the Red Army from officers or men. The death sentence was imposed for desertion or disloyalty. In the heady revolutionary days before Trotsky took over, the traditional forms of army discipline had been greatly relaxed. Graded ranks, special uniforms, saluting and deferential titles had been dropped as belonging to the reactionary past. Trotsky, however, had no truck with such fanciful experiments. He insisted that the demands of war meant that discipline had to be tighter not looser.

Although the term 'officer' was replaced by 'commander', in all other key respects the Red Army returned to the customary forms of rank and address, with the word 'Comrade' usually prefixing the standard terms, as in 'Comrade Captain'. The practice of electing officers, which had come into favour in the democratic atmosphere of the February Revolution, was abandoned, as were soldiers' committees.

Political commissars
Party workers who permanently accompanied the officers and reported on their political correctness.

Key term

The original photo of Lenin addressing a crowd in Moscow in May 1920 also shows Trotsky and Kamenev on the steps of the podium. This photo later became notorious when in Stalin's time it was either airbrushed or clipped to remove Trotsky and Kamenev from it. Despite such later attempts to deny Trotsky's role in the revolution he had undoubtedly been Lenin's right-hand man between 1917 and 1924.

Conscription

Trotsky responded to the Civil War's increasing demand for manpower by enforcing **conscription** in those areas under Bolshevik control. (The Whites did the same in their areas.) Under the slogan 'Everything for the Front', Trotsky justified the severity of the Red Army's methods by referring to the dangers that Russia faced on all sides. Those individuals whose social or political background made them suspect as fighting men were nevertheless conscripted, being formed into labour battalions for back-breaking service behind the lines, digging trenches, loading ammunition and pulling heavy guns.

Most of the peasants who were drafted into the Red Army proved reluctant warriors, and were not regarded as reliable in a crisis. Desertions were commonplace, in spite of the heavy penalties. The Bolsheviks judged that the only dependable units were those drawn predominantly from among the workers. Such units became in practice the élite corps of the Red Army. Heroic stories of the workers as defenders of the revolution quickly became legends.

Morale

Not everything was achieved by coercion; there were idealists among the troops who believed sincerely in the Communist mission to create a new proletarian world. Theirs was a vital contribution to the relatively high morale of the Reds. Although, by the standards of the European armies of the time, the Red Army was short of equipment and expertise, within Russia it soon came to outstrip its White opponents in its efficiency and sense of purpose.

Key debate

> Were Lenin's terror tactics a temporary response to a desperate situation or an expression of Russian Communism's true character?

Whether the terror was justified remains a matter of dispute. One argument is that the extreme measures which Lenin's government adopted were the only response possible to the problems confronting the Bolsheviks after the October Revolution, in particular the need to win a desperate civil war.

An opposing view is that repression was not a reaction to circumstances but was a defining characteristic of **Marxism–Leninism**, a creed which regarded itself as uniquely superior to all other ideologies. An extension of this argument is that there was something essentially authoritarian about Lenin himself. He did not know how to act in any other way. He had always accepted the necessity of terror as an instrument of political control. Before 1917 he had often made it clear that a Marxist revolution could not survive if it were not prepared to smash its enemies:

Marxism–Leninism The notion that Marx's theory of class war as interpreted by Lenin was a supremely accurate and unchallengeable piece of scientific analysis.

Key term

> Coercion is necessary for the transition from capitalism to socialism. There is absolutely no contradiction between Soviet democracy and the exercise of dictatorial powers.

A particular point, which a number of modern historians have stressed, is how popular the Terror was with many peasants and workers. It offered them a chance to get their own back on their previous exploiters, who, now that the Bolsheviks had taken over, were themselves the victims. This process has been described as 'looting the looters'. It is possible to argue, therefore, that rather than being imposed from the top, the Red Terror was a Bolshevik response to what was already happening in revolutionary Russia. The attack upon privilege in the form of mobs' ransacking the homes of landlords and nobles and plundering churches gave the cue to Lenin and the Bolsheviks to turn it all into a systemised programme of terror. Orlando Figes, a modern authority, writes:

> There is no doubt that the Terror struck a deep chord in the Russian civil war mentality, and that it had a strange mass appeal … People even called their daughters Terrora.

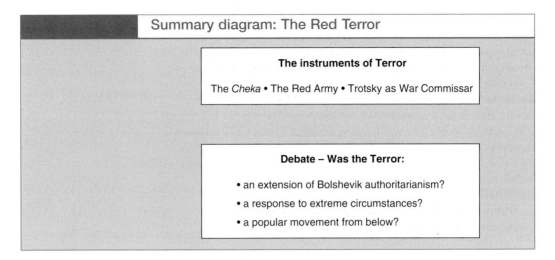

Summary diagram: The Red Terror

The instruments of Terror

The *Cheka* • The Red Army • Trotsky as War Commissar

Debate – Was the Terror:

• an extension of Bolshevik authoritarianism?

• a response to extreme circumstances?

• a popular movement from below?

Key question
Why was War Communism introduced?

5 | War Communism 1918–21

War Communism is best understood as another aspect of the Red Terror. It was a series of harshly restrictive economic measures that Lenin began to introduce in the summer of 1918 to replace the system of state capitalism that the Bolsheviks had operated during their first nine months in power.

The chief reason for adopting it was the desperate situation created by the Civil War. Lenin judged that the White menace could be met only by a tightening of authority in those regions that the Reds controlled (approximately 30 of the 50 provinces of European Russia). The change in strategy has to be seen, therefore, as part of the terror that the Bolsheviks imposed in these years. Every aspect of life – social, political and economic – had to be subordinated to the task of winning the Civil War.

Key question
What was the impact of War Communism on industry?

Industry

The first step towards War Communism as a formal policy was taken in June 1918. The existence of the *Cheka* and the Red Army enabled Lenin to embark on a policy of **centralisation**, knowing that he had the means of enforcing it. By that time, there had also been a considerable increase in Bolshevik influence in the factories, a result of the infiltration of the workers' committees by political commissars. This development helped prepare the way for the issuing of the **Decree on Nationalisation** in June 1918, which within two years brought practically all the major industrial enterprises in Russia under central government control.

However, nationalisation by itself did nothing to increase production. It was imposed at a time of severe industrial disruption, which had been caused initially by the strains of the war of 1914–17 but which worsened during the Civil War. Military needs came first when supplies were being distributed. The result was that many industries were starved of essential resources.

Key terms

Centralisation
The concentration of political and economic power at the centre.

Decree on Nationalisation
Announced the take-over by the State of the larger industrial concerns in Russia.

The situation was made more serious by the factories' being deprived of manpower. This was a result of both military conscription and the flight from the urban areas of large numbers of inhabitants, who left either in search of food or to escape the Civil War. The populations of Petrograd and Moscow dropped by a half between 1918 and 1921.

The problems for industry were deepened by severe inflation. The scarcity of goods and the government's policy of continuing to print currency notes effectively destroyed the value of money. By the end of 1920, the rouble had fallen to one per cent of its worth in 1917. All this meant that while War Communism tightened the Bolshevik grip on industry it did not lead to economic growth. Table 1.2 below shows the failure of War Communism in economic terms.

Table 1.2: A comparison of industrial output in 1913 and in 1921

	1913	1921
Index of gross industrial output	100	31
Index of large-scale industrial output	100	21
Electricity (million kWh)	2039	520
Coal (million tons)	29	8.9
Oil (million tons)	9.2	3.8
Steel (million tons)	4.3	0.18
Imports [at 1913 rouble value (millions)]	1374	208
Exports [at 1913 rouble value (millions)]	1520	20

Agriculture

For Lenin, a major purpose of War Communism was to tighten government control over agriculture and force the peasants to provide more food. But the peasants proved difficult. As a naturally conservative class, they were resistant to central government, whether tsarist or Bolshevik. The government blamed the resistance on the **Kulaks** who, it was claimed, were hoarding their grain stocks in order to keep prices artificially high. This was untrue. There was little hoarding. The truth was that the peasants saw no point in producing more food until the government, which had become the main grain purchaser, was willing to pay a fair price for it.

Grain requisitioning and famine

However, exasperated by the peasants' refusal to conform, the government condemned them as counter-revolutionaries and resorted to coercion. *Cheka* requisition units were sent into the countryside to take the grain by force. In August 1918, the people's commissar for food issued the following orders:

> The tasks of the requisition detachments are to: harvest winter grain in former landlord-owned estates; harvest grain on the land of notorious Kulaks; every food requisition detachment is to consist of not less than 75 men and two or three machine guns. The political commissar's duties are to ensure that the detachment carries out its duties and is full of revolutionary enthusiasm and discipline.

Key question
What was the impact of War Communism on agriculture?

Kulaks
The Bolshevik term for the class of rich exploiting peasants. The notion was largely a myth. The Kulaks were simply the more efficient farmers who were marginally more prosperous than the bulk of the peasants.

Key term

Between 1918 and 1921, the requisition squads systematically terrorised the countryside. The Kulaks were targeted for particularly brutal treatment. Lenin ordered that they were to be 'mercilessly suppressed'. In a letter of 1920, he gave instructions that 100 Kulaks were to be hanged in public in order to terrify the population 'for hundreds of miles around'.

Yet the result was largely the reverse of the one intended. Even less food became available. Knowing that any surplus would simply be confiscated, the peasant produced only the barest minimum to feed himself and his family. Nevertheless, throughout the period of War Communism, the Bolsheviks persisted in their belief that grain hoarding was the basic problem. Official reports continued to speak of 'concealment everywhere, in the hopes of selling grain to town speculators at fabulous prices'.

Key question
Why was the Russian famine of 1921 so severe?

Famine

By 1921, the combination of requisitioning, drought and the general disruption of war had created a national famine. The grain harvests in 1920 and 1921 produced less than half that gathered in 1913. Even *Pravda* admitted in 1921 that one in five of the population was starving.

Matters became so desperate that the Bolsheviks, while careful to blame the Kulaks and the Whites, were prepared to admit there was a famine and to accept foreign assistance. A number of countries supplied Russia with aid. The outstanding contribution came from the USA, which through the **American Relief Association (ARA)**, provided food for some 10 million Russians. Despite such efforts, foreign help came too late to prevent mass starvation. Of the 10 million fatalities of the Civil War period, over half starved to death. Lenin resented having to accept aid from the ARA and ordered it to withdraw from Russia in 1923 after two years' work there, during which time it had spent over $60 million on relief.

Lenin positively welcomed the famine as providing an opportunity to increase his attack on the Orthodox Church (see page 36). In a letter of 1922, he ordered the Politburo to exploit the famine by shooting priests, 'the more, the better'. He went on:

> It is precisely now and only now when in the starving regions people are eating human flesh and thousands of corpses are littering the roads that we can carry out the confiscation of the church valuables with the most savage and merciless energy.

Key terms

Pravda (the truth)
The Bolshevik newspaper dating from 1912 that, after October 1917, became a principal means of spreading government propaganda.

American Relief Association (ARA)
Formed by Herbert Hoover (a future President of the USA, 1928–32) to provide food and medical supplies for post-war Europe.

End of War Communism

By 1921, the grim economic situation had undermined the original justification for War Communism. During its operation, industrial and agricultural production had fallen alarmingly. Yet, this did not mean the policy necessarily became unpopular among the Bolsheviks themselves. Indeed, there were many in the party who, far from regarding it as a temporary measure to meet an extreme situation, believed that it represented true revolutionary communism. The party's leading economists, Nikolai Bukharin and Yevgeny Preobrazhensky, urged that War Communism should be retained as the permanent economic policy of the Bolshevik government. They saw it as true socialism in action since it involved:

- The centralising of industry
- The ending of private ownership
- The persecution of the peasants.

Lenin himself clung to War Communism as long as he could. However, the failure of the economy to recover and the scale of the famine led him to consider possible alternatives. He was finally convinced of the need for change by widespread anti-Bolshevik risings in 1920–1. These were a direct reaction against the brutality of requisitioning. One in particular made Lenin re-think his whole policy. This was the Kronstadt Rising of 1921, the most serious challenge to Bolshevik control since the October Revolution.

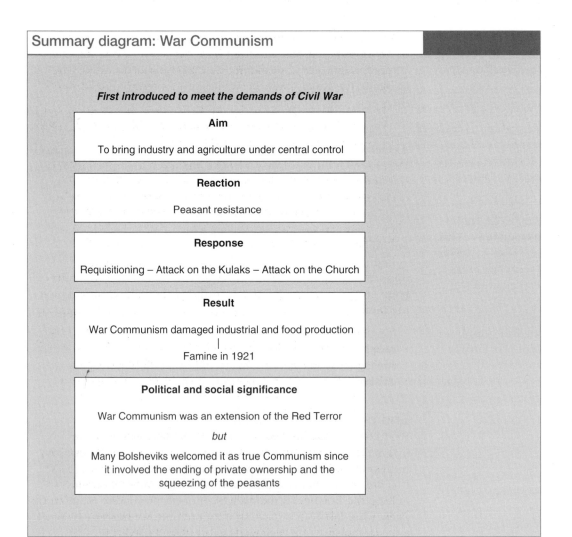

Summary diagram: War Communism

First introduced to meet the demands of Civil War

Aim

To bring industry and agriculture under central control

Reaction

Peasant resistance

Response

Requisitioning – Attack on the Kulaks – Attack on the Church

Result

War Communism damaged industrial and food production
|
Famine in 1921

Political and social significance

War Communism was an extension of the Red Terror

but

Many Bolsheviks welcomed it as true Communism since it involved the ending of private ownership and the squeezing of the peasants

6 | The Kronstadt Rising 1921

Key question
What circumstances led to the rising?

Key terms

Labour commissar
Equivalent to a minister of labour, responsible for industry and its workers.

Non-partisan
Politically neutral, belonging to no party.

Martial law
The whole of the population being placed under military discipline.

The policy of War Communism was maintained even after the victory of the Red Army in the Civil War. The systematic use of terror by the *Cheka*, the spying on factory workers by political commissars, and the enforced requisitioning of peasant grain stocks all continued. As a short-term measure the policy had produced the conformity Lenin wanted, but its severity had increased Bolshevik unpopularity. Throughout 1920 there were outbreaks of resistance, scattered across the Red-held areas of Russia.

As long as unrest was confined to the peasants and to the Bolsheviks' political enemies it was a containable problem. What became deeply worrying to Lenin in 1921 was the development of opposition to War Communism within the party itself. Two prominent Bolsheviks, Alexander Shlyapnikov, the **labour commissar**, and Alexandra Kollontai, the outstanding woman in the party (see page 37), led a 'Workers' Opposition' movement against the excesses of War Communism. Kollontai produced a pamphlet in which she accused the party leaders of losing touch with the proletariat:

> The workers ask – who are we? Are we really the prop of the class dictatorship, or just an obedient flock that serves as a support for those, who, having severed all ties with the masses, carry out their own policy and build up industry without any regard to our opinions?

Picking up the cue given by the Workers' Opposition, groups of workers in Petrograd went on strike early in 1921, justifying their actions in an angrily worded proclamation:

> The workers and peasants need freedom. They don't want to live by the decrees of the Bolsheviks; they want to control their own destinies. Comrades, preserve revolutionary order! Determinedly and in an organised manner demand: liberation of all the arrested Socialists and **non-partisan** working men; abolition of **martial law**; freedom of speech, press and assembly for all who labour.

By February 1921, thousands of workers had crossed from Petrograd to the naval base on Kronstadt, an island a few miles offshore in the Gulf of Finland. There they linked up with the sailors and dockyard workers to demonstrate for greater freedom. They demanded that in a workers' state the workers should be better, not worse, off than in tsarist times. In an attempt to pacify the strikers, Lenin sent a team of political commissars to Kronstadt. They were greeted with loud jeers. Petrechenko, a spokesman for the demonstrators, rounded bitterly on the commissars at a public meeting:

> You are comfortable; you are warm; you commissars live in the palaces … Comrades, look around you and you will see that we have fallen into a terrible mire. We were pulled into this mire by a group of Communist bureaucrats, who, under the mask of Communism, have feathered their nests in our republic. I call on you, Comrades, drive out these false Communists who set worker against peasant and peasant against worker. Enough shooting of our brothers!

The Kronstadt manifesto

Early in March, the sailors and workers of Kronstadt produced a manifesto which included the following demands:

Key question
Why was the rising so disturbing for Lenin and the Bolsheviks?

1. New elections to the Soviets, to be held by secret ballot.
2. Freedom of speech and of the press.
3. Freedom of assembly.
4. Rights for trade unions and release of imprisoned trade unionists.
5. Ending of the right of Communists to be the only permitted socialist political party.
6. The release of left-wing political prisoners.
7. Ending of special food rations for Communist Party members.
8. Freedom for individuals to bring food from the country into the towns without confiscation.
9. Withdrawal of political commissars from the factories.
10. Ending of the Communist Party monopoly of the press.

It was not the demands themselves that frightened the Bolsheviks; it was the people who had drafted them – the workers and sailors of Kronstadt. They had been the great supporters of the Bolsheviks in 1917. Trotsky had referred to them as 'the heroes of the Revolution'. It was these same heroes who were now insisting that the Bolshevik government return to the promises that had inspired the Revolution. For all the efforts of the Bolshevik press to brand the Kronstadt protesters as White agents, the truth was that they were genuine socialists who had previously been wholly loyal to Lenin's government, but who had become appalled by the regime's betrayal of the workers' cause.

Suppression of the rising

Angered by the growing number of strikers and their increasing demands, Trotsky ordered the Red Army under General Tukhachevsky to cross the late winter ice linking Kronstadt to Petrograd and crush 'the tools of former tsarist generals and agents of the interventionists'. An ultimatum was issued to the demonstrators. When this was rejected, Tukhachevsky gave the signal for his force, made up of Red Army units and *Cheka* detachments, to attack. After an artillery bombardment, 60,000 Red troops stormed the Kronstadt base. The sailors and workers resisted fiercely. Savage fighting occurred before they were finally overcome. Tukhachevsky reported back to Trotsky:

Key question
How did the government deal with the rising?

> The sailors fought like wild beasts. I cannot understand where they found the might for such rage. Each house where they were located had to be taken by storm. An entire company fought for an hour to capture one house and when the house was captured it was found to contain two or three soldiers at a machine-gun. They seemed half-dead, but they snatched their revolvers and gasped, 'We didn't shoot enough at you bastards.'

Immediately after the rising had been suppressed, the ringleaders who had survived were condemned as White reactionaries and shot. In the succeeding months the *Cheka* hunted down and executed those rebels who had escaped from Kronstadt. Lenin justified the severity on the grounds that the rising had been the work of the bourgeois enemies of the October Revolution: 'Both the Mensheviks and the Socialist Revolutionaries declared the Kronstadt movement to be their own.'

However, as well as being a propagandist, Lenin was also a realist. He took the lesson of Kronstadt to heart. To avoid the scandal and embarrassment of another open challenge to his party and government, he decided it was time to soften the severity of War Communism.

At the Tenth Conference of the Communist Party, which opened in March 1921, Lenin declared that the Kronstadt Rising had 'lit up reality like a lightning flash'. This was the prelude to his introduction of the New Economic Policy (NEP), a move intended to tackle the famine and in doing so to lessen the opposition to Bolshevism. However, this was to be a purely economic adjustment. Lenin was not prepared to make political concessions: communist control was to be made even tighter.

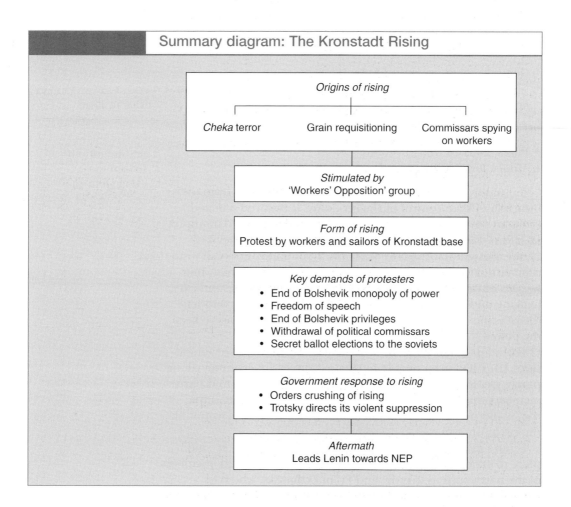

Summary diagram: The Kronstadt Rising

Origins of rising

Cheka terror | Grain requisitioning | Commissars spying on workers

Stimulated by
'Workers' Opposition' group

Form of rising
Protest by workers and sailors of Kronstadt base

Key demands of protesters
- End of Bolshevik monopoly of power
- Freedom of speech
- End of Bolshevik privileges
- Withdrawal of political commissars
- Secret ballot elections to the soviets

Government response to rising
- Orders crushing of rising
- Trotsky directs its violent suppression

Aftermath
Leads Lenin towards NEP

7 | The New Economic Policy (NEP)

Key question
What were Lenin's motives in introducing NEP?

As with the policy it replaced, NEP was intended by Lenin primarily to meet Russia's urgent need for food. Whatever the purity of the revolutionary theory behind War Communism, it had clearly failed to deliver the goods. State terror had not forced the peasants into producing larger grain stocks. Pragmatic as ever, Lenin judged that, if the peasants could not be forced, they must be persuaded. The stick had not worked so now was the time for the carrot. He told the delegates at the 1921 Party Congress:

> We must try to satisfy the demands of the peasants who are dissatisfied, discontented, and cannot be otherwise. In essence the small farmer can be satisfied with two things. First of all, there must be a certain amount of freedom for the small private proprietor; and, secondly, commodities and products must be provided.

Despite the deep disagreements that were soon to emerge within the Bolshevik Party over NEP, the grim economic situation in Russia led the delegates to give unanimous support to Lenin's proposals when they were first introduced. The decree making NEP official government policy was published in the spring of 1921. Its essential features were:

- Central economic control to be relaxed.
- The requisitioning of grain to be abandoned and replaced by a **tax in kind**.
- The peasants to be allowed to keep their food surpluses and sell them for a profit.
- Public markets to be restored.
- Money to be reintroduced as a means of trading.

Tax in kind
The surrendering by the peasant of a certain amount of his produce, equivalent to a fixed sum of money.

Key term

Lenin was aware that the new policy marked a retreat from the principle of state control of the economy. It restored a mixed economy in which certain features of capitalism existed alongside socialism. Knowing how uneasy this made many Bolsheviks, Lenin stressed that the NEP was only a temporary concession to capitalism and that the party still controlled 'the commanding heights of the economy', by which he meant large-scale industry, banking and foreign trade. He added: 'we are prepared to let the peasants have their little bit of capitalism as long as we keep the power.'

   The adoption of NEP showed that the Bolshevik government since 1917 had been unable to create a successful economy along purely ideological lines. Lenin admitted as much. He told party members that it made no sense for Bolsheviks to pretend that they could pursue an economic policy which took no account of the circumstances.

   Lenin's realism demanded that political theory take second place to economic necessity. It was this that troubled the members of the party, such as Trotsky and Preobrazhensky, who had regarded the repressive measures of war communism as the proper revolutionary strategy for the Bolsheviks to follow. To their mind, bashing the peasants was exactly what the Bolsheviks should be doing since it advanced the revolution. It disturbed them, therefore, that the peasants were being given in to and that capitalist ways were being tolerated. Trotsky described NEP as 'the first sign of the degeneration of Bolshevism'.

A main complaint was that the reintroduction of money and private trading was creating a new class of profiteers whom they derisively dubbed **'Nepmen'**. It was the profiteering that Victor Serge, a representative of the Left Bolsheviks, had in mind when he described the immediate social effects of NEP: 'The cities we ruled over assumed a foreign aspect; we felt ourselves sinking into the mire. Money lubricated and befouled the entire machine just as under capitalism'.

Party unity

Key question
How did Lenin prevent the party's splitting over NEP?

NEP became such a contentious issue among the Bolsheviks that Lenin took firm steps to prevent the party being torn apart over it. At the Tenth Party Congress in 1921, at which the NEP had been formally announced, he introduced a resolution 'On Party Unity'. The key passage read:

> The Congress orders the immediate dissolution, without exception, of all groups that have been formed on the basis of some platform or other, and instructs all organisations to be very strict in ensuring that no manifestations of **factionalism** of any sort be tolerated. Failure to comply with this resolution of the Congress is to entail unconditional and immediate expulsion from the party.

Key terms

Nepmen
Those who stood to gain from the free trading permitted under the new policy, e.g. rich peasants, retailers, traders.

Factionalism
The forming within the party of groups with a particular complaint or grievance.

The object of this proposal was to prevent 'factions' within the party from criticising government or Central Committee decisions. An accompanying resolution condemned the 'Workers' Opposition', the group which had been involved in the Kronstadt Rising. These two resolutions on party unity provided a highly effective means of stifling criticism of the NEP.

At the same time as Lenin condemned factionalism, he also declared that all political parties other than the Bolsheviks were now outlawed in Soviet Russia. 'Marxism teaches that only the Communist Party is capable of organising the proletariat and the whole mass of the working people.' This was the logical climax of the policy, begun in 1918, of suppressing all opposition to Bolshevik rule. Lenin's announcements at this critical juncture made it extremely difficult for doubting members to criticise NEP openly, since this would appear to be challenging the party itself.

What also helped to preserve Bolshevik unity was the decision by Nicolai Bukharin, the outstanding Bolshevik economist, to abandon his opposition to NEP and become its most enthusiastic supporter. His new approach was expressed in his appeal to the peasants: 'Enrich yourselves under the NEP'.

Bukharin believed that the greater income the peasants would have, as a result of selling their surplus grain, would stimulate industry since their extra money would be spent on buying manufactured goods. It is significant that during the final two years of Lenin's life, when he became increasingly exhausted by a series of crippling strokes, it was Bukharin who was his closest colleague. The last two articles published under Lenin's name, 'On Co-operation' and 'Better Fewer, But Better', were justifications of the NEP. Both were the work of Bukharin.

Success of the NEP

In the end, the most convincing reason for the party to accept the NEP proved to be a statistical one. The production figures suggested that the policy worked. By the time of Lenin's death in 1924, the Soviet economy had begun to make a marked recovery. Table 1.3 indicates the scale of this.

Key question
How far did NEP meet Russia's needs?

Table 1.3: Growth under the NEP

	1921	1922	1923	1924
Grain harvest (million tons)	37.6	50.3	56.6	51.4
Value of factory output (in millions of roubles)	2004	2619	4005	4660
Electricity (million kWh)	520	775	1146	1562
Average monthly wage of urban worker (in roubles)	10.2	12.2	15.9	20.8

Lenin's claim that under the NEP the Bolsheviks would still control 'the commanding heights of the economy' was shown to be substantially correct by the census of 1923. Figure 1.4 and Table 1.4 indicate that, in broad terms, the NEP had produced an economic balance: while agriculture and trade were largely in private hands, the State dominated Russian industry.

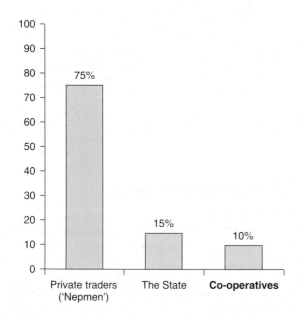

Figure 1.4: Share of trade

Co-operatives
Groups of workers or farmers working together on their own enterprise.

Key term

Table 1.4: Balance between main types of enterprise

	Proportion of industrial workforce	Average number of workers in each factory
Private enterprises	12%	2
State enterprises	85%	155
Co-operatives	3%	15

The NEP was not a total success. Its opponents criticised it on the grounds that the balance it appeared to have achieved was notional rather than real. The fact was that industry failed to expand as quickly as agriculture. The 'Nepmen' may have done well, but there was high unemployment in the urban areas. NEP would continue to be a matter of division among the Bolsheviks long after Lenin's death. Yet despite the disputes, it remained official Soviet policy until it was finally jettisoned by Stalin in 1928 when introducing his collectivisation schemes (see page 70).

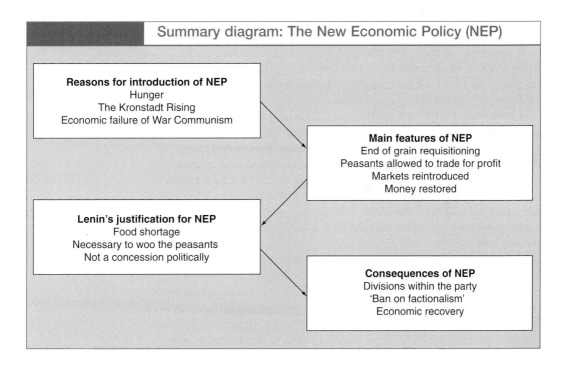

Summary diagram: The New Economic Policy (NEP)

Reasons for introduction of NEP
Hunger
The Kronstadt Rising
Economic failure of War Communism

Main features of NEP
End of grain requisitioning
Peasants allowed to trade for profit
Markets reintroduced
Money restored

Lenin's justification for NEP
Food shortage
Necessary to woo the peasants
Not a concession politically

Consequences of NEP
Divisions within the party
'Ban on factionalism'
Economic recovery

Key question
What place did culture have in Lenin's Russia?

8 | Soviet Society under Lenin

Culture and the arts

In Russia after the Revolution there was much talk of creating a new type of human being. The claim was that the Bolshevik triumph had liberated the people from the weaknesses that had tainted all previous societies. The people were now ready to be moulded into a new species. A Latin term was even invented to describe it – '*Homo sovieticus*', soviet man. Lenin was reported to have said 'Man can be made whatever we want him to be'. Trotsky claimed that the aim of the Communist State was 'to produce a new, "improved" version of man'.

The critical aspect of what Lenin and Trotsky believed was that this process would not happen of its own accord. It would have to be directed; people would have to be moulded; culture would have to be shaped. This further emphasised the dominant role of the State. The result was that, after a brief period of apparent artistic freedom, culture came under State control. The outstanding example of this was the **Proletkult** movement.

The Proletkult movement

In theory, this was the spontaneous creation by the workers of a new Russian culture. In practice, there was little genuine contribution from ordinary people. Cultural expression was the preserve of a small artistic establishment – writers, composers, artists and film-makers.

Proletkult pre-dated the Revolution. It had begun earlier in the century as a movement led by Anatoli Lunarcharsky with the aim and mission of educating the masses. Lenin saw in it a means of extending Bolshevik control. In 1917 he appointed Lunarcharsky as **Commissar of Enlightenment**. Lunarcharsky saw his role as using Proletkult as 'a source of agitation and propaganda'. The purpose was to attack and destroy the reactionary prejudices and attitudes of pre-revolutionary Russia.

It had been Lenin's original hope that after October 1917 the new revolutionary Russia would see a spontaneous flowering of culture. The word culture is not easy to define precisely. In one obvious sense it refers to the refined aspects of life, such as music, art, sculpture and writing. But, in the sense that Marx and Lenin understood culture, these things did not exist separately. They were an expression of the class structure of society itself. That was what Trotsky meant when he said that 'every ruling class creates its own culture'. Just as a feudal society has a feudal culture and a bourgeois society a bourgeois culture, so, too, a proletarian society, such as Russia now was, must have a proletarian culture.

The works of writers and artists, therefore, would now express the values of revolutionary Russia. If they did not then they would be unacceptable. As with politics and economics, culture and artistic expression had to serve the State. There was to be no place for free expression and individualism in Soviet culture. Lenin was clear that 'the purpose of art and literature is to serve the people'.

There were some Bolsheviks who believed that a new people's culture would grow naturally out of the existing conditions. Lenin now rejected this; he was no longer prepared to wait for such an evolution. The task was to eradicate the remnants of Russia's cultural past and construct a new, wholly socialist form. That is why he approved of Proletkult's willingness to see its role not as narrowly cultural but as covering all aspects of life including politics and religion. By 1922 a range of Proletkult artistic and sporting organisations had been set up across Russia. These included:

Key terms

Proletkult
Proletarian culture.

Commissar of Enlightenment
Equivalent to an arts minister.

- writers' circles
- amateur dramatic groups – including street theatre
- art studios
- poetry workshops
- musical appreciation societies.

Many of these were based in factories; there was even a 'Proletarian University', especially set up in Moscow for factory workers. On the surface all this seemed to indicate a flowering of workers' culture, but the hard fact was that the art, music, architecture and literature that ordinary people were supposed to enjoy were dictated by the **intelligentsia**. It was they who decided what the workers' tastes should be and who enjoyed such artistic freedom as prevailed after 1917. And even here restrictions soon set in.

By 1920, Lenin had become concerned by developments. The artistic control he had originally looked for seemed too loose. He did not want Proletkult to become an independent organisation within the state. He instructed that it be brought under much tighter supervision within Lunarcharsky's Commissariat of the Enlightenment. As a result, Proletkult by 1922 had been largely disbanded.

Key term

Intelligentsia
The group in society distinguished by their intellectual or creative abilities, e.g. writers, artists, composers, academics.

The campaign against the intelligentsia

Proletkult's fate was part of the campaign that Lenin launched in 1922 against the intelligentsia, his last major initiative before he died. Angered by criticisms from writers and university teachers about his policies of War Communism and NEP, he ordered the GPU (the new title of the *Cheka*) to impose strict censorship on the press and on academic publications. Branded variously as 'counter-revolutionaries, spies, and corrupters of student youth' hundreds of writers and university dons were imprisoned or sent into exile.

It was not a totally dark picture:

- Literacy rose from 43 per cent to 51 per cent.
- Some of the arts did reach a wider audience and works of artistic merit were produced.
- Experiment with form was allowable; hence abstract art was permitted.

But the content and meaning or a message of a work had to be socialist. This meant all work, whether a poem, a play, a novel, a sculpture or an opera, had to be pro-government. Anything critical of the Communist system, however well dressed up or packaged, was not tolerated.

This puritan attitude was typified by Lenin himself. As a younger man he had loved classical music, particularly Beethoven's late string quartets which sent him into raptures. But his reaction made him feel ashamed; he was allowing himself to be seduced by a bourgeois notion of beauty. He resolved to give up Beethoven and dedicate himself single-mindedly to revolutionary study.

Religion

Karl Marx had described religion as 'the opium of the people'. He was not being simply dismissive; he was making a profound historical point. His argument was that religious belief and worship were what people turned to in order to deaden the pain of life. Since all periods of history were times of conflict, suffering was ever present. Only with the victory of the proletariat would people understand there was no longer any need to believe in God and the afterlife. They would then realise that religion was a mere superstition used by class oppressors to keep the people down.

Having come to power, Lenin put this Marxist notion into action. Revolutionary Russia was to be a secular state with no place for organised religion. This intention was immediately declared in the Decree on Separation of Church and State. This measure had two aims: to break the hold of the clergy and to undermine the religious faith of the peasants for whom the Bolsheviks had a particular distaste as representing the most backward features of old Russia. The main terms of the Decree were:

- Church properties were no longer to be owned by the clergy, but by the local Soviets from whom churches would have to be rented for public worship.
- Clergy were no longer paid salaries or pensions by the state.
- The Church was no longer to have a central organisation with authority over local congregations.
- Religious teaching was forbidden in schools.

Over the next three years the Bolsheviks built on this decree to wage war against the Orthodox Church. Its leaders such as Metropolitan (Archbishop) Benjamin, its chief spokesman in Moscow, who dared to speak out against the regime and its methods were subjected to a **show trial** before being imprisoned. By the time of Lenin's death in 1924, over 300 bishops had been executed and some 10,000 priests imprisoned or exiled. The head of the Church, Patriarch Tikhon, at first resisted bravely, issuing powerful denunciations of the godless attacks upon the Church, but he then broke under the stress and became totally subservient to the regime, which used him thereafter as a puppet.

It soon became common practice for churches and monasteries to be looted and desecrated by the GPU acting under government direction. Such moves were backed by a widespread propaganda campaign to ridicule religion and the Church. The press poured out daily mockeries. Plays and street theatre presentations, sometimes subtly, more often crudely, jeered at the absurdities of faith and worship. Judaism and Islam did not escape. Those faiths, too, were pilloried.

Religion was too deeply embedded in Russian tradition for it to be totally eradicated in this way, but it was driven underground. Peasants continued to pray and worship as their forebears had but they could no longer risk doing it publicly.

Key question
Why were the Bolsheviks so determined to destroy religious faith?

Key date
Decree on Separation of Church and State: 20 January 1918

Key term
Show trial
A special public court hearing, meant as a propaganda exercise in which the accused, whose guilt is assumed, are paraded as enemies of the people.

Key question
How did the status of
women change in
Bolshevik Russia?

Women and the family

It was a firm Marxist belief that women were abused under
capitalism. The principal instrument of their subjection was
marriage. This one-sided social contract turned women into
victims since it made them, in effect, the property of their
husbands. It was the perfect example of the exploitative capitalist
system. It was not surprising, therefore, that on taking power the
Bolsheviks should have taken immediate steps to raise the status
of women and undermine marriage as an institution. In the two
years after 1917, decrees had been introduced which included
such innovations as:

Alexandra Kollontai 1872–1952

1872	– Born to a well-to-do military family
1906	– Became a Menshevik
1914–17	– Travelled in Scandinavia and the USA
1915	– Joined the Bolsheviks
1918	– Opposed the Brest-Litovsk Treaty
1919	– Wrote *The New Morality and the Working Class*
1920	– Head of the Women's section of the Central Committee
1921	– Joined the Workers' Opposition – opposed the crushing of the Kronstadt Rising
1923	– Soviet representative in Norway
1926	– Soviet representative in Mexico
1943–45	– Soviet ambassador to Sweden
1952	– Died

The outstanding woman in the party was Alexandra Kollontai.
She was the voice of early Russian feminism and a pioneer
among Bolshevik women. Her life was a dramatic one.
Rebellious and unconventional by nature, she married
frequently and had countless affairs, including a fling with the
King of Sweden. In her writings she advanced the idea that
women need to be liberated sexually, politically and
psychologically. She argued that free love was the only
relationship that guaranteed equality for women. For her,
the family was a prison; children should be reared by society
at large.

Kollontai was undoubtedly a fascinating woman and an
important international feminist, but she was atypical as a
Bolshevik. It might be thought that, given the views of
Kollontai and the general desire of the Bolsheviks to eradicate
old values, revolutionary Russia would become a haven of
immorality and sexual licence. It did not quite work that way.
The Bolsheviks were an odd mixture of permissiveness and
puritanism. Lenin was unimpressed by Kollontai's feminism.
He found her emphasis on free love and casual relationships
unwelcome in a society that, under his direction, was aiming at
socialist conformity.

- legal divorce if either partner requested it
- recognition of illegitimate children as full citizens
- legalisation of abortion
- the state to be responsible for the raising of children.

These changes derived from the notion that 'love' was a bourgeois concept based on a false view of the relations between the sexes and between parents and children. It was believed that, once such romantic nonsense was recognised for what it was, a structured, ordered society would follow.

However, plans for setting up large boarding schools where children would be permanently removed from their parents and brought up in social equality were soon dropped. It was simply too costly. There were also growing doubts about whether the attack on the family was well advised.

It is always easier to be revolutionary in political matters than in social ones. The family was the traditional social unit in Russia and it proved impossible to replace it simply on the basis of a theory. Where would the carers of the young come from? Were there not deep emotional bonds between parents and children with which it would be dangerous to tamper? It was an area where Marxism–Leninism did not have any workable answers. It is significant that in a later period Stalin strongly disapproved of divorce and insisted on the social value of the family as the basic unit in Soviet society (see page 169).

9 | Lenin's Legacy

Key question
What plans had Lenin made for his succession?

Between 1922 and 1924 Lenin suffered a series of strokes that left him partially paralysed and unable to speak. Because he was so unwell during what proved to be the last two years of his life, he had no opportunity to prepare for his succession. He gave no clear indication as to the type of government that should follow him. There were suggestions that he favoured some form of collective leadership, but this cannot be known for sure since he left no precise instructions. What he did leave was a set of comments on the character of his leading Bolshevik colleagues. These notes, which date from December 1922 and became known as 'Lenin's testament', were highly critical. On the basis of what he said, there was no outstanding colleague worthy of taking up the reins of leadership. He was especially severe on Joseph Stalin (see page 47).

The problem was that Lenin not only failed to name a replacement; he effectively prevented any other choice being made by pointing out the weaknesses in all the other likely candidates, Trotsky, Kamenev, Zinoviev and Bukharin. The result was that at Lenin's death in January 1924 the 'Testament' had still not been made public.

Perhaps aware of the problem that he was leaving the party, Lenin, in his last writings in 1923, warned the comrades against allowing the party and government to lose their revolutionary character by becoming mired in routine and bureaucracy.

'Our state apparatus is so deplorable, so wretched.' It was a sign of his failing grasp that he did not realise that he, more than anyone, was responsible for the growth of the bureaucracy that he now condemned.

Absolutism versus democracy

Key question
How had Lenin exercised power after 1917?

Although Lenin rejected the Russian past, he remained very much its heir. He had as little time for democracy as the tsars had. The rule of the Bolsheviks was a continuation of the absolutist tradition in Russia. The Civil War and the foreign interventions, by intensifying the threat to the Bolshevik government, provided it with the excuse for demanding total conformity from the masses and the party as the price of the Revolution's survival. The forcible dissolution of the Constituent Assembly in 1918, the Terror, and the crushing of the Kronstadt revolt in 1921 were clear proof that Bolshevik control was intended to be absolute. Rather than marking a complete break with the past, 1917 was the replacement of one form of state authoritarianism with another.

Lenin was careful always to describe his policies as democratic, but for him the term had a particular meaning. Democracy was not to be reckoned as a matter of numbers but as a method of party rule. Because the Party was the vehicle of historical change, its role was not to win large-scale backing, but to direct the Revolution from above, regardless of the scale of popular support. 'No revolution', Lenin wrote, 'ever waits for formal majorities'. Moreover, since authority flowed from the centre downwards, it was the role of the leaders to lead, the duty of the party members to follow. The special term describing this was 'democratic centralism'. Lenin defined it in these terms:

> Classes are led by parties, and parties are led by individuals who are called leaders. This is the ABC. The will of a class is sometimes fulfilled by a dictator. Soviet socialist democracy is not in the least incompatible with individual rule and dictatorship. What is necessary is individual rule, the recognition of the dictatorial powers of one man. All phrases about equal rights are nonsense.

Foreign relations

Key question
What problems did Lenin leave the Soviet Union in its relations with the outside world?

A vital factor to stress when assessing Lenin's leadership of Russia is that he regarded himself primarily as an **international revolutionary**. Originally he had expected that the successful Bolshevik seizure of power in October 1917 would be the first stage in a worldwide proletarian uprising. When this proved mistaken, he had to adapt to a situation in which Bolshevik Russia became an isolated revolutionary state, beset by internal and external enemies.

Lenin responded by making another major adjustment to Marxist theory. Marx had taught that proletarian revolution would be an international class movement. Yet the 1917 Revolution had been the work not of a class, but of a party, and had been restricted to one nation. Lenin explained this in terms

Key term

International revolutionary
A Marxist willing to sacrifice national interests for the worldwide rising of the workers.

of a delayed revolution: the international rising would occur at some point in the future; in the interim Soviet Russia must consolidate its own individual revolution. This placed the Bolshevik government and its international agency, the Comintern, in an ambiguous position. What was their essential role to be? At Lenin's death in 1924, this question – whether Soviet Russia's primary aim was world revolution or national survival – was still unresolved.

Authoritarianism

Key question
What were the main features of Lenin's legacy?

Lenin's greatest legacy to Soviet Russia was authoritarianism. He returned Russia to the absolutism that it had known under the tsars. In that sense Bolshevism was a continuation of, not a break with, Russia's past. The main results of Lenin's authoritarian rule after 1917 were:

- The one-party state – all parties other than the Bolsheviks had been outlawed.
- The bureaucratic state – despite the Bolsheviks' original belief in the withering away of the State, central power increased under Lenin and the number of government institutions and officials grew.
- The police state – the *Cheka* was the first of a series of secret police organisations in Soviet Russia whose task was to impose government control over the people.
- The ban on factionalism – prevented criticism of leadership within the party, in effect a prohibition of free speech.
- The destruction of the trade unions – with Lenin's encouragement, Trotsky had destroyed the independence of the trade unions with the result that the Russian workers were entirely at the mercy of the State.
- The politicising of the law – under Lenin the law was not operated as a means of protecting society and the individual but as an extension of political control. He declared that the task of the courts was to apply revolutionary justice. 'The court is not to eliminate terror but to legitimise it'.
- The system of **purges** and show trials which were to become a notorious feature of Stalinism (see page 92) had first been created under Lenin. Outstanding examples of these were the public trials of the Moscow clergy between April and July 1922 and of the SRs between June and August of the same year.

Purge
In theory a means of purifying the Communist Party. In practice, it was a terror tactic by which Stalin removed anyone regarded as a threat to his authority.

Key term

- Concentration camps – at the time of Lenin's death there were 315 such camps. Developed as part of the Red Terror they held White prisoners of war, rebel peasants, Kulaks, and political prisoners, such as SRs, who were considered a threat to Soviet authority.
- Prohibition of public worship – the Orthodox churches had been looted then closed, their clergy arrested or dispersed and atheism adopted as a replacement for religious belief.

The basic apparatus of Stalin's later oppression was in place at Lenin's death.

Summary diagram: Lenin's legacy

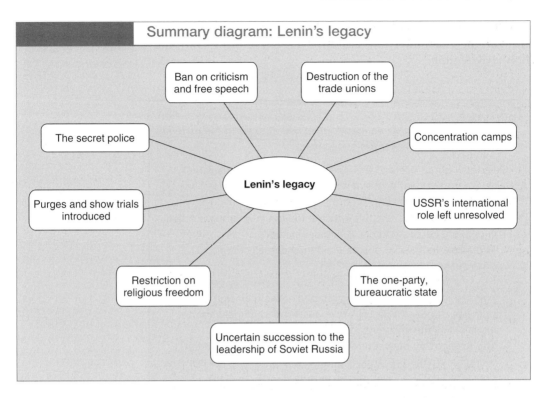

- Ban on criticism and free speech
- Destruction of the trade unions
- The secret police
- Concentration camps
- **Lenin's legacy**
- Purges and show trials introduced
- USSR's international role left unresolved
- Restriction on religious freedom
- The one-party, bureaucratic state
- Uncertain succession to the leadership of Soviet Russia

Study Guide: AS Questions

In the style of AQA

Read the following source and then answer the question that follows.

Adapted from Richard Pipes, The Russian Revolution 1899–1919, *1990.*

The dispersal of the Constituent Assembly was in many respects more important than the October *coup* that had been carried out behind the smokescreen of 'All power to the Soviets.'

Explain briefly what is meant by 'the Soviets' in the context of the October Revolution in Russia. (3 marks)

> *Exam tips*
> *The cross-references are intended to take you straight to the material that will help you to answer the question.*
>
> Here you need to make clear what the Soviets actually were, i.e. the elected councils of soldiers and workers (page 3). Then go on to stress that from April 1917 onwards Lenin had committed the Bolsheviks to the overthrow of the Provisional Government (page 6). However, since his party had too little influence at this stage, he planned to take power under the cloak of the Soviets. Bolshevik infiltration of the Soviets meant that Soviet power would in fact be Bolshevik power. In October when the Bolsheviks took over they did so officially in the name of the Soviets (page 7).

In the style of Edexcel

Why did the allied interventions, 1918–21, fail to bring down the Bolshevik regime?   (15 marks)

Exam tips

The cross-references are intended to take you straight to the material that will help you to answer the question.

- Be careful not to misread this as a question on the Russian Civil War. Clearly that war is relevant and will come into the answer, but the weight of the question is on the allied interventions.
- You must explain the reasons why the foreign interventions failed. The different causes you could explore include:
  - The Allies' motives and aims – did they actually intend to destroy the Bolsheviks (page 13)?
  - How the interventions were carried out – were they centrally planned, co-ordinated and committed? Was their purpose primarily military (page 15)? Your answer should help you to explain why the interventions were ineffective.
  - The relationship between the interventions and the civil war. Were the Whites ever truly aligned with the interventionists in a concerted anti-Red war effort (page 15)?
  - The strengths of the Reds (see page 12).
  - It would give quality to your answer if you were to place the reasons for failure in what you judge to be their order of importance.

Study Guide: A2 Question

In the style of OCR

Study the following four passages **A**, **B**, **C** and **D**, on Lenin and the NEP, and answer the question that follows.

A

From: J. Nettl, The Soviet Achievement, *published in 1967, an historian who argues that, in introducing the NEP, Lenin gave priority to the short-term political needs of the Bolsheviks.*

Whatever the arguments about the theoretical merits of the NEP Lenin, its determined champion, knew that change had become essential and that this froze all arguments in a vacuum of sheer irrelevance. Lenin has often been described as a superb tactician and his enemies have accused him of being willing to sacrifice his principles to practical advantage whenever necessary. By 1921, the maintenance of Soviet power had become the main preoccupation of the Bolsheviks and Lenin certainly felt the regime was in danger unless a period of consolidation and construction took place. He knew better than others to what extent this implied a retreat and he always referred to the NEP as such.

B

From: S. Cohen, Bukharin and the Bolshevik Revolution, *published in 1971, an historian who argues that Lenin believed that War Communism was discredited and that the NEP would be the basis of Soviet policy for many years to come.*

Lenin frankly presented the New Economic Policy to his followers as a retreat born of the failure of War communism. But he tried to legitimise the NEP by stating that it had been adopted 'seriously and for a long time', by describing it as a return to his correct aborted policies of early 1918 and, as if to convince the party it was no longer on the run, by announcing shortly that the retreat had come to an end. Meantime, he began discrediting methods associated with War communism: the time of 'furious assaults' was past; the notion that 'all tasks can be solved by Communist decrees' was 'Communist delusions'. And Lenin revived the concept of gradual reform which he preached until he died.

C

From: O. Figes, A People's Tragedy: The Russian Revolution 1890–24, *published in 1996, an historian who argues that Lenin's support for the NEP was based on a combination of Marxist ideology and the realities of Soviet society.*

As Lenin saw it, the NEP was more than a temporary concession to the market in order to get the country back on its feet. It was a fundamental if rather ill-formulated attempt to redefine the role of socialism in a backward peasant country where, largely as a result of his own party's *coup d'état* [seizure of power by a small group] in 1917, the 'bourgeois revolution' had not been completed. Only 'in countries of developed capitalism' was it possible to make an 'immediate transition to socialism', Lenin had told the Tenth Party Congress. Soviet Russia was thus confronted with the task of 'building communism with bourgeois hands', of basing socialism on the market. Lenin remained full of doubts: at times he expressed fears that the regime would be drowned in a sea of petty peasant capitalism. But in the main he saw the market – regulated by the state and gradually socialised through co-operatives – as the only way to socialism. Whereas the Bolsheviks had up till now lived by the slogan 'the less market, the more socialism', Lenin was moving towards the slogan 'the more market, the more socialism'.

D

From: D. Volkogonov, The Rise and Fall of the Soviet Empire, *published in 1998, a post-Communist Russian historian who argues that Lenin saw NEP as a short-term move, forced on the Bolsheviks by Soviet Russia's economic crisis.*

Reckless nationalisation, constant requisitioning and confiscation proved unable to feed starving Russia. With gritted teeth, therefore, Lenin recognised the disastrous consequences of Bolshevik practice, heeded the advice of more sober heads in his inner circle and softened the policy towards private ownership. He made it perfectly plain, however, that the New Economic Policy was 'a definite gesture, a definite movement. We are now withdrawing, as if retreating, but we are doing it in order to retreat and then take a run and leap forward more strongly'. Lenin's view of the NEP was purely tactical. He wrote on 3 March 1922, 'it would be the biggest mistake to think that the NEP put an end to terror. We shall return to terror and economic terror'. But to give him his due, when he faced the total collapse of War communism, Lenin was able to display astonishing tactical ability by rejecting – temporarily – what he had held sacred.

Using these four passages and your own knowledge, explain why the Communists' adoption of the NEP in 1921 has caused controversy amongst historians. (30 marks)

Source: OCR, June 2002

Exam tips

The cross-references are intended to take you straight to the material that will help you to answer the question.

What the four passages show are the differences among four modern historians regarding NEP. Your task is to evaluate the views offered by the passages.

- Passage A, written by someone sympathetic to Russian Communism, sees Lenin as adopting NEP out of necessity to meet the immediate problems confronting Russia in 1921. It was a practical not an ideological move.
- Passage B, in contrast, regards NEP as a permanent move on Lenin's part. He intended it to be part of a calmer, more considered approach to Russia's problems rather than the hectic, hurried dash of War Communism.
- Passage C also regards NEP as more than a temporary measure. Lenin was a realist who wanted to combine socialist ideals with the market. NEP was Lenin's intended way of advancing socialism by using certain features of the capitalist system that were known to work.
- Volkogonov in Passage D differs. He interprets NEP as something forced on Lenin rather than chosen by him.

These are the types of distinction to make in your reading of the extracts. Where your own knowledge comes in is in putting NEP in its historical perspective. You can measure the views of the four writers against the background to NEP. Features to highlight might include:

- The terrible famine of the early 1920s (see page 25).
- The resistance to War Communism and Bolshevism as shown in the Kronstadt Rising – for Lenin a 'lightning flash' (see page 29).
- The ban on factionalism which accompanied the introduction of NEP at the Tenth Party Congress (see page 31).

How do these factors support or challenge each of the passages? Evaluate the passages by making cross-references between them and judging them in the light of your own knowledge of NEP. And remember – there is a controversy among historians over NEP because there was a Bolshevik controversy over it in the first place. Did NEP represent a betrayal or an advance of Communism?

2 Stalin's Rise to Power 1924–9

POINTS TO CONSIDER

When Lenin died in 1924 he left no obvious successor. Few Russian Communists gave thought to Stalin as a likely leader. Yet five years later, after a bitter power struggle, it was Stalin who had outmanoeuvred his rivals and established his authority over the party and the nation. How he achieved this is the subject of this chapter whose main themes are:

- The roots of Stalin's power
- The power struggle after Lenin's death
- The defeat of Trotsky and the Left
- The defeat of the Right

Key dates

1924	Death of Lenin – Politburo declared USSR to be ruled by a collective leadership
1925	Trotsky lost his position as War Commissar Kamenev and Zinoviev headed 'the United Opposition'
1926	Trotsky joined Kamenev and Zinoviev in the Left political bloc, which was defeated by Stalin's supporters
1927	Stalin persuaded Congress to expel Trotsky from the CPSU
1928	Stalin attacked the Right (led by Tomsky, Bukharin and Rykov) over agricultural policy
1929	The leading figures on the Right finally defeated by Stalin and demoted in the CPSU Trotsky exiled from the USSR

1 | The Roots of Stalin's Power

Most historians used to accept that Stalin's pre-1924 career was unimportant. A description of him by **Nicolai Sukhanov**, dating from 1922, as a 'dull, grey blank', was regarded as accurate. But recent research in the Soviet archives, which were opened to scholars after the collapse of the USSR in the early 1990s, has indicated that the notion of Stalin as a nonentity is far from the truth. A leading British authority, Robert Service, has shown that Stalin was very highly regarded by Lenin and played a central role in the Bolshevik Party.

Key question
How significant was Stalin's career before 1924?

Nicolai Sukhanov
An anti-Bolshevik who wrote one of the most influential accounts of the Revolution.

Key term

Before 1917 the Bolshevik Party had been only a few thousand strong and Lenin had known the great majority of members personally. He had been impressed by Stalin's organising ability and willingness to obey orders. He once described him as 'that wonderful Georgian', a reference to his work as an agitator among the non-Russian peoples. With Lenin's backing Stalin had risen by 1912 to become one of the six members of the Central Committee, the policy-making body of the Bolshevik Party. He had also helped to found the Party's newspaper, *Pravda*.

The October Revolution and Civil War

Having spent the war years, 1914–17, in exile in Siberia, Stalin returned to Petrograd in March 1917. His role in the October Revolution is difficult to disentangle. Official accounts, written after he had taken power, were a mixture of distortion and invention, with any unflattering episodes totally omitted. What is reasonably certain is that Stalin was loyal to Lenin after the latter's return to Petrograd in April 1917. Lenin instructed the Bolsheviks to abandon all co-operation with other parties and to devote themselves to preparing for a seizure of power. As a Leninist, Stalin was opposed to the **'October deserters'**, such as Kamenev and Zinoviev (see page 60).

During the period of crisis and civil war that accompanied the efforts of the Bolsheviks to consolidate their authority after 1917, Stalin's non-Russian background proved invaluable. His knowledge of the minority peoples of the old Russian Empire led to his being appointed **Commissar for Nationalities**. Lenin had believed that Stalin, a Georgian, was particularly well qualified for this role. As Commissar, Stalin became the ruthless Bolshevik organiser for the whole of the Caucasus region during the Civil War from 1918 to 1920. This led to a number of disputes with Trotsky, the Bolshevik Commissar for War. Superficially the quarrels were about strategy and tactics, but at a deeper level they were a clash of wills. They proved to be the beginning of a deep personal rivalry between Stalin and Trotsky.

Lenin's testament

Although Stalin had been totally loyal to Lenin, there were two particular occasions when he had aroused Lenin's anger. After the Civil War had ended, Stalin, despite being a Georgian, had been off-hand and dismissive in discussions with the representatives from Georgia. Lenin, anxious to gain the support of the national minorities for the Bolshevik regime, had to intervene personally to prevent the Georgians leaving in a huff. On another occasion, in a more directly personal matter, Lenin learned from his wife, Krupskaya, that in a row over the Georgian question Stalin had subjected her to 'a storm of the coarsest abuse', telling her to keep her nose out of State affairs, and calling her 'a whore'. The very day that Lenin was informed of this, 22 December 1922, he dictated his testament as a direct response.

Key terms

October deserters
Those Bolsheviks who in October 1917, believing that the Party was not yet strong enough, had advised against a Bolshevik rising.

Commissar for Nationalities
Minister responsible for liaising with the non-Russian national minorities.

His main criticism read: 'Comrade Stalin, since becoming General Secretary of the Party in 1922, has concentrated enormous power in his hands; and I am not sure he always knows how to exercise that power with sufficient caution.' In a later post-script, Lenin again stressed Stalin's rudeness, which was unacceptable in a General Secretary who had to be a person of tact so as to prevent divisions developing within the party. Lenin went on to urge the comrades 'to think about ways of removing Comrade Stalin from that position.' But this was not done. Lenin was too ill during the last year of his life to be politically active. At his death in January 1924, he had still not taken any formal steps to remove Stalin, and the 'Testament' had not been made public.

Death of Lenin: 21 January 1924

Key date

Profile: Joseph Stalin (career to 1924)

1879	– Born in Georgia
1899	– His revolutionary activities led to expulsion from Tiflis seminary
1905	– Met Lenin for first time
1912	– Adopted the name Stalin
	– Became a member of the Central Committee of the Bolshevik Party
	– Helped to found *Pravda*
1914–17	– In exile in Siberia
1917	– Returned to Petrograd
	– People's Commissar for Nationalities
1919	– Liaison Officer between Politburo and Orgburo
	– Head of the Workers' and Peasants' Inspectorate
1922	– General Secretary of the Communist (Bolshevik) Party
1924	– Delivered the oration at Lenin's funeral

Stalin, meaning 'man of steel', was not his real name. It was simply the last in a series of aliases that Joseph Vissarionovich Djugashvili adopted in order to avoid detection as a revolutionary. He was born in Georgia, a rugged province in the south of the Russian Empire, renowned for the fierceness of its people. Blood feuds and family vendettas were common. Georgia had only recently been incorporated into the Russian Empire. Tsarist government officials often wrote in exasperation of the difficulties of trying to control a savage people who refused to accept their subordination to Russia.

Stalin came from Georgian stock. His drunken father eked out a miserable existence as a cobbler and the family appears to have lived in constant poverty. There have been suggestions that both Stalin's admiration of things Russian and his contempt for middle-class intellectuals derived from a sense of resentment over his humble Georgian origins. Stalin's mother was a particularly devout woman and it was largely through her influence that her son was enrolled as a student in a Georgian-Orthodox seminary in Tbilisi (Tiflis). This did not show religious fervour on Stalin's part. The fact was that at this time in imperial Russia attendance at a church academy was the only way to obtain a Russian-style education, an essential requirement for anyone from the provinces who had ambition. Stalin seems to have been attracted less by theology than by the political ideas with which he came into contact.

In the seminary records for 1899 there is an entry beside Stalin's name that reads 'expelled for not attending lessons – reasons unknown'. We now know the reasons; he had become involved in the Georgian resistance movement, agitating against tsarist control. His anti-government activities drew him into the Social Democratic Workers' Party. From the time of his expulsion from the seminary to the Revolution of 1917 Stalin was a committed follower of Lenin. He threw himself into the task of raising funds for the Bolsheviks; his specialities were bank hold-ups and train robberies. By 1917 he had been arrested eight times and had been sentenced to various periods of imprisonment and exile. Afterwards he tended to despise those revolutionaries who had escaped such experiences by fleeing to the relative comfort of self-imposed exile abroad.

Stalin's position in 1924

Key question
How had Stalin been able to rise up the Bolshevik ranks?

In the uncertain atmosphere that followed Lenin's death, a number of pieces of luck helped Stalin promote his own claims. However, it would be wrong to ascribe his success wholly to good fortune. The luck had to be used. Stalin may have lacked brilliance, but he did not lack ability. His particular qualities of perseverance and willingness to undertake laborious administrative work were ideally suited to the times.

The government of Soviet Russia, as it had developed by 1924, had two main features: the **Council of Peoples' Commissars**, and the **Secretariat**. Both bodies were staffed and controlled by the Bolshevik Party. It has to be stressed that the vital characteristic of this governmental system was that the Party ruled. By 1922 Soviet Russia was a one-party state. Membership of that one party was essential for all who held government posts at whatever level.

As the government grew in scope, certain posts, which initially had not been considered especially significant, began to provide their holders with the levers of power. This had not been the intention, but was the unforeseen result of the emerging pattern of Bolshevik rule. It was in this context that Stalin's previous appointments to key posts in both government and Party proved vital. These had been:

Key terms

Council of Peoples' Commissars
A cabinet of ministers, responsible for creating government policies.

Secretariat
A form of civil service, responsible for carrying out those policies.

- People's Commissar for Nationalities (1917)
  In this post Stalin was in charge of the officials in the many regions and republics that made up the USSR (the official title of the Soviet state after 1922).

- Liaison Officer between Politburo and Orgburo (1919)
  This post placed him in a unique position to monitor both the Party's policy and the Party's personnel.
- Head of the Workers' and Peasants' Inspectorate (1919)
  This position entitled him to oversee the work of all government departments.
- General Secretary of the Communist Party (1922)
  In this position, he recorded and conveyed Party policy.
  This enabled him to build up personal files on all the members of the Party. Nothing of note happened that Stalin did not know about.

Stalin became the indispensable link in the chain of command in the Communist Party and the Soviet government. Above all, what these posts gave him was the power of **patronage**. He used this authority to place his own supporters in key positions. Since they then owed their place to him, Stalin could count on their support in the voting in the various committees which made up the organisation of the party and the government.

Such were the levers in Stalin's possession during the party in-fighting over the succession to Lenin. No other contender came anywhere near matching Stalin in his hold on the party machine. Whatever the ability of the individuals or groups who opposed him, he could always outvote and outmanoeuvre them.

Patronage
The right to appoint individuals to official posts in the Party and government.

CPSU
The Communist Party of the Soviet Union

The Lenin enrolment

Stalin had also gained advantage from recent changes in the structure of the Communist Party. Between 1923 and 1925 the Party had set out to increase the number of true proletarians in its ranks. This was known as 'the Lenin enrolment'. It resulted in the membership of the **CPSU** rising from 340,000 in 1922 to 600,000 by 1925.

The new members were predominantly poorly educated and politically unsophisticated, but they were fully aware that the many privileges which came with party membership depended on their being loyal to those who had first invited them into the Bolshevik ranks. The task of vetting 'the Lenin enrolment' had fallen largely to the officials in the Secretariat who worked directly under Stalin as General Secretary. In this way, the expansion of the Party added to his growing power of patronage. It provided him with a reliable body of votes in the various Party committees at local and central level.

Key question
What was the significance for Stalin of 'the Lenin enrolment'?

Attack on factionalism

Another lasting feature of Lenin's period that proved of great value to Stalin was what had become known as the 'attack upon factionalism'. This referred to Lenin's condemnation in 1921 of divisions within the Party (see page 31). What this rejection of 'factionalism' effectively did was to frustrate any serious attempt to criticise Party decisions or policies. It became extremely difficult to mount any form of legitimate opposition within the CPSU. Stalin benefited directly from the ban on criticism of the

Key question
How did Lenin's 'attack upon factionalism' help Stalin?

Party line. The charge of 'factionalism' provided him with a ready weapon for resisting challenges to the authority he had begun to exercise.

Key question
How did the 'Lenin legacy' benefit Stalin?

The Lenin legacy

There was an accompanying factor that legitimised Stalin's position. Stalin became heir to the 'Lenin legacy'. By this is meant the tradition of authority and leadership that Lenin had established during his lifetime, and the veneration in which he was held after his death. It is no exaggeration to say that in the eyes of the Communist Party, Lenin became a god. His actions and decisions became unchallengeable, and all arguments and disputes within the Party were settled by reference to his statements and writings. Lenin became the measure of the correctness of Soviet theory and practice. Soviet Communism became Leninism. After 1924, if a Party member could assume the mantle of Lenin and appear to carry on Lenin's work, he would establish a formidable claim to power. This is exactly what Stalin began to do.

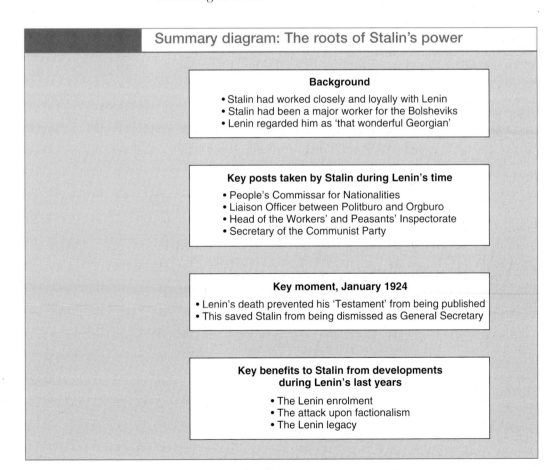

Summary diagram: The roots of Stalin's power

Background
- Stalin had worked closely and loyally with Lenin
- Stalin had been a major worker for the Bolsheviks
- Lenin regarded him as 'that wonderful Georgian'

Key posts taken by Stalin during Lenin's time
- People's Commissar for Nationalities
- Liaison Officer between Politburo and Orgburo
- Head of the Workers' and Peasants' Inspectorate
- Secretary of the Communist Party

Key moment, January 1924
- Lenin's death prevented his 'Testament' from being published
- This saved Stalin from being dismissed as General Secretary

Key benefits to Stalin from developments during Lenin's last years
- The Lenin enrolment
- The attack upon factionalism
- The Lenin legacy

2 | The Power Struggle after Lenin's Death

Lenin's funeral

Immediately after Lenin's death, the **Politburo** publicly proclaimed their intention to continue as a collective leadership, but behind the scenes the competition for individual authority had already begun. In the manoeuvring, Stalin gained an advantage by being the one to deliver the oration at Lenin's funeral. The sight of Stalin as leading mourner suggested a continuity between him and Lenin, an impression heightened by the contents of his speech in which, in the name of the Party, he humbly dedicated himself to follow in the tradition of the departed leader:

> In leaving us, Comrade Lenin commanded us to keep the unity of our Party. We swear to thee, Comrade Lenin, to honour thy command. In leaving us, Comrade Lenin ordered us to maintain and strengthen the dictatorship of the proletariat. We swear to thee, Comrade Lenin, to exert our full strength in honouring thy command.

Since Stalin's speech was the first crucial move to promote himself as Lenin's successor, it was to be expected that Trotsky, his chief rival, would try to counter it in some way. Yet Trotsky was not even present at the funeral. It was a very conspicuous absence, and it is difficult to understand why Trotsky did not appreciate the importance of appearances following Lenin's death in January 1924. Initially he, not Stalin, had been offered the opportunity of making the major speech at the funeral. But not only did he decline this, he also failed to attend the ceremony itself. His excuse was that Stalin had given him the wrong date, but this simply was not true. The documentation shows that he learned the real date early enough for him to have reached Moscow with time to spare. Instead he continued his planned journey and was on holiday on the day of the funeral. This was hardly the image of a dedicated Leninist.

What makes Trotsky's behaviour even odder is that he was well aware of the danger Stalin represented. In 1924 he prophesied that Stalin would become 'the dictator of the USSR'. He also gave a remarkable analysis of the basis of Stalin's power in the Party:

> He is needed by all of them; by the tired radicals, by the bureaucrats, by the Nepmen, the upstarts, by all the worms that are crawling out of the upturned soil of the manured revolution. He knows how to meet them on their own ground, he speaks their language and he knows how to lead them. He has the deserved reputation of an old revolutionary. He has will and daring. Right now he is organising around himself the sneaks of the Party, the artful dodgers.

This was a bitter but strikingly accurate assessment of how Stalin had made a large part of the Party dependent on him. But logically such awareness on Trotsky's part should have made him eager to prevent Stalin from stealing an advantage. His reluctance to act is a fascinating feature of Trotsky's puzzling character.

Key question
What were Stalin's advantages in his leadership struggle with Trotsky?

Politburo
The inner cabinet of the ruling Central Committee of CPSU – at the time of Lenin's death it consisted of Trotsky, Stalin, Rykov, Tomsky, Kamenev and Zinoviev.

Key term

Key question
What were Trotsky's
weaknesses?

Trotsky's character

Trotsky had a complex personality. He was one of those figures in history who may be described as having been their own worst enemy. Despite his many gifts and intellectual brilliance, he had serious weaknesses that undermined his chances of success. At times, he was unreasonably self-assured; at other critical times, he suffered from diffidence and lack of judgement. An example of this had occurred earlier, at the time of Stalin's mishandling of the Georgian question. Lenin's anger with Stalin had offered Trotsky a golden opportunity for undermining Stalin's position, but for some reason Trotsky had declined to attack.

A possible clue to his reluctance is that he felt inhibited by his Jewishness. Trotsky knew that, in a nation such as Russia with its deeply ingrained **anti-Semitism**, his race made him an outsider. A remarkable example of his awareness of this occurred in 1917, when Lenin offered him the post of Deputy Chairman of the Soviet government. Trotsky rejected it on the grounds that his appointment would be an embarrassment to Lenin and the government. 'It would', he said, 'give enemies grounds for claiming that the country was ruled by a Jew'. It may be that similar reasoning in January 1924 allowed Stalin to gain an advantage over him.

Key date
Lenin's Testament
suppressed:
May 1924

Suppression of Lenin's testament

A dangerous hurdle in Stalin's way was Lenin's 'Testament'. If it were to be published, Stalin would be gravely damaged by its contents. However, here, as so often during this period, fortune favoured him. Had the document been made public, not only would Lenin's criticisms of Stalin have been revealed, but also those concerning Trotsky, Zinoviev and Kamenev. Nearly all the members of the Politburo had reason for suppressing the 'Testament'.

When the Central Committee was presented with the document in May 1924, they realised that it was too damning broadly to be used exclusively against any one individual. They agreed to its being shelved indefinitely. Trotsky, for obvious personal reasons, went along with the decision, but in doing so he was declining yet another opportunity to challenge Stalin's right to power. In fact it was Trotsky, not Stalin, whom the Politburo regarded as the greater danger.

Key terms

Anti-Semitism
Hatred of the
Jewish race – for
centuries Russia
had been notorious
for the virulence of
her anti-Jewish
attitude and
policies.

Triumvirate
A ruling or
influential bloc of
three persons.

Attitudes towards Trotsky

Kamenev and Zinoviev joined Stalin in an unofficial **triumvirate** within the Politburo. Their aim was to isolate Trotsky by exploiting his unpopularity with large sections of the Party. The 'Lenin enrolment' helped them in this. The new proletarian members were hardly the type of men to be impressed by the cultured Trotsky. The seemingly down-to-earth Stalin was much more to their liking.

The attitude of Party members towards Trotsky was an important factor in the weakening of his position. Colleagues tended to regard Trotsky as dangerously ambitious and Stalin as reliably self-effacing. This was because Trotsky was flamboyant

Profile: Lev Trotsky 1879–1940

1879	– Born into a Ukrainian Jewish family
1898	– Convicted of revolutionary activities and exiled to Siberia
1902	– Adopted the name Trotsky
	– Escaped from exile and joined Lenin in London
1903	– Sided with the Mensheviks in the SD split
1905	– Became Chairman of St Petersburg Soviet
1906	– Exiled again to Siberia
1907	– Escaped again and fled abroad
1907–17	– Lived in various European countries and the USA
1917	– Returned to Petrograd after the February Revolution
	– The principal organiser of the October *coup*
	– Appointed Foreign Affairs Commissar
1918	– Negotiated the Brest-Litovsk Treaty
1918–20	– As War Commissar, created the Red Army
1921	– Suppressed the Kronstadt Rising
	– Destroyed the trade unions in Russia
1924–27	– Outmanoeuvred in the power struggle with Stalin
1927	– Sentenced to internal exile at Alma Ata
1929	– Banished from USSR
1929–40	– Lived in various countries
	– Wrote on revolutionary theory, in opposition to Stalin
1940	– Assassinated in Mexico on Stalin's orders

Early career

Trotsky's real name was Leon (Lev) Bronstein. He was born into a Jewish landowning family in the Ukraine in 1879. Rebellious from an early age, he sided with the peasants on his family's estate. Yet, like Lenin, he rejected '**economism**', the attempt to raise the standards of peasants and workers by improving their conditions. He wanted to intensify class warfare by exploiting grievances, not to lessen it by introducing reforms.

Key term

Economism
Putting the improvement of the workers' conditions before the need for revolution.

As a revolutionary, Trotsky's sympathies lay with the Mensheviks and it was as a Menshevik that he became president of the St Petersburg Soviet during the 1905 Revolution. His activities led to his arrest and exile. Between 1907 and 1917 he lived in a variety of foreign countries, developing his theory of 'permanent revolution' (see page 58).

Following the collapse of tsardom in the February Revolution, Trotsky returned to Petrograd and immediately joined the Bolshevik Party. He became chairman of the Petrograd Soviet and it was from this position that he organised the Bolshevik rising, which overthrew the Provisional Government in October 1917.

Commissar for Foreign Affairs

In the Bolshevik government that then took over, Trotsky became Commissar for Foreign Affairs. He was the chief negotiator in the Russo-German talks that resulted in Russia's withdrawal from the war in 1918 under the Brest-Litovsk Treaty.

Commissar for War

He then became Commissar for War, and achieved what was arguably the greatest success of his career, the victory of the Red Army in the Civil War of 1918–20. As a hardliner, Trotsky fully supported Lenin's repressive policy of War Communism. He plotted the destruction of the Russian trade unions, and in 1921 ordered the suppression of the rebellious Kronstadt workers.

Exile

Trotsky was never fully accepted by his fellow Bolsheviks, which enabled Stalin to isolate him after 1924. In 1929 Trotsky was exiled from the USSR. He spent his last 11 years in a variety of countries. In 1939 he founded the Fourth International, a movement of anti-Stalin Marxists drawn from some 30 countries. Trotsky's end came in 1940 in Mexico City, when a Soviet agent acting on Stalin's direct orders killed him by driving an ice-pick into his head.

and brilliant, while his rival was unspectacular and methodical. Trotsky was the type of person who attracted either admiration or distaste, but seldom loyalty. That was why he lacked a genuine following. It is true that he was highly regarded by the Red Army, whose creator he had been, but this was never matched by any comparable political support. Trotsky failed to build a power base within the Party. This invariably gave him the appearance of an outsider.

Adding to his difficulties in this regard was the doubt about his commitment to Bolshevism. Until 1917, as Lenin had noted in his 'Testament', Trotsky had belonged to the Mensheviks. This led to the suspicion that his conversion had been a matter of expediency rather than conviction. Many of the old-guard Bolsheviks regarded Trotsky as a Menshevik turncoat who could not be trusted.

Key question
What did Trotsky mean by 'bureaucratisation'?

Bureaucratisation

Despite the attacks upon him, Trotsky attempted to fight back. The issue he chose was bureaucratisation. He defined this as the abandonment of genuine discussion within the party and the growth in the centralised power of the Secretariat, which was able to make decisions and operate policies without reference to ordinary Party members.

Trotsky had good reason to think he had chosen a powerful cause. After all, Lenin himself in his last writings had warned the Party against the creeping dangers of bureaucracy. Accordingly, Trotsky pressed his views in the Party Congresses and in the meetings of the Central Committee and the Politburo. His condemnation of the growth of bureaucracy was coupled with an appeal for a return to **'Party democracy'**. He expanded his arguments in a series of essays, the most controversial of which was *Lessons of October*, in which he criticised Kamenev and Zinoviev for their past disagreements with Lenin. The assault was

Key term

Party democracy
Trotsky was not pressing for democracy in the full sense of all party members having a say. His aim was to condemn the centralising of power from which Stalin had gained such benefit.

ill judged, since it invited retaliation in kind. Trotsky's Menshevik past and his divergence from Leninism were highlighted in a number of books and pamphlets, most notably Kamenev's, *Lenin or Trotsky*.

As a contribution to the power struggle Trotsky's campaign for greater party democracy was misjudged. Trotsky's censures on bureaucracy left Stalin largely unscathed. In trying to expose bureaucratic tendencies in the Communist Party, Trotsky overlooked the essential fact that Bolshevik rule since 1917 had always been a bureaucracy. It was because the Soviet state functioned as a bureaucracy that Party members received privileges in political and public life. Trotsky's line was hardly likely to gain significant support from Party members who had a vested interest in bureaucracy.

The NEP

Trotsky's reputation was further damaged by the issue of the New Economic Policy (see page 30). NEP went back to 1921 when Lenin had introduced it as a replacement for the severe economic controls, known as War Communism (see page 23). Lenin admitted that NEP was a relaxing of strict socialism, but had indicated that he regarded it as a temporary measure.

Key question
How was Trotsky weakened by the issue of NEP?

However, at the time of his death in 1924 the question was already being asked as to whether the NEP was to last indefinitely. The Party members who were unhappy with it saw its continuation as a betrayal of revolutionary principle. They objected to the policy of giving preferential treatment to the peasantry. The peasants, they argued, were being allowed to slow the pace of Soviet Russia's advance as a truly proletarian state, which had been the whole object of the 1917 Revolution. Critics of the NEP were broadly referred to as **Left Communists**, while those who supported it were known as **Right Communists**.

It is important not to exaggerate the difference of principle between Left and Right over NEP. Although fierce disputes were to arise, initially the disagreement was simply about timing: how long should the NEP be allowed to run?

However, in the power struggle of the 1920s these minor differences deepened into questions of political correctness and Party loyalty. A rival's attitude towards the NEP might be a weakness to be exploited; if it could be established that his views indicated deviant Marxist thinking it became possible to destroy his position in the Party.

Stalin did precisely this. He used Trotsky's attitude towards the NEP as a way of undermining him. Trotsky had backed Lenin in 1921, but there were strong rumours that his support had not been genuine and that he regarded NEP as a deviation from true socialism. It was certainly the case that in 1923 Trotsky had led a group of Party members, known from their number as 'the Platform of 46', in openly criticising *Gosplan* for its 'flagrant errors of economic policy'. Trotsky's charge was that the government had placed the interests of the Nepmen above those of the Revolution and the Russian people. He urged a return to a

Key terms

Left Communists
Those members of the party who opposed the continuation of NEP.

Right Communists
Those members of the party who favoured the continuation of NEP.

Gosplan
The government body responsible for national economic planning.

much tighter state control of industry and warned that under NEP the revolutionary gains made under War Communism would be lost.

Stalin was quick to suggest to Party members, who already looked on Trotsky as a disruptive force, that he was, indeed, suspect. The interesting point here is that Stalin's own view of NEP was far from clear at this stage. He had loyally supported Lenin's introduction of it in 1921, but had given little indication as to whether, or for how long, it should be retained after Lenin's death. He preferred to keep his own views to himself and play on the differences between his colleagues.

Modernisation

Key question
Why was there a Left–Right division over the question of how the USSR should modernise?

The NEP debate was one aspect of the question of how the Soviet Union should plan for the future. This would have been a demanding issue regardless of whether there had been a power struggle. What the rivalry for leadership did was to intensify the argument. The USSR was a poor country. If it were to modernise and overcome its poverty it would have to industrialise. Recent history had shown that a strong industrial base was an absolute essential for a modern state and there was little disagreement among Soviet Communists about that. The quarrel was not over whether the USSR should industrialise, but over how and at what speed.

History had further shown that the industrial expansion that had taken place in the previous century, in such countries as Germany and Britain, had relied on a ready supply of resources and the availability of capital for investment. Russia was rich in natural resources, but these had yet to be effectively exploited, and it certainly did not possess large amounts of capital. Nor could it easily borrow any; after 1917 the Bolsheviks had rejected capitalist methods of finance. Moreover, even if the Bolsheviks had been willing to borrow, there were few countries after 1917 willing to risk the dangers of investing in revolutionary Russia.

The only usable resource, therefore, was the Russian people themselves, 80 per cent of whom were peasants. If the Soviet Union was to industrialise, it would have to be done by persuading or forcing the peasant population to produce a food surplus that could then be sold abroad to raise capital for industrial investment. Both Left and Right agreed that this was the only solution, but, whereas the Right were content to rely on persuasion, the Left demanded that the peasantry be forced into line.

It was Trotsky who most clearly represented the view of the Left on this. He wanted the peasants to be coerced into co-operating. However, for him the industrialisation debate was secondary to the far more demanding question of Soviet Russia's role as the organiser of international revolution. His views on this created a wide divergence between him and Stalin, expressed in terms of a clash between the opposed notions of 'Permanent Revolution' and 'Socialism in One Country'.

'Permanent Revolution'

What inspired Trotsky's politics was his belief in 'Permanent Revolution' made up of a number of key ideas:

Key question
What were the essential features of Trotsky's concept of 'Permanent Revolution'?

- Revolution was not as a single event but a permanent (continuous) process in which risings took place from country to country.
- The events in Russia since 1917 were simply a first step towards a worldwide proletarian revolution.
- Individual nations did not matter. The interests of the international working class were paramount.
- True revolutionary socialism could be achieved in the USSR only if an international uprising took place.

Trotsky believed that the USSR could not survive alone in a hostile world. With her vast peasant population and undeveloped proletariat, Russia would prove 'incapable of holding her own against conservative Europe'. He contended that the immediate task of the USSR was 'to export revolution'. That was the only way to guarantee its survival.

It should be stressed that at no point did Trotsky call for the Soviet Union to be sacrificed to some theoretical notion of world revolution. His argument was an opposite one; unless there was international revolution the Soviet Union would go under. Stalin, however, ignored the subtlety of his opponent's reasoning. He chose to portray Trotsky as someone intent on damaging the Soviet Union.

'Socialism in One Country'

Stalin countered Trotsky's notion of 'Permanent Revolution' with his own concept of 'Socialism in One Country'. He meant by this that the nation's first task was to consolidate Lenin's revolution and the rule of the CPSU by turning the USSR into a modern state, capable of defending itself against its internal and external enemies. The Soviet Union, therefore must work:

Key question
What were the essential features of Stalin's 'Socialism in One Country'?

- To overcome its present agricultural and industrial problems by its own unaided efforts.
- To go on to build a modern state, the equal of any nation in the world.
- To make the survival of the Soviet Union an absolute priority, even if this meant suspending efforts to create international revolution.

The contrast between this programme and Trotsky's was used by Stalin to characterise his rival as an enemy of the Soviet Union. Trotsky's ideas were condemned as an affront to Lenin and the Bolshevik Revolution. An image was created of Trotsky as an isolated figure, a posturing Jewish intellectual, whose vague notions of international revolution threatened the security of the Soviet Union.

Trotsky's position was further weakened by the fact that throughout the 1920s the Soviet Union had a constant fear of invasion by the combined capitalist nations. Although this fear was ill-founded, the tense atmosphere it created made Trotsky's notion of the USSR's engaging in foreign revolutionary wars appear even more irresponsible. A number of historians, including E.H. Carr and Isaac Deutscher, have remarked on Stalin's ability to rally support and silence opponents at critical moments by assuming the role of the great Russian patriot concerned to save the nation from the grave dangers that threatened it.

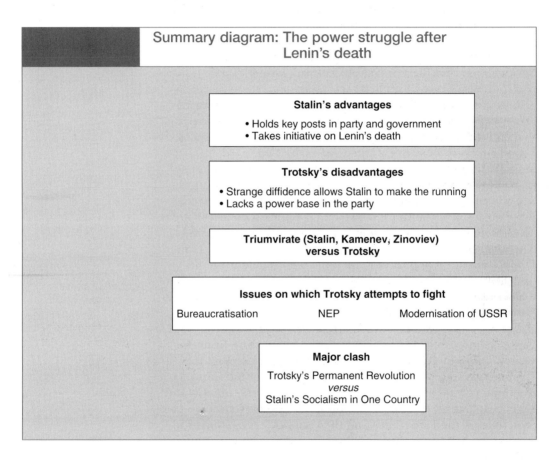

Summary diagram: The power struggle after Lenin's death

Stalin's advantages
- Holds key posts in party and government
- Takes initiative on Lenin's death

Trotsky's disadvantages
- Strange diffidence allows Stalin to make the running
- Lacks a power base in the party

Triumvirate (Stalin, Kamenev, Zinoviev) versus Trotsky

Issues on which Trotsky attempts to fight

Bureaucratisation   NEP   Modernisation of USSR

Major clash
Trotsky's Permanent Revolution
versus
Stalin's Socialism in One Country

Key question
What were the basic weaknesses of the Left in their challenge to Stalin?

Key term

'To deliver the votes'
To use one's control of the party machine to gain majority support in key votes.

3 | The Defeat of Trotsky and the Left

Trotsky's failure in the propaganda war of the 1920s meant that he was in no position to persuade either the Politburo or the Central Committee to vote for his proposals. Stalin's ability **'to deliver the votes'** in the crucial divisions was decisive. Following a vote against him in the 1925 Party Congress, Trotsky was relieved of his position as Commissar for War. Lev Kamenev and Grigory Zinoviev, the respective Chairmen of the Moscow and

Leningrad Soviets, played a key part in this. They used their influence over the local Party organisations to ensure that it was a pro-Stalin, anti-Trotsky, Congress that gathered.

Kamenev and Zinoviev

Kamenev and Zinoviev had been motivated by a personal dislike of Trotsky, who at various times had tried to embarrass them by reminding the Party of their failure to support Lenin in October 1917. Now it was their turn to be ousted. With Trotsky weakened, Stalin turned to the problem of how to deal with these two key figures, whom he now saw as potential rivals.

In the event, they created a trap for themselves. In 1925 Kamenev and Zinoviev, worried by the USSR's economic backwardness, publicly stated that it would require the victory of proletarian revolution in the capitalist nations in order for the Soviet Union to achieve socialism. Zinoviev wrote:

> When the time comes for the revolution in other countries and the proletariat comes to our aid, then we shall again go over to the offensive. For the time being we have only a little breathing space.

He called for the NEP to be abandoned, for restrictions to be reimposed on the peasants, and for enforced industrialisation.

It was understandable that Kamenev and Zinoviev, respective party bosses in the Soviet Union's only genuinely industrial areas, Moscow and Leningrad, should have thought in these terms. Their viewpoint formed the basis of what was termed the **United Opposition** but it appeared to be indistinguishable from old Trotskyism. It was no surprise, therefore, when Trotsky joined his former opponents in 1926 to form a 'Trotskyite–Kamenevite–Zinovievite' opposition bloc.

Again, Stalin's control of the Party machine proved critical. The Party Congress declined to be influenced by pressure from the United Opposition. Stalin's chief backers among the Right Communists were Aleksei Rykov, the Chairman of the Central Committee, Mikhail Tomsky, the leader of the trade unions, and Nicolai Bukharin, the editor of *Pravda* and the outstanding economist in the Party. They and their supporters combined to outvote the bloc. Kamenev and Zinoviev were dismissed from their posts as Soviet Chairmen, to be replaced by two of Stalin's staunchest allies, Molotov in Moscow and Kirov in Leningrad. Soon afterwards, Trotsky was expelled from both the Politburo and the Central Committee.

Trotsky exiled

Trotsky still did not admit defeat. In 1927, on the tenth anniversary of the Bolshevik rising, he tried to rally support in a direct challenge to Stalin's authority. Even fewer members of Congress than before were prepared to side with him and he was again outvoted. His complete failure led to the acceptance by Congress of Stalin's proposal that Trotsky be expelled from the

Key date

CPSU Congress votes against Trotsky: 1925

Key terms

Leningrad
Petrograd had been renamed in Lenin's honour.

United Opposition
The group led by Kamenev and Zinoviev, sometimes known as the New Opposition, who called for an end to NEP and the adoption of an industrialisation programme.

Key dates

Trotsky dismissed from Central Committee: October 1927

Trotsky dismissed from Communist Party: November 1927

Trotsky sent into internal exile: January 1928

Trotsky exiled from the Soviet Union: January 1929

Party altogether. An internal exile order against him in 1927 was followed two years later by total exile from the USSR.

Stalin's victory over Trotsky was not primarily a matter of ability or principle. Stalin won because Trotsky lacked a power base. Trotsky's superiority as a speaker and writer, and his greater intellectual gifts, counted for little when set against Stalin's grip on the Party machine. It is difficult to see how, after 1924, Trotsky could have ever mounted a serious challenge to his rival. Even had his own particular failings not stopped him from acting at vital moments, Trotsky never had control of the political system as it operated in Soviet Russia. Politics is the art of the possible. After 1924 all the possibilities belonged to Stalin and he used them.

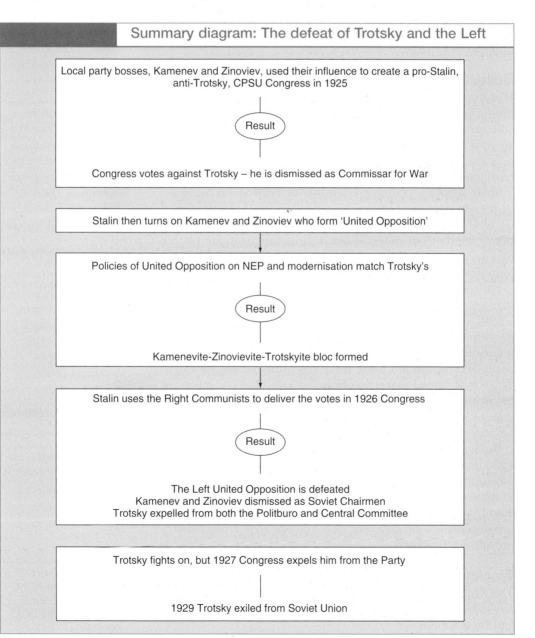

Summary diagram: The defeat of Trotsky and the Left

Local party bosses, Kamenev and Zinoviev, used their influence to create a pro-Stalin, anti-Trotsky, CPSU Congress in 1925

Result

Congress votes against Trotsky – he is dismissed as Commissar for War

Stalin then turns on Kamenev and Zinoviev who form 'United Opposition'

Policies of United Opposition on NEP and modernisation match Trotsky's

Result

Kamenevite-Zinovievite-Trotskyite bloc formed

Stalin uses the Right Communists to deliver the votes in 1926 Congress

Result

The Left United Opposition is defeated
Kamenev and Zinoviev dismissed as Soviet Chairmen
Trotsky expelled from both the Politburo and Central Committee

Trotsky fights on, but 1927 Congress expels him from the Party

1929 Trotsky exiled from Soviet Union

4 | The Defeat of the Right

Although Stalin's victory over the Right Opposition is best studied as a feature of his industrialisation programme (see page 76), it is important also to see it as the last stage in the consolidation of his authority over the Party and over the USSR. The defeat of the Right marks the end of any serious attempt to limit his power. From the late 1920s to his death in 1953 he would become increasingly dictatorial.

The major representatives of the Right were Rykov, Tomsky and Bukharin, the three who had loyally served Stalin in his outflanking of Trotsky and the Left. Politically the Right were by no means as challenging to Stalin as the Trotskyite bloc had been. What made Stalin move against them was that they stood in the way of the industrial and agricultural schemes that he began to implement in 1928.

Key question
What was the attitude of the Right towards NEP and industrialisation?

Collectivisation and industrialisation

Historians are uncertain as to when Stalin finally decided that the answer to the Soviet Union's growth problem was to impose **collectivisation** and **industrialisation**. It is unlikely to have been an early decision; the probability is that it was another piece of opportunism. Having defeated the Left politically he may then have felt free to adopt their economic policies.

Some scholars have suggested that in 1928 Stalin became genuinely concerned about the serious grain shortage and decided that the only way to avoid a crisis was to resort to the drastic methods of collectivisation. It no longer mattered that this had been the very solution that the Left had advanced, since they were now scattered.

For some time it had been the view of Bukharin and the Right that it was unnecessary to force the pace of industrialisation in the USSR. They argued that it would be less disruptive to let industry develop its own momentum. The State should assist, but it should not direct. Similarly, the peasants should not be controlled and oppressed; this would make them resentful and less productive. The Right agreed that it was from the land that the means of financing industrialisation would have to come, but they stressed that, by offering the peasants the chance to become prosperous, far more grain would be produced for sale abroad.

Bukharin argued in the Politburo and at the Party Congress in 1928 that Stalin's aggressive policy of **State grain procurements** was counter-productive. He declared that there were alternatives to these repressive policies. Bukharin was prepared to state openly what everybody knew, but was afraid to admit: that Stalin's programme was no different from the one that Trotsky had previously advocated.

Key terms

Collectivisation
The taking over by the Soviet State of the land and property previously owned by the peasants accompanied by the requirement that the peasants now live and work communally.

Industrialisation
The introduction of a vast scheme for the building of factories which would produce heavy goods such as iron and steel.

State grain procurements
Enforced collections of fixed quotas of grain from the peasants.

Weaknesses of the Right

The Right suffered from a number of weaknesses, which Stalin was able to exploit: these related to their ideas, their organisation and their support.

Key question
Why were the Right unable to mount a successful challenge to Stalin?

Ideas

- Their economic arguments were not unsound, but in the invasion-scared atmosphere of the late 1920s they appeared timid and unrealistic.
- Their plea for a soft line with the peasants did not accord with the Party's needs. The threatening times were judged as requiring a dedicated resistance to the enemies of Revolution both within the USSR and outside.
- Stalin was able to suggest that the Right were guilty of underestimating the crisis facing the Party and the Soviet Union. He declared that it was a time for closing the ranks in keeping with the tradition of 1917.

Stalin showed a shrewd understanding of the mentality of Party members. The majority were far more likely to respond to the call for a return to a hard-line policy, such as had helped them survive the desperate days of the Civil War, than they were to risk the Revolution itself by untimely concessions to a peasantry that had no real place in the proletarian future. The Party of Marx and Lenin would not be well served by the policies of the Right.

Organisation

- The difficulty experienced by the Right in advancing their views was the same as that which had confronted the Left. How could they impress their ideas upon the Party while Stalin remained master of the Party's organisation?
- Bukharin and his colleagues wanted to remain good Party men and it was this sense of loyalty that weakened them in their attempts to oppose Stalin. Fearful of creating 'factionalism', they hoped that they could win the whole Party round to their way of thinking without causing deep divisions. On occasion they were sharply outspoken, Bukharin particularly so, but their basic approach was conciliatory.

All this played into Stalin's hands. Since it was largely his supporters who were responsible for drafting and distributing Party information, it was not difficult for Stalin to portray the Right as a weak and irresponsible clique.

Support

- The Right's only substantial support lay in the trade unions, whose Central Council was chaired by Tomsky, and in the CPSU's Moscow branch where Uglanov, an admirer of Bukharin, was the leader.
- When Stalin realised that these might be a source of opposition he acted quickly and decisively. He sent the ruthless and ambitious young Politburo member, Lazar Kaganovich, to undertake a purge of the suspect trade unionists.
- The Right proved totally incapable of organising resistance to this political blitz. Molotov, Stalin's faithful henchman, was dispatched to Moscow where he enlisted the support of the pro-Stalin members to achieve a similar purge of the local Party officials.

By early 1929 the Right had been trounced beyond recovery. Tomsky was no longer the national trade union leader; Uglanov had been replaced in the Moscow Party organisation; Rykov had been superseded as Premier by Molotov, and Bukharin had been voted out as Chairman of the Comintern and had lost his place in the Politburo. Tomsky, Rykov and Bukharin, the main trio of the 'Right Opportunists' as they were termed by the Stalinist press, were allowed to remain in the Party but only after they had publicly admitted the error of their ways. Stalin's triumph over both Left and Right was complete. The grey blank was about to become the red tsar.

Study Guide: AS Questions

In the style of AQA
Read the following source and then answer the questions that follow.

Adapted from: Richard Overy, The Dictators: Hitler's Germany, Stalin's Russia, *2004.*

The five years between 1924 and 1929 were decisive in Stalin's career. During this period he exploited his position as General Secretary to outmanoeuvre and outdistance his colleagues. His first weapon was to appropriate Lenin's legacy.

(a) What is meant by 'Lenin's legacy' in the context of the USSR between 1924 and 1929? (3 marks)
(b) Explain why Trotsky was unable to mount a successful bid for the leadership of the USSR in the late 1920s. (7 marks)
(c) 'It was Stalin's control of the party machine more than any other factor that explains why he overcame his rivals for power.' Explain why you agree or disagree with this statement. (15 marks)

Exam tips
The cross-references are intended to take you straight to the material that will help you to answer the questions.

(a) This requires only a brief answer. Check back (page 51) to remind yourself of the context. Explain what the term means by referring to the structure of government that Lenin had created (page 50) and the ways of exercising power that he bequeathed to those who came after him.

(b) This needs a fuller answer but do not be tempted into writing a full essay. The following points should help you to develop your answer:

- Trotsky's personal and political deficiencies (pages 53–4).
- Stalin's party posts (pages 49–50).
- Stalin's strength of purpose and political skills (pages 56–7).
- Stalin's exploitation of Lenin's legacy (pages 51–2).
- Trotsky's unpopularity and lack of a power base (pages 53–4).

Remember not merely to list your points. The question requires you to explain the reasons.

(c) Pages 49–51 will help you here. The choice to agree or disagree is yours, but you must explain your decision.
Points to consider:

- What is meant by Stalin's control of the party machine?
- What powers did this control give him over his rivals?
- Who were Stalin's main rivals?

Note that the question requires you to compare the importance of Stalin's control of the party machine with other factors. So while it is important that you concentrate on the machine you must also evaluate other factors. These might include:

- Trotsky's character weaknesses and political limitations (pages 52–4).
- The inability of the Left Opposition to persuade the party or 'to deliver the votes' (page 57).
- Stalin's skill and luck in playing off his rivals against each other (pages 60–2).
- The Right Opposition's lack of organisation and resolve (pages 62–3).
- The divisions among Stalin's rivals regarding government and party policy (page 63).
- The way the 'Lenin legacy' worked to Stalin's advantage and against Trotsky and the other rivals (page 51).

In the style of OCR

Assess the reasons why Stalin's political rivals were unable to prevent his rise to power.

Source: OCR, January 2003

Exam tips

The cross-references are intended to take you straight to the material that will help you to answer the question.

Spend time making sure you fully grasp the question and its terms. Notice that, although Stalin appears to be the central figure, the question is asking you to concentrate on his political rivals. Your task, therefore, is to examine why they were unable to prevent his eventually filling Lenin's place as the dominant figure in Soviet government. You could, of course, describe Stalin's attributes and skills and then make a strong comparison by explaining how none of his rivals could match him in these respects. But, whatever approach you choose, you do need to identify who his rivals were and their limitations.

  Trotsky (page 53) will obviously loom large, but do not restrict your answer to him. The Left and Right Opposition (pages 59 and 62) deserve attention and analysis. Note that the key instruction in the question is *Assess*. It would not be sufficient for you simply to describe the failure of the opposition to him. You are required to explain the reasons why it failed. The following points may help to structure your thoughts.

- Trotsky's character weaknesses, political limitations and lack of a power base (pages 53 and 59).
- Stalin's control of the party machine by 1924 (page 24).
- The divisions among Stalin's rivals regarding government and party policy (page 57).
- The way the 'Lenin legacy' worked to Stalin's advantage and against Trotsky and the other rivals (pages 50–1).
- The importance of the ban on factionalism (page 50).
- The inability of the Left Opposition to persuade the party or 'to deliver the votes' (page 59).
- Stalin's skill and luck in playing off his rivals against each other (pages 60–2).
- The Right Opposition's lack of organisation and resolve (pages 62–3).

Take care not merely to list your points. Weight them according to the importance you think they have, and emphasise the ones that you regard as being particularly significant. Try to integrate and relate them so that they meet the requirement to 'Assess the reasons …'. You can do this by assessing them against each other and by putting them in what you think is their order of priority. Make certain that you explain and justify your selection.

Study Guide: A2 Question

In the style of Edexcel
Using the evidence of Sources 1, 2 and 3, and your own knowledge, explain the process that enabled Stalin, by 1929, to have emerged as Lenin's successor.

Source: Edexcel, June 2002

Source 1
From: L. Trotsky, On the Suppressed Testament of Lenin, published in December 1932.

Lenin undoubtedly valued highly certain of Stalin's characteristics: his firmness of character, tenacity, stubbornness, even ruthlessness and craftiness – qualities necessary in war. But Lenin was far from thinking these gifts were sufficient for the leadership of the party and the state. Lenin saw in Stalin a revolutionist, but not a statesman of the grand style. Theory had too high an importance for Lenin in a political struggle. Nobody considered Stalin a theoretician and he was never brought into discussion of the problems of the International Workers' Movement. Finally, Stalin was neither a writer nor an orator in the strict sense of the word. His articles were laden not only with theoretical blunders but also with crude sins against the Russian language. In the eyes of Lenin, Stalin's value was wholly in the sphere of party organisation and machine manoeuvring, but in his position as General Secretary he became the dispenser of favour and fortune.

Source 2

From: Stephen F. Cohen, Bukharin and the Bolshevik Revolution, *published in 1974, writing about 1925–6.*

Bukharin's accession to the co-leadership helped Stalin, lending his popularity to a man opposed as much out of personal dislikes as for policy differences. Now, however, Zinoviev and Kamenev had abandoned Stalin and were shortly to join with Trotsky. 'It's enough for you and Zinoviev to appear on the same platform, and the Party will find its true Central Committee', Kamenev assured Trotsky. Such a development was Stalin's nightmare. The least illustrious, he was now opposed and denounced by three of the five heirs of Lenin, a prospect made more serious by Lenin's still unpublished but widely known Testament.

Source 3

From: a speech by J.V. Stalin to the Central Committee, April 1929.

What can there be in common between Bukharin's theory that Kulaks will grow into Socialism and Lenin's theory of dictatorship as a fierce class struggle? Obviously, there is not, nor can there be, anything in common between them.

Exam tips

The cross-references are intended to take you straight to the material that will help you to answer the question.

Your response should be led by a careful analysis of the sources. Make and support a judgement about how Stalin emerged as Lenin's successor by using the material in the sources and your own knowledge. Pages 52–64 will be of help here. Ask yourself:

- What the sources tell you about Stalin, Trotsky, Zinoviev and Kamenev, and Bukharin.
- How this relates to your own knowledge of the power struggle between 1924 and 1929.
- How the sources help in your understanding of Stalin's strength and the weakness of the Left and Right opposition.

Use this material to trace the process by which Stalin took over. Remember not merely to describe but to *explain*. Use the sources not just as information but as evidence. For example, you might use the details in Source 1 to illustrate Trotsky's own position and attitude as well as Stalin's.

Stalin and the Soviet Economy

1 | Stalin's Economic Aims

In the late 1920s Stalin decided to impose on the USSR a crash programme of reform of the Soviet economy. Agriculture and industry were to be revolutionised. The pretext for this had been provided in 1926 by a critical resolution of the Party Congress that aimed at fundamentally altering the Soviet economy. Stalin planned to turn that resolution into reality.

His economic policy had one essential aim: the modernisation of the Soviet economy, and two essential methods: collectivisation and industrialisation. From 1928 onwards, with the introduction of collectivisation and industrialisation, the Soviet State took over the running of the nation's economy. Stalin called this momentous decision 'the second revolution' to indicate that it was as important a stage in Soviet history as the original 1917 Revolution had been. It is also frequently defined as a 'revolution from above.'

Revolution from above

In theory, 1917 had been a revolution from below. The Bolshevik-led proletariat had begun the construction of a state in which the workers ruled. Bukharin and the Right had used this notion to argue that, since the USSR was now a proletarian society, the economy should be left to develop at its own pace, without interference from the government. But Stalin's economic programme ended such thinking. The State would now command and direct the economy from above.

A central planning agency, known as *Gosplan* (see page 56), had been created earlier under Lenin. However, what was different about Stalin's schemes was their scale and thoroughness. Under Stalin, State control was to be total. There was an important political aspect to this. He saw in a hard-line policy the best means of confirming his authority over Party and government.

When he introduced his radical economic changes Stalin claimed that they marked as significant a stage in Soviet Communism as had Lenin's fateful decision to sanction the October rising in 1917. This comparison was obviously intended to enhance his own status as a revolutionary leader following in the footsteps of Lenin.

Modernisation

Yet it would be wrong to regard Stalin's policy as wholly a matter of **political expediency**. Judging from his speeches and actions after 1928, he had become convinced that the needs of Soviet Russia could be met only by modernisation. By that, Stalin meant bringing his economically backward nation up to a level of industrial production that would enable it to catch up with and then overtake the advanced economies of western Europe and the USA.

He believed that the survival of the revolution and of Soviet Russia depended on the nation's ability to turn itself into a modern industrial society within the shortest possible time. He told the Soviet people: 'Either we do it, or we shall be crushed.'

Key term

Political expediency
Pursuing a course of action with the primary aim of gaining a political advantage.

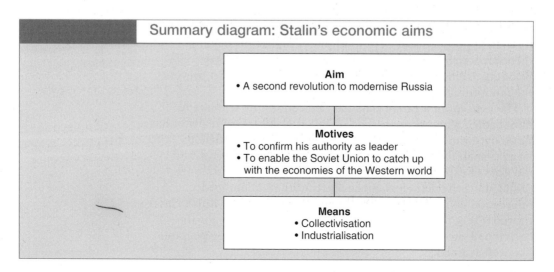

Summary diagram: Stalin's economic aims

Aim
• A second revolution to modernise Russia

Motives
• To confirm his authority as leader
• To enable the Soviet Union to catch up with the economies of the Western world

Means
• Collectivisation
• Industrialisation

2 | Collectivisation

Stalin judged that the only way to raise the money for Soviet industry was to use the land. The necessary first step towards this was the collectivisation of Russian agriculture. This involved taking the land from the peasants and giving it all to the State. The peasants would no longer farm the land for their own individual profit. Instead they would pool their efforts and receive a wage. Stalin calculated that this change would allow the Soviet Union to use the collective profits from the land to finance a massive industrialisation programme. For him, the needs of the land were always subordinate to those of industry.

Key question
How did Stalin plan to pay for industrialisation?

Two types of farm

Stalin defined collectivisation as 'the setting up of **collective farms** and **state farms** in order to squeeze out all capitalist elements from the land'. In practice, there was little difference between the two. Both types of farm were to be the means by which private peasant-ownership would be ended and agriculture made to serve the interests of the Soviet State. The plan was to group between 50 and 100 holdings into one unit. The reasoning was that large farms would be more efficient and would develop the effective use of agricultural machinery. Indeed, the motorised tractor became the outstanding symbol of this mechanisation of Soviet farming.

It was reckoned that efficient farming would have two vital results. It would create surplus food supplies that could be sold abroad to raise capital for Soviet industry. It would also decrease the number of rural workers needed and so release workers for the new factories.

Key terms

Collective farms
Run as co-operatives in which the peasants pooled their resources and shared the labour and the wages.

State farms
Peasants worked directly for the State, which paid them a wage.

The Kulaks

When introducing collectivisation in 1928, Stalin claimed that it was 'voluntary', the free and eager choice of the peasants. But the truth was it was forced on a very reluctant peasantry. In a major propaganda offensive, he identified a class of Kulaks who were holding back the workers' revolution by monopolising the best land and employing cheap peasant labour to farm it. By hoarding their farm produce they kept food prices high, thus making themselves rich at the expense of the workers and poorer peasants. Unless they were broken as a class, they would prevent the modernisation of the USSR.

The concept of a Kulak class has been shown by scholars to have been a Stalinist myth. The so-called Kulaks were really only those hard-working peasants who had proved more efficient farmers than their neighbours. In no sense did they constitute the class of exploiting landowners described in Stalinist propaganda. Nonetheless, given the tradition of landlord oppression going back to tsarist times, the notion of a Kulak class proved a very powerful one and provided the grounds for the coercion of the peasantry as a whole – middle and poor peasants – as well as Kulaks.

Key question
What was Stalin's motivation in persecuting the Kulaks?

Surplus peasants and grain

As a revolutionary, Stalin had little sympathy for the peasants. Communist theory taught that the days of the peasantry as a revolutionary social force had passed. The future belonged to the urban workers. October 1917 had been the first stage in the triumph of this proletarian class. Therefore, it was perfectly fitting that the peasantry should, in a time of national crisis, bow to the demands of industrialisation. Stalin used a simple formula. The USSR needed industrial investment and manpower. The land could provide both. Surplus grain would be sold abroad to raise investment funds for industry; surplus peasants would become factory workers.

One part of the formula was correct; for generations the Russian countryside had been overpopulated, creating a chronic land shortage. The other part was a gross distortion. There was no grain surplus. Indeed, the opposite was the case. Even in the best years of the NEP, food production had seldom matched needs. Yet Stalin insisted that the problem was not the lack of food but its poor distribution; food shortages were the result of grain hoarding by the rich peasants. This argument was then used to explain the urgent need for collectivisation as a way of securing adequate food supplies. It also provided the moral grounds for the onslaught on the Kulaks, who were condemned as enemies of the Soviet nation in its struggle to modernise itself in the face of international, capitalist hostility.

De-Kulakisation

In some regions the poorer peasants undertook 'de-Kulakisation' with enthusiasm, since it provided them with an excuse to settle

Oppression of the Kulaks in Russia. Here we see members of the communist youth league unearthing bags of grain hidden by Kulaks in a cemetery near Odessa.

An anti-Kulak demonstration on a collective farm in 1930. The banner reads: 'Liquidate the Kulaks as a class'.

old scores and to give vent to local jealousies. Land and property were seized from the minority of better-off peasants, and they and their families were physically attacked. Such treatment was often the prelude to arrest and deportation by **OGPU** anti-Kulak squads, authorised by Stalin and modelled on the gangs that had persecuted the peasants during the State-organised Terror of the Civil War period (1918–20).

The renewal of terror also served as a warning to the mass of the peasantry of the likely consequences of resisting the State reorganisation of Soviet agriculture. The destruction of the Kulaks was thus an integral part of the whole collectivisation process. As a Soviet official later admitted: 'most Party officers thought that the whole point of de-Kulakisation was its value as an administrative measure, speeding up tempos of collectivisation'.

Resistance to collectivisation

In the period between December 1929 and March 1930, nearly half the peasant farms in the USSR were collectivised. Yet peasants in their millions resisted. Civil war broke out in the countryside. Such was the turmoil that Stalin called a halt, blaming the troubles on over-zealous officials who had become 'dizzy with success'. Many of the peasants were allowed to return to their original holdings. However, the delay was only temporary. Having cleared his name, Stalin restarted collectivisation in a more determined, if somewhat slower, manner. By the end of the 1930s virtually the whole of the peasantry had been collectivised (see Figure 3.1).

Key term

OGPU
Succeeded the GPU as the State security force. In turn it became the NKVD and then the KGB.

Key question
What were the effects of collectivisation on the peasantry?

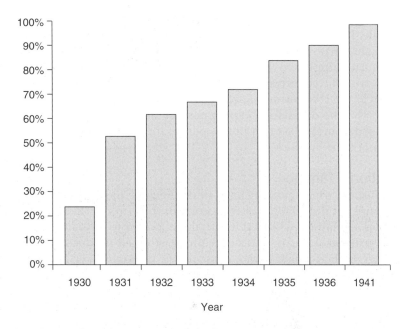

Figure 3.1: Cumulative percentage of peasant holdings collectivised in the USSR, 1930–41

Upheaval and starvation

Behind these remarkable figures lay the story of a massive social upheaval. Bewildered and confused, the peasants either would not or could not co-operate in the deliberate destruction of their traditional way of life. The consequences were increasingly tragic. The majority of peasants ate their seed corn and slaughtered their livestock. There were no crops left to reap or animals to rear.

The Soviet authorities responded with still fiercer coercion, but this simply made matters worse: imprisonment, deportation and execution could not replenish the barns or restock the herds. Special contingents of party workers were sent from the towns to restore food production levels by working on the land themselves. But their ignorance of farming only added to the disruption. By a bitter irony, even as starvation set in, the little grain that was available was being exported as 'surplus' to obtain the foreign capital that industry demanded. By 1932 the situation on the land was catastrophic.

Table 3.1: The fall in food consumption (in kilograms per head)

	Bread	Potatoes	Meat and lard	Butter
1928	250.4	141.1	24.8	1.35
1932	214.6	125.0	11.2	0.7

Table 3.2: The fall in livestock (in millions)

	Horses	Cattle	Pigs	Sheep and goats
1928	33	70	26	146
1932	15	34	9	42

The figures in Tables 3.1 and 3.2 (page 73) refer to the USSR as a whole. In the urban areas there was more food available. Indeed, a major purpose of the grain requisition squads was to maintain adequate supplies to the industrial regions. This meant that the misery in the countryside was proportionally greater, with areas such as the Ukraine and Kazhakstan suffering particularly severely. The devastation experienced by the Kazhaks can be gauged from the fact that in this period they lost nearly 90 per cent of their livestock.

National famine

Starvation, which in many parts of the Soviet Union persisted throughout the 1930s, was at its worst in the years 1932–3, when a national famine occurred. Collectivisation led to despair among the peasants. In many areas they simply stopped producing, either as an act of desperate resistance or through sheer inability to adapt to the violently enforced land system. Hungry and embittered, they made for the towns in huge numbers. It had, of course, been part of Stalin's collectivisation plan to move the peasants into the industrial regions. However, so great was the migration that a system of internal passports had to be introduced in an effort to control the flow.

Despite overwhelming evidence of the tragedy that had overtaken the USSR, the official Stalinist line was that there was no famine. In the whole of the contemporary Soviet press there were only two oblique references to it. This conspiracy of silence was of more than political significance. As well as protecting the image of Stalin the great planner, it effectively prevented the introduction of measures to remedy the distress. Since the famine did not officially exist, Soviet Russia could not publicly take steps to relieve it. For the same reason, it could not appeal, as had been done during an earlier Russian famine in 1921 (see page 25), for aid from the outside world.

Thus what Isaac Deutscher, the historian and former Trotskyist, called 'the first purely man-made famine in history' went unacknowledged in order to avoid discrediting Stalin. Not for the last time, large numbers of the Soviet people were sacrificed on the altar of Stalin's reputation. There was a strong rumour that Stalin's second wife, Nadezhda Alliluyeva, had been driven to suicide by the knowledge that it was her husband's brutal policies that had caused the famine. Shortly before her death she had railed at Stalin: 'You are a tormentor, that's what you are. You torment your own son. You torment your wife. You torment the whole Russian people.'

The success of collectivisation

Even allowing for the occasional progressive aspect of collectivisation, such as the spread of the mechanised tractors, the overall picture remained bleak. The mass of the peasantry had been uprooted and left bewildered. Despite severe reprisals and coercion, the peasants were unable to produce the surplus food that Stalin demanded. By 1939 Soviet agricultural productivity

Key question
Why could the famine of the early 1930s not be dealt with effectively?

Key date
National famine: 1932–3

Key question
How successful had collectivisation proven to be by 1939?

had barely returned to the level recorded for Tsarist Russia in 1913. But the most damning consideration still remains the man-made famine, which in the 1930s killed between 10 and 15 million peasants.

Yet, leaving aside questions of human suffering, the hard fact is that Stalin's policies did force a large number of peasants to leave the land and go into the factories. There they provided the workforce that enabled the industrialisation programme to be started.

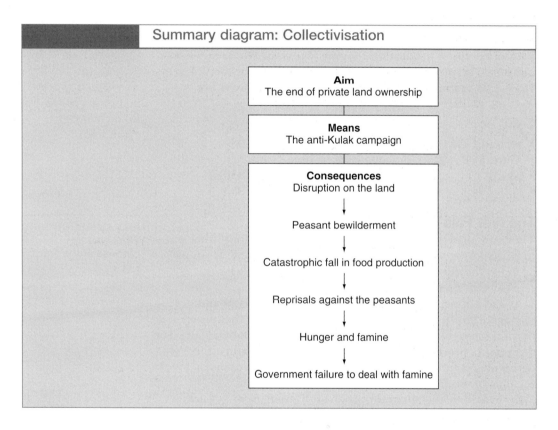

Summary diagram: Collectivisation

Aim
The end of private land ownership

Means
The anti-Kulak campaign

Consequences
Disruption on the land
↓
Peasant bewilderment
↓
Catastrophic fall in food production
↓
Reprisals against the peasants
↓
Hunger and famine
↓
Government failure to deal with famine

Key question
What were Stalin's aims for Soviet industry in the 1930s?

3 | Industrialisation

Stalin described his industrialisation plans for the USSR as an attempt to establish a war economy. He declared that he was making war on the failings of Russia's past and on the class enemies within the nation. He also claimed that he was preparing the USSR for war against its capitalist foes abroad. This was not simply martial imagery. Stalin regarded iron, steel and oil as the sinews of war. Their successful production would guarantee the strength and readiness of the nation to face its enemies.

For Stalin, therefore, industry meant heavy industry. He believed that the industrial revolutions which had made Western Europe and North America so strong had been based on iron and steel production. So, the USSR must adopt a similar industrial pattern in its drive towards modernisation. The difference would be that, whereas the West had taken the capitalist road, the USSR would follow the path of socialism.

Stalin had grounds for his optimism. It so happened that the Soviet industrialisation drive in the 1930s coincided with the **Depression** in the Western world. Stalin claimed that the USSR was introducing into its own economy the technical successes of Western industrialisation but was rejecting the destructive capitalist system that went with them. Socialist planning would enable the USSR to avoid the errors that had begun to undermine the Western economies.

Soviet industrialisation under Stalin took the form of a series of Five-Year Plans (FYPs). *Gosplan* was required by Stalin to draw up a list of quotas of production ranging across the whole of Soviet industry. The process began in 1928 and, except for the war years 1941–5, lasted until Stalin's death in 1953. There were five separate plans:

- First FYP   October 1928 to December 1932
- Second FYP   January 1933 to December 1937
- Third FYP   January 1938 to June 1941
- Fourth FYP   January 1946 to December 1950
- Fifth FYP   January 1951 to December 1955

Key term

Depression
A period of economic stagnation that began in the USA in 1929 and lasted throughout the 1930s. It affected the whole of the industrial world and was interpreted by Marxists as the beginning of the final collapse of capitalism.

The first Five-Year Plan 1928–32

The term 'plan' is misleading. The first FYP laid down what was to be achieved, but did not say how it was to be done. It simply assumed the quotas would be met. What the first FYP represented, therefore, was a set of targets rather than a plan.

As had happened with collectivisation, local officials and managers falsified their production figures to give the impression they had met their targets when, in fact, they had fallen short. For this reason, precise statistics for the first FYP are difficult to determine. A further complication is that three quite distinct versions of the first FYP eventually appeared.

Impressed by the apparent progress of the Plan in its early stages, Stalin encouraged the formulation of an 'optimal' plan which reassessed targets upwards. These new quotas were hopelessly unrealistic and stood no chance of being reached. Nonetheless, on the basis of the supposed achievements of this 'optimal' plan the figures were revised still higher. Western analysts suggest the figures in Table 3.3 as the closest approximation to the real figures.

Key question
What was the purpose of the first FYP?

Table 3.3: Industrial output

Product (in million tons)	1927–8 First plan	1932–3 'Optimal'	1932 Revised	1932 Actual
Coal	35.0	75.0	95–105	64.0
Oil	11.7	21.7	40–55	21.4
Iron ore	6.7	20.2	24–32	12.1
Pig iron	3.2	10.0	15–16	6.2

'The Five-Year Plan' – a propaganda wall poster of the 1930s, depicting Stalin as the heroic creator of a powerful, industrialised, Soviet Union. He is overcoming the forces of religion, international capitalism, and Russian conservatism and backwardness.

Propaganda

The importance of these figures should not be exaggerated. At the time it was the grand design, not the detail, that mattered. The Plan was a huge propaganda project, which aimed at convincing the Soviet people that they were personally engaged in a vast industrial enterprise. By their own efforts, they were changing the character of the society in which they lived and providing it with the means of achieving greatness.

Nor, was it all a matter of State coercion, widely used though that was. There was, among the young especially, an enthusiasm and a commitment that suggested that many Soviet citizens believed they were genuinely building a new and better world. The sense of the Soviet people as masters of their own fate was expressed in the slogan, 'There is no fortress that we Bolsheviks cannot storm'.

Cultural revolution

The term 'cultural revolution' is an appropriate description of the significance of what was being undertaken under Stalin's leadership. Two renowned Western analysts of Soviet affairs, Alec Nove and Sheila Fitzpatrick, have laid stress on this aspect. They see behind the economic changes of this period a real attempt being made to create a new type of individual, *Homo sovieticus* (Soviet man), as if a new species had come into being. Stalin told a gathering of Soviet writers that they should regard themselves as 'engineers of the human soul' (see page 155).

Successes and achievements

Key question
How far did the first FYP achieve its objectives?

No matter how badly the figures may have been rigged at the time, the first FYP was an extraordinary achievement overall. Coal, iron and electrical power supply all increased in huge proportions. The production of steel and chemicals was less impressive, while the output of finished textiles actually declined.

A striking feature of the Plan was the low priority it gave to improving the material lives of the Soviet people. No effort was made to reward the workers by providing them with affordable consumer goods. Living conditions actually deteriorated in this period. Accommodation in the towns and cities remained sub-standard.

The Soviet authorities' neglect of basic social needs was not accidental. The Plan had never been intended to raise living standards. Its purpose was collective, not individual. It called for sacrifice on the part of the workers in the construction of a socialist state, which would be able to sustain itself economically and militarily against the enmity of the outside world.

Resistance and sabotage

It was Stalin's presentation of the FYP as a defence of the USSR against international hostility that enabled him to brand resistance to the Plan as 'sabotage'. A series of public trials of industrial 'wreckers', including a number of foreign workers, was used to impress the Party and the masses of the futility of protesting against the industrialisation programme. In 1928 in a prelude to the first FYP, Stalin claimed to have discovered an anti-Soviet conspiracy among the mining engineers of Shakhty in the Donbass region. Their subsequent public trial was intended to frighten the workers into line. It also showed that the privileged position of the skilled workers, the 'bourgeois experts', was to be tolerated no longer.

This attack upon the experts was part of a pattern in the first FYP, which emphasised quantity at the expense of quality. The push towards sheer volume of output was intended to prove the correctness of Stalin's grand economic schemes. Sheila Fitzpatrick has termed this 'gigantomania', the worship of size for its own sake. This may be interpreted as a shrewd judgement on Stalin's part. He knew that the untrained peasants who now filled the factories would not turn immediately into skilled workers. It made sense, therefore, at least in the short term, to ignore the question of quality and to emphasise quantity. The result very often was that machines, factories, and even whole enterprises were ruined because of the workers' lack of basic skills.

Stalin was seemingly untroubled by this. His notions of industrial 'saboteurs' and 'wreckers' allowed him to place the blame for poor quality and under-production on managers and workers who were not prepared to play their proper part in re-building the nation. He used OGPU agents and Party **cadres** to terrorise the workforce. 'Sabotage' became a blanket term used to denounce anyone considered not to be pulling his weight. The simplest errors, such as being late for work or mislaying tools, could lead to such a charge.

At a higher level, those factory managers or foremen who did not meet their production quotas might find themselves on public trial as enemies of the Soviet state. In such an atmosphere, fear

Key question
Why was there so little resistance to the FYP?

Key term

Cadres
Party members who were sent into factories and onto construction sites to spy and report back on managers and workers.

and recrimination flourished. Doctoring official returns and inflating output figures became normal practice. Everybody at every level was engaged in a huge game of pretence. This was why Soviet statistics for industrial growth were so unreliable and why it was possible for Stalin to claim in mid-course that since the first FYP had already met its initial targets, it would be shortened to a four-year plan. In Stalin's industrial revolution appearances were everything. This was where the logic of 'gigantomania' had led.

Key question
How far was the first FYP planned from the top?

Stalin: the master-planner?

The industrial policies of this time had been described as 'the Stalinist blue-print' or 'Stalin's economic model'. Modern scholars are, however, wary of using such terms. Norman Stone, for example, interprets Stalin's policies not as far-sighted strategy but as 'simply putting one foot in front of the other as he went along'. Despite the growing tendency in all official Soviet documents of the 1930s to include a fulsome reference to Stalin, the master-planner, there was in fact very little planning from the top.

Stalin's government exhorted, cajoled and bullied the workers into ever greater efforts towards ever greater production, but such planning as there was occurred not at national but at local level. It was the regional and site managers who, struggling desperately to make sense of the instructions they were given from on high, formulated the actual schemes for reaching their given production quotas. This was why it was so easy for Stalin and his Kremlin colleagues to accuse lesser officials of sabotage while themselves avoiding any taint of incompetence.

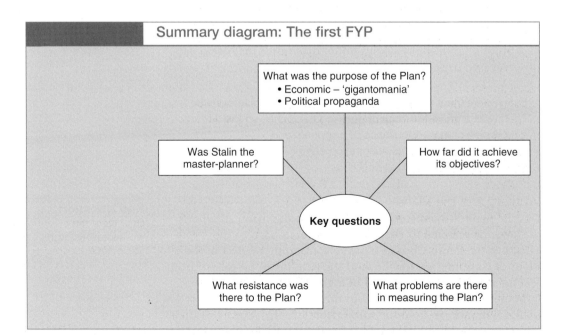

Summary diagram: The first FYP

What was the purpose of the Plan?
• Economic – 'gigantomania'
• Political propaganda

Was Stalin the master-planner?

How far did it achieve its objectives?

Key questions

What resistance was there to the Plan?

What problems are there in measuring the Plan?

The second and third Five-Year Plans

Although the second and third FYPs were modelled on the pattern of the first, the targets set for them were more realistic. Nevertheless, they still revealed the same lack of co-ordination that had characterised the first. Over-production occurred in some parts of the economy, under-production in others, which often resulted in whole branches of industry being held up for lack of vital supplies. For example, some projects had too little timber at times, while at other times enough timber but insufficient steel. Spare parts were hard to come by, which often meant that broken machines stood unrepaired and idle for long periods.

The hardest struggle was to sustain a proper supply of materials; this often led to fierce competition between regions and sectors of industry, all of them anxious to escape the charge of failing to achieve their targets. As a result there was hoarding of resources and a lack of co-operation between the various parts of the industrial system. Complaints about poor standards, carefully veiled so as not to appear critical of Stalin and the Plan, were frequent. What successes there were occurred again in heavy industry where the second FYP began to reap the benefit of the creation of large-scale plants under the first FYP.

Scapegoats

The reluctance to tell the full truth hindered genuine industrial growth. Since no-one was willing to admit there was an error in the planning, faults went unchecked until serious breakdowns occurred. Then followed the familiar search for scapegoats. It was during the period of the second and third FYPs that Stalin's political purges were at their fiercest. In such an all-pervading atmosphere of terror the mere accusation of 'sabotage' was taken as a proof of guilt. Productivity suffered as result. As Alec Nove observes (see page 85):

> Everywhere there were said to be spies, wreckers, diversionists. There was a grave shortage of qualified personnel, so the deportation of many thousands of engineers and technologists to distant concentration camps represented a severe loss.

Workers and the Plans

Despite Stalin's statements to the contrary, the living standards of the workers failed to rise. This was due, in part, to the effects of the famine, but also to the continuing neglect in the Plans of consumer goods. Beyond the comfort to be gained from feeling that they were engaged in a great national enterprise, a theme constantly emphasised in the Soviet press, there were few material rewards to help the workers endure the severity of their conditions. Moreover, they had to accept their lot without complaint.

Key question
What were the main strengths and weaknesses of the second and third Five-Year Plans?

Second FYP: 1933–7
Third FYP: 1938–41

Key dates

Key question
How were the workers affected by the FYPs?

The Stakhanovite movement, 1935

The Party's control of newspapers, cinema and radio meant that only a favourable view of the Plans was ever presented. The official line was that all was well and the workers were happy. Support for this claim was provided by the Stakhanovite movement, which was exploited by the authorities to inspire or shame workers into raising their production levels still higher. It was officially claimed in August 1935 that Alexei Stakhanov, a miner in the Donbass region, had produced in one five-hour shift over 14 times his required quota of coal. Whatever the truth of the story, his feat was seized on by the authorities as a glorious example of what was possible in a Soviet Union guided by the great and wise Joseph Stalin.

Workers' rights

After 1917, the Russian trade unions had become powerless. In Bolshevik theory, in a truly socialist state such as Russia now was, there was no distinction between the interests of government and those of the workers. Therefore, there was no longer any need for a separate trade union movement. In 1920 Trotsky had taken violent steps to destroy the independence of the unions and bring them directly under Bolshevik control. The result was that after 1920 the unions were simply the means by which the Bolshevik government enforced its requirements upon the workers.

Under Stalin's industrialisation programme any semblance of workers' rights disappeared. Strikes were prohibited and the traditional demands for better pay and conditions were regarded as selfishly inappropriate in a time of national crisis. A code of 'labour discipline' was drawn up, demanding maximum effort and output; failure to conform was punishable by a range of penalties from loss of wages to imprisonment in forced labour camps. On paper, wages improved during the second FYP, but in real terms, with food rationing and high prices, living standards were lower in 1937 than they had been in 1928.

Living and working conditions

Throughout the period of the FYPs, the Soviet government asserted that the nation was under siege. It claimed that unless priority was given to defence needs, the very existence of the USSR was at risk. Set against such a threat, workers' material interests were of little significance. For workers to demand improved conditions at a time when the Soviet Union was fighting for survival was unthinkable; they would be betraying the nation. It was small wonder, then, that food remained scarce and expensive and severe overcrowding persisted.

Nearly all workers lived in overcrowded apartments. Public housing policy did produce a large number of tenement blocks in towns and cities. These were usually five-storey structures with no lifts. Quite apart from their architectural ugliness they were a hazard to health. So great was the overcrowding that it was common for young families to live with their in-laws and equally common for four or five families to share a single lavatory and a single kitchen, which was often no more than an alcove with a gas-ring. There were rotas for the use of these facilities. Queuing to relieve oneself or to cook was part of the daily routine.

There was money available, but the government spent it not on improving social conditions but on armaments. Between 1933 and 1937, defence expenditure rose from four to 17 per cent of the overall industrial budget. By 1940, under the terms of the third FYP, which renewed the commitment to heavy industrial development, this proportion had reached 33 per cent.

Despite the official adulation of Stalin for his great diplomatic triumph in achieving the Non-aggression Pact with Nazi Germany in August 1939 (see page 119) there was no relaxation within the Soviet Union of the war atmosphere. Indeed, the conditions of the ordinary people became even harsher. An official decree of 1940 empowered Stalin's government to encroach even further on workers' liberties. Direction of labour, enforced settlement of undeveloped areas, and severe penalties for slacking and absenteeism: these were some of the measures imposed under the decree.

In 1941, when the German invasion effectively destroyed the third FYP, the conditions of the Soviet industrial workers were marginally lower than in 1928. Yet whatever the hardship of the workers, the fact was that in 1941 the USSR was economically strong enough to engage in an ultimately successful military struggle of unprecedented duration and intensity. In Soviet propaganda, this was what mattered, not minor questions of living standards. The USSR's triumph over Nazism would later be claimed as the ultimate proof of the wisdom of Stalin's enforced industrialisation programme.

The German invasion and occupation of Russia: June 1941 **Key date**

Yet despite their victory in war, the Soviet people received few material rewards for their prodigious efforts. Stalin's post-war concerns remained industrial recovery and national defence. The annual budgets down to his death in 1953 showed a decline in the amount dedicated to improving living conditions. Rationing was formally ended in 1947 but this was not a real sign that shortages had been overcome; a widespread black-market, officially condemned but tolerated in practice, was necessary for the workers to supplement their meagre resources. Accommodation was scarcer and conditions in the factories were grimmer than they had been in wartime. Real wages were not permitted to rise above subsistence level and the rigours of the 'Labour Code' were not relaxed. When Stalin died in 1953 the lot of the Russian worker was harder than at any time since 1917.

Labour Code
Severe regulations imposed on the workers.

Key term

Key question
How successful were
Stalin's economic
reforms?

Strengths of the reforms

In judging the scale of Stalin's achievement it is helpful to cite such statistics relating to industrial output during the period of the first three FYPs as are reliable. The data in Table 3.4 are drawn from the work of the economic historian E. Zaleski, whose findings are based on careful analysis of Soviet and Western sources.

Table 3.4: Industrial output during the first three FYPs

	1927	1930	1932	1935	1937	1940
Coal (million tons)	35	60	64	100	128	150
Steel (million tons)	3	5	6	13	18	18
Oil (million tons)	12	17	21	24	26	26
Electricity (million kWh)	18	22	20	45	80	90

They indicate a remarkable increase in production overall. In a little over 12 years, coal production had grown five times, steel six, and oil output had more than doubled. Perhaps the most impressive statistic is the one showing that electricity generation had quintupled. These four key products provided the basis for the military economy, which enabled the USSR not only to survive four years of German occupation but eventually to amass sufficient resources to turn the tables and drive the German army out of Soviet territory. The climax of this was the Soviet defeat of Germany in May 1945.

Key question
What were the
limitations of Stalin's
reforms?

Weaknesses

Stalin's economic reforms succeeded in the traditional areas of heavy industry. In those sectors where unskilled and forced labour could be easily used, as in the building of large projects such as factories, bridges, refineries and canals, the results were impressive.

However, the Soviet economy itself remained unbalanced. Stalin gave little thought to developing an overall economic strategy. Nor were modern industrial methods adopted. Old, wasteful techniques, such as using massed labour rather than efficient machines, continued to be used. Vital financial and material resources were wasted.

Stalin's love of what he called 'the Grand Projects of Communism' meant that no real attention was paid to producing quality goods that could then be profitably sold abroad to raise the money the USSR so badly needed. The simple fact was that Stalin's policies had deprived the Soviet Union of any chance to compete with the modernising economies of Europe and the USA.

The other major failing of the policies was their inability to increase agricultural productivity or to raise the living standards

of the Soviet workers. Stalin's neglect of agriculture, which continued to be deprived of funds since it was regarded as wholly secondary to the needs of industry, proved very damaging. The lack of agricultural growth resulted in constant food shortages, which could be met only by buying foreign supplies. This drained the USSR's limited financial resources.

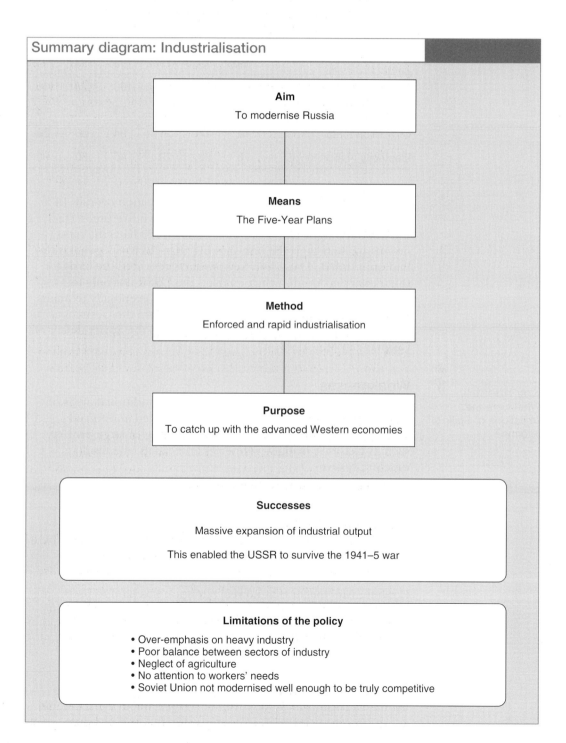

Summary diagram: Industrialisation

Aim

To modernise Russia

Means

The Five-Year Plans

Method

Enforced and rapid industrialisation

Purpose

To catch up with the advanced Western economies

Successes

Massive expansion of industrial output

This enabled the USSR to survive the 1941–5 war

Limitations of the policy

- Over-emphasis on heavy industry
- Poor balance between sectors of industry
- Neglect of agriculture
- No attention to workers' needs
- Soviet Union not modernised well enough to be truly competitive

4 | The Key Debate

Many historians have contributed to the analysis of Stalin's economic policies, which remain a lively area of discussion. The central question that scholars address is:

> Did the policies benefit the Soviet Union and its people or were they introduced by Stalin primarily to consolidate his political hold on the USSR?

Alec Nove

Argued strongly that Stalin's collectivisation and industrialisation programmes were bad economics. They caused upheaval on the land and misery to the peasants without producing the industrial growth that the USSR needed. Furthermore, the condition of the industrial workers deteriorated under Stalin's policies. The living standards of Soviet factory-workers in 1953 were barely higher than in 1928, while those of farm-workers were actually lower than in 1913.

Robert Conquest

An especially sharp critic of Stalin's totalitarianism, he remarked: 'Stalinism is one way of attaining industrialisation, just as cannibalism is one way of attaining a high protein diet'.

Leonard Shapiro

Contended that had the industrial growth under the tsars continued uninterrupted beyond 1914 it would have reached no less a level of expansion by 1941 than that achieved by Stalin's terror strategy.

Norman Stone

Has supported this projection by arguing that without the expertise and basic industrial structures that already existed in Russia before 1917 the Five-Year Plans would have been unable to reach the level of success that they did.

Sheila Fitzpatrick

Broadly agreed with Nove's and Conquest's criticisms; she added that Stalin's 'gigantomania', his obsession with large-scale projects, distorted the economy at a critical time when what was needed was proper investment and planning. She stressed, however, that Stalin's policies need to be seen in a broad social and political context. Harsh though Stalin was, he was trying to bring stability to a Soviet Russia that had known only turmoil and division since 1917.

Dmitri Volkogonov

Dmitri Volkogonov, who saw things at first hand as a soldier and administrator in 1930s' Russia, suggested that the real purpose of

Stalin's policies was only incidentally economic; the Soviet leader was aiming at removing all opposition to himself by making his economic policies a test of loyalty. To question his plans was to challenge his authority.

Peter Gattrell

An interesting viewpoint was offered by Peter Gattrell, who built on the arguments first put forward by E.H. Carr. He acknowledged that Stalin was certainly severe and destructive in his treatment of people but pointed out that the outcome of collectivisation and industrialisation was an economy strong enough to sustain the USSR through four years of the most demanding of modern wars. Gattrell suggested that, hard though it is for the Western liberal mind to accept, it may be that Russia could not have been modernised by any other methods except those used by Stalin.

Some key books in the debate
E.H. Carr, *A History of Soviet Russia* (Macmillan, 1979).
Robert Conquest, *The Great Terror: Stalin's Purge of the Thirties* (Penguin, 1971).
Robert Conquest, *Harvest of Sorrow* (Macmillan, 1988).
Sheila Fitzpatrick, *The Cultural Front: Power and Culture in Revolutionary Russia* (Cornell, 1992).
Sheila Fitzpatrick (ed), *Stalinism: New Directions* (Routledge, 2000).
Peter Gattrell, *Under Command: The Soviet Economy 1924–53* (Routledge, 1992).
Alec Nove, *An Economic History of the USSR* (Penguin, 1972).
Alec Nove, *Stalinism and After* (Allen and Unwin, 1975).
Leonard Shapiro, *The Communist Party of the Soviet Union* (Routledge, 1970).
Norman Stone, *The Eastern Front* (Penguin Books, 1998).
Dmitri Volkogonov, *The Rise and Fall of the Soviet Empire* (HarperCollins, 1998).
Dmitri Volkogonov, *Stalin: Triumph and Tragedy* (Weidenfeld and Nicholson, 1991).

Study Guide: AS Questions

In the style of AQA

Read the following source and answer the questions that follow.

Adapted from: a contemporary account of the migration from the rural to urban areas.

Agricultural technicians … were arrested in thousands and made to appear in huge sabotage trials so that responsibility might be unloaded on somebody.

(a) What is meant by sabotage in the context of the USSR in the 1930s? (3 marks)
(b) Explain why migration from rural to urban areas was so great in the 1930s. (7 marks)
(c) 'Stalin's collectivisation and industrial programmes were bad economics in the USSR in the 1930s.' Explain why you agree or disagree with this statement. (15 marks)

Exam tips
The cross-references are intended to take you straight to the material that will help you to answer the questions.

(a) You should provide a brief explanation of the meaning of sabotage, linked to the context. These could include:

- Examples of 'sabotage' charges, e.g. simple errors such as mislaying tools with the supposed purpose of slowing down production, not meeting quotas (pages 78–9).
- The 'sabotage' concept used as a technique for enforcing the Five-Year Plans (pages 79–80).

(b) You have to demonstrate explicit understanding of a range of factors and draw conclusions about their relative significance, for example:

- The ways in which it was a planned policy (pages 71–2).
- The ways in which it was a result of the famine (pages 74–5).
- Remember to show how your factors inter-relate and provide some overall judgement.

(c) You should evaluate the extent to which Stalin's policies were bad economics by:

- Debating the definition of bad economics in the context of Stalin's 1930s' regime.
- Showing support for and against the argument.
- Showing an appreciation of the aims and outcomes of Stalin's economic policies (pages 68–79).

Remember in your answer to do two essential things:
- Show the points where you agree or disagree with the statement.
- Make it clear why you find the statement convincing or otherwise by explaining your decision.

In the style of Edexcel

Study Sources 1 and 2 below and then answer the questions that follow.

Source 1

(Stalin speaking in 1929)

We are advancing full steam ahead along the path of industrialisation – to socialism, leaving behind the age long Russian backwardness. We are becoming a country of metal, a country of automobiles, a country of tractors. And when we have put the USSR on the automobile, and the peasant on the tractor, let the worthy capitalists, who boast so loudly of their civilisation, try to overtake us. We shall see which countries may then be classified as backward and which as advanced.

Source 2

(Stalin speaking in 1931)

To slow down the tempo of industrialisation would mean falling behind. And those who fall behind get beaten. The history of old Russia shows that she was continually beaten because of her military, cultural, political, industrial and agricultural backwardness. We are fifty or a hundred years behind the advanced countries. We must make good this distance in ten years. Either we do it, or they will crush us.

Study Sources 1 and 2

(a) What reasons for industrialisation does Stalin advance in these Sources 1 and 2? (10 marks)

(b) What contribution did collectivisation of agriculture make to the process of industrialisation? (14 marks)

(c) Did the lives of the mass of the Russian people improve or worsen as a result of Stalin's economic policies between 1929 and 1941? Explain your answer. (36 marks)

Source: Edexcel specimen paper, 2000

Exam tips

The cross-references are intended to take you straight to the material that will help you to answer the questions.

(a) The answer is to be found entirely within Sources 1 and 2. The key requirement is for you to show that you understand the sources and also that you grasp what is implied in them. In other words you need not only to refer to what Stalin says directly but also to go below the surface to tease out Stalin's deeper motives or objectives in regard to his industrialisation programme. However, avoid the temptation to write a full essay. Keep your answer to the point.

(b) In this question you have to use your own knowledge to explain the link between the collectivisation of agriculture and of industrialisation (pages 68–76). A key word is 'contribution', which invites you not simply to describe the link but to examine its implications. This requires an analysis of the significance of the relationship and connection between the two economic policies. In assessing the contribution it would be helpful if you were to make an informed judgement on how far collectivisation fulfilled Stalin's original hope that it would provide a source for industrial investment.

(c) This question carries the greatest number of marks, so deserves the greatest amount of time devoted to it. You have to call on your own knowledge to describe the conditions created by Stalin's policies and then make a judgement as to whether things were better or worse for the mass of the Russians in 1941 compared with 1929. Be careful to make sure that your verdict on whether conditions improved or worsened follows logically and directly from the evidence that you introduce and the criteria that you use to examine it. Use the information in this chapter (pages 80–4) and in Chapter 7 (pages 163–71) to help you.

In the style of OCR

To what extent did Stalin bring about change in the USSR in the 1930s?

Source: OCR specimen paper 2000

Exam tips

The cross-references are intended to take you straight to the material that will help you to answer the questions.

You should examine the various strategies used by Stalin and evaluate the importance of each. The critical need is for you to consider *the extent* of the change they brought about and their limits. Strategies include:

- The FYPs (pages 76–84).
- Collectivisation (pages 70–6).
- Use of propaganda (pages 77–81).
- Use of terror (pages 100–4).

Do not merely list the various strategies and changes they brought about. The question requires that you come to a firm conclusion based on the analysis that you have presented.

Study Guide: A2 Question

In the style of AQA

'Stalin's industrial programme had three motives: the modernisation of the USSR, the creation of a siege economy, and the consolidation of his political power.'

Assess the relative importance of each of these factors. (20 marks)

Exam tip

The cross-references are intended to take you straight to the material that will help you to answer the question.

Make sure you consider all three motives in the quotation, so as to be able to assess their importance in the light of your own knowledge. These sub-questions will help direct your thoughts:

- How was industrialisation meant to create a modern economy? (pages 75–84).
- How was industrialisation intended to provide the USSR with security and the means of defending itself in a hostile world? (pages 78–83).
- In what ways did Stalin use industrialisation to tighten his political grip on the USSR? (pages 77–9 and 100).

Note that you are not being asked whether you agree with the quotation. Take it as a given. Your key task is to evaluate the relative importance of the three factors. This means you need to place them in order of importance and explain your grading of them. You are, of course, entitled to claim they were each of equal weight. But you must explain why you think this.

4 Stalin's Purges

POINTS TO CONSIDER
With his defeat by 1929 of the Left and Right Bolsheviks, Stalin had achieved personal power in the Soviet Union. He went on to consolidate that power to the point of absolute control by a series of purges that continued until his death in 1953. In this chapter these are examined as:

- The early purges
- The post-Kirov purges 1934–6
- The Great Purge 1936–9
- The later purges 1941–53
- The purges as a study in Stalin's use of power

Key dates

1932	The trial of the Ryutin group
1933	The purges begun under Yezhov's direction
1934	The assassination of Kirov
	Intensification of the purges under Yagoda
1935	Yezhov, Vyshinsky and Beria took over organising the purges
1936–9	The 'Great Purge' of the Party, the army and the people
1937–38	The Yezhovschina persecutions in the localities
1941–5	Purges used to remove those accused of undermining the war effort
1945	Purging of Soviet people believed to have supported Germany
1949	The 'Leningrad Affair' led to a further purge of the Party
1953	The 'doctors' plot', which began a purge of the medical profession, was ended by the death of Stalin

1 | The Early Purges

Key question
What form did the early purges take?

Having gained personal power in the Soviet Union by 1929, Stalin spent the rest of his life consolidating and extending his authority. The purge was his principal weapon for achieving this.

The Stalinist purges, which began in 1932, were not unprecedented. Under Lenin, in the early 1920s, tens of thousands of 'anti-Bolsheviks' had been imprisoned in labour camps. Public trials, such as the Shakhty affair had been held during the early stages of the first Five-Year Plan as a way of exposing industrial 'saboteurs' (see page 78).

Even at this early stage, prosecutions had not been restricted to industrial enemies. In 1932 the trial of the **Ryutin group** had taken place. Ryutin and his supporters were publicly tried and expelled from the Party. This was the prelude to the first major purge of the CPSU by Stalin. Between 1933 and 1934 nearly one million members, over a third of the total membership, were excluded from the Party on the grounds that they were 'Ryutinites'. The purge was organised by Nicolai Yezhov, the poisonous chief of the Control Commission, the branch of the Central Committee responsible for Party discipline.

Nature of the purges

At the beginning, Party purges were not as violent or as deadly as they later became. The usual procedure was to oblige members to hand in their **Party cards** for checking, at which point any suspect individuals would not have their cards returned to them. This amounted to expulsion since, without cards, members were denied access to all Party activities. Furthermore, they and their families then lost their privileges in regard to employment, housing and food rations. The threat of expulsion was enough to force members to conform to official Party policy.

Under such a system, it became progressively more difficult to mount effective opposition. Despite this, attempts were made in the early 1930s to criticise Stalin, as the Ryutin affair illustrates. These efforts were ineffectual, but they led Stalin to believe that organised resistance to him was still possible.

The year 1934 is an important date in Stalin's rise to absolute authority, marking the point at which he began the systematic terrorising, not of obvious political opponents, but of colleagues and Party members. It is difficult to explain precisely why Stalin initiated such a terror. Historians accept that they are dealing with behaviour that goes beyond reason and logic. Stalin was deeply suspicious by nature and suffered from increasing **paranoia** as he grew older. Right up to his death in 1953 he continued to believe he was under threat from actual or potential enemies.

Such thinking meant everyone was suspect and no-one was safe. Purges became not so much a series of episodes as a permanent condition of Soviet political life. Terror was all-pervading. Its intensity varied from time to time, but it was an ever-present reality throughout the remainder of Stalin's life.

2 | The Post-Kirov Purges 1934–6

In Leningrad on 1 December 1934, a man named Leonid Nicolaev walked into the Communist Party headquarters, and shot dead Sergei Kirov, the secretary of the Leningrad Soviet. The apparent motive was revenge; Kirov had been having an affair with the killer's wife. But dramatic though the incident was

Key terms

Ryutin group
These were the followers of M.N. Ryutin, a Right Communist, who had published an attack on Stalin, describing him as 'the evil genius who had brought the Revolution to the verge of destruction'.

Party card
An official CPSU document granting membership and guaranteeing privileges to the holder. It was a prized possession in Soviet Russia.

Paranoia
A persecution complex, a conviction in the sufferer that he is surrounded by enemies intent on harming him.

Key date

Beginning of the purges as a systematic terror system: 1934

Key question
In what sense did the post-Kirov purges mark 'Stalin's victory over the Party'?

in itself, its significance went far beyond the tale of a jealous husband shooting his wife's lover. There is a strong probability that the murder of Kirov had been approved, if not planned, by Stalin himself.

Nikita Khrushchev, in his secret speech of 1956 (see page 175), stated that Stalin was almost certainly behind the murder. However, a special study concluded in 1993 that while Stalin may well have been guilty, the evidence against him consists of 'unverified facts, rumours and conjectures'.

Whatever the truth concerning Stalin's involvement, it was certainly the case that the murder worked directly to his advantage. Kirov had been a highly popular figure in the Party. A strikingly handsome Russian, he had made a strong impression at the 17th Party Congress in 1934 and had been elected to the Politburo. He was known to be unhappy with the speed and scale of Stalin's industrialisation drive. He was also opposed to extreme measures being used as a means of disciplining Party members. If organised opposition to Stalin were to form within the Party, Kirov was the outstanding individual around whom dissatisfied members might rally. That danger to Stalin had now been removed.

Stalin was quick to exploit the situation. Within two hours of learning of Kirov's murder he had signed a **'Decree against terrorist acts'** (also known as the 1st December Decree). Under the guise of hunting down those involved in Kirov's murder, a fresh purge of the Party was begun. Stalin claimed that the assassination had been organised by a wide circle of Trotskyites and Leftists, who must all be brought to account. There followed a large-scale round-up of suspected conspirators, who were then imprisoned or executed.

The atmosphere was captured in an account by Victor Serge, one of the suspects who managed to flee from the USSR at this time:

> The shot fired by Nikolaev ushered in an era of panic and savagery. The immediate response was the execution of 114 people, then the execution of Nikolaev and his friends; then the arrest and imprisonment of the whole of the former Zinoviev and Kamenev tendency, close on 3000 persons; then the mass deportation of tens of thousands of Leningrad citizens, simultaneously with hundreds of arrests among those already deported and the opening of fresh secret trials in the prisons.

Party membership

It was an interesting coincidence that just as Stalin's path to power had been smoothed 10 years earlier by 'the Lenin Enrolment' (see page 50), so in 1934 his successful purge was made a great deal easier by a recent major shift in the make-up of the Party. During the previous three years, in 'the Stalin Enrolment', the CPSU had recruited a higher proportion of skilled workers and industrial managers than at any time since 1917.

Stalin encouraged this as a means of tightening the links between the Party and those actually operating the first Five-Year

Key date

Assassination of Kirov: 1 December 1934

Key term

Decree against terrorist acts
Gave the NKVD limitless powers in pursuing the enemies of the State and the Party.

Key question
What was the relationship between the growth in Party membership and the purges?

Plan, but it also had the effect of bringing in a large number of members who joined the Party primarily to advance their careers. Acutely aware that they owed their privileged position directly to Stalin's patronage, the new members eagerly supported the elimination of the anti-Stalinist elements in the Party. After all, it improved their own chances of promotion. The competition for good jobs in Soviet Russia was invariably fierce. Purges always left positions to be filled. As the chief dispenser of positions, Stalin knew that the self-interest of these new Party members would keep them loyal to him. As Norman Stone, a Western analyst of the Soviet Union, memorably put it:

> It was characteristic of Stalin to have his own allies 'marked' by their own subordinates: in Stalin's system identical thugs kept on replacing each other, like so many Russian dolls.

The full-scale purge that followed Kirov's murder in 1934 was the work of Gengrikh Yagoda, head of the **NKVD**. In 1935 Kirov's key post as Party boss in Leningrad was filled by Andrei Zhdanov, described by one contemporary Communist, who managed to escape the purges, as 'a toady without an idea in his head'. The equivalent position in Moscow was filled by another ardent Stalinist, Nikita Khrushchev. In recognition of his strident courtroom bullying of 'oppositionists' in the earlier purge trials, Andrei Vyshinsky, a reformed Menshevik, was appointed State Prosecutor.

    Stalin's fellow-Georgian, Lavrenti Beria, was entrusted with overseeing State security in the national-minority areas of the USSR. With another of Stalin's protégés, Alexander Poskrebyshev, in charge of the Secretariat, there was no significant area of the Soviet bureaucracy that Stalin did not control. Public or Party opinion meant nothing when set against Stalin's grip on the key personnel and functions in Party and government. There had been rumours, around the time of the second FYP (see page 80), of a possible move to oust him from the position of Secretary General. These were silenced in the aftermath of the Kirov affair.

NKVD
The State secret police, a successor of the *Cheka* and a forerunner of the KGB.

Key term

Victims

The outstanding feature of the post-Kirov purge was the status of many of its victims. Prominent among those arrested were Kamenev and Zinoviev, who, along with Stalin, had formed the triumvirate after Lenin's death in 1924 and who had been the leading Left Bolsheviks in the power struggle of the 1920s. At the time of their arrest in 1935 they were not accused of involvement in Kirov's assassination, only of having engaged in 'opposition', a charge that had no precise meaning, and, therefore could not be answered. However, the significance of their arrest and imprisonment was plain to all: no Party members, whatever their rank or revolutionary pedigree, were safe.

    Arbitrary arrest and summary execution became the norm. In the post-Stalin years it was admitted by Khrushchev that the Decree against terrorist acts had become the justification for 'broad acts which contravened socialist justice', a euphemism for

Key question
Who were the victims of the post-Kirov purge?

mass murder. An impression of this can be gained from glancing at the fate of the representatives at the Party Congress of 1934.

- Of the 1996 delegates who attended, 1108 were executed during the next three years.
- In addition, out of the 139 Central Committee members elected at that gathering all but 41 of them were put to death during the purges.

Leonard Shapiro, in his study of the CPSU, described these events as 'Stalin's victory over the Party'. From this point on, the Soviet Communist Party was entirely under his control. It ceased, in effect, to have a separate existence. Stalin had become the Party.

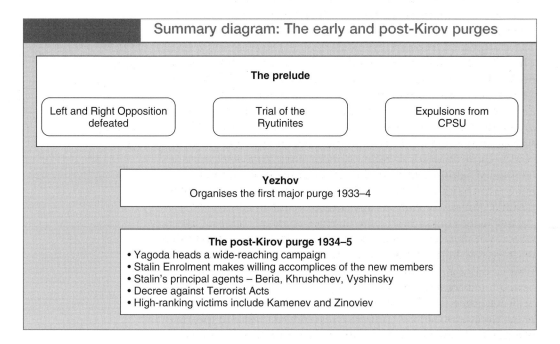

Summary diagram: The early and post-Kirov purges

The prelude

Left and Right Opposition defeated

Trial of the Ryutinites

Expulsions from CPSU

Yezhov
Organises the first major purge 1933–4

The post-Kirov purge 1934–5
- Yagoda heads a wide-reaching campaign
- Stalin Enrolment makes willing accomplices of the new members
- Stalin's principal agents – Beria, Khrushchev, Vyshinsky
- Decree against Terrorist Acts
- High-ranking victims include Kamenev and Zinoviev

3 | The Great Purge 1936–9

Key question
Was there any logic to the Great Purge?

It might be expected that once Stalin's absolute supremacy over the Party had been established the purges would stop. But they did not; they increased in intensity. Stalin declared that the Soviet Union was in 'a state of siege' and called for still greater vigilance in unmasking the enemies within. In 1936 a progressive terrorising of the Soviet Union began which affected the entire population, but took its most dramatic form in the public show trials of Stalin's former Bolshevik colleagues. The one-time heroes of the 1917 Revolution and the Civil War were arrested, tried and imprisoned or executed as enemies of the State. Remarkably, the great majority went to their death after confessing their guilt and accepting the truth of the charges levelled against them. Such was the scale of the persecution at this time, and so high ranking were the victims, that it has gone down in history as 'the Great Purge' or the 'Great Terror'.

The descriptions applied to the accused during the purges bore little relation to political reality. 'Right', 'Left' and Centre' opposition blocs were identified and the groupings invariably had the catch-all term 'Trotskyite' tagged on to them, but such words were convenient prosecution labels rather than definitions of a genuine political opposition. They were intended to isolate those in the Communist Party and the Soviet State whom Stalin wished to destroy.

Stalin's terror programme breaks down conveniently into three sections:

(a) The purge of the Party
(b) The purge of the armed services
(c) The purge of the people.

a) The purge of the Party

The purging of the Left

Key question
Why was there so little resistance from the Party members who were purged?

The prelude to the Great Purge of 1936 was a secret letter sent from CPSU headquarters, warning all the local Party branches of a terrorist conspiracy by 'the Trotskyite–Kamenevite–Zinovievite–Leftist Counter-Revolutionary Bloc' and instructing Party officials to begin rooting out suspected agents and sympathisers. Once this campaign of denunciation and expulsion had been set in motion in the country at large, Kamenev and Zinoviev were put on public trial in Moscow, charged with involvement in Kirov's murder and with plotting to overthrow the Soviet State. Both men pleaded guilty and read out abject confessions in court.

The obvious question is: 'why did they confess?' After all, these men were tough Bolsheviks. No doubt, as was later revealed during de-Stalinisation, physical and mental torture was used. Possibly more important was their sense of demoralisation at having been accused and disgraced by the Party to which they had dedicated their lives and which could do no wrong. In a curious sense, their admission of guilt was a last act of loyalty to the Party.

Whatever their reasons, the fact that they did confess made it extremely difficult for other victims to plead their own innocence. If the great ones of State and Party were prepared to accept their fate, on what grounds could lesser men resist? The psychological impact of the public confessions of such figures as Kamenev and Zinoviev was profound. It helped to create an atmosphere in which innocent victims cravenly submitted in open court to false charges, and went to their death begging the Party's forgiveness.

It also shows Stalin's astuteness in insisting on a policy of public trials. There is little doubt that he had the power to conduct the purges without using legal proceedings. However, by making the victims deliver humiliating confessions in open court, Stalin was able to reveal the scale of the conspiracy against him and to prove the need for the purging to continue.

The purging of the Right

This soon became evident after Kamenev and Zinoviev, along with 14 other Bolsheviks, had been duly executed in keeping with Vyshinsky's notorious demand as Prosecutor that they be shot 'like the mad dogs they are'. The details that the condemned had revealed in their confessions were used to prepare the next major strike, the attack upon 'the Right deviationists'. Bukharin, Rykov and Tomsky were put under investigation, but not yet formally charged. The delay was caused by the reluctance of some of the older Bolsheviks in the Politburo to denounce their comrades. Stalin intervened personally to speed up the process. Yagoda, who was considered to have been too lenient in his recent handling of the 'Trotskyite–Zinovievite bloc', was replaced as head of the NKVD by the less scrupulous Yezhov whose name, like Vyshinsky's, was to become a byword for terror.

The 'Anti-Soviet Trotskyist Centre'

Meanwhile, the case for proceeding against Bukharin and the Right was strengthened by the revelations at a further show trial in 1937, at which 17 Communists, denounced collectively as the 'Anti-Soviet Trotskyist Centre', were charged with spying for Nazi Germany. The accused included Radek and Pyatakov, the former favourites of Lenin, and Sokolnikov, Stalin's Commissar for Finance during the first FYP. Radek's grovelling confession in which he incriminated his close colleagues, including his friend Bukharin, saved him from the death sentence imposed on all but three of the other defendants. He died two years later, however, in an Arctic labour camp.

Yezhov and Vyshinsky now had the evidence they needed. In 1938, in the third of the major show trials, Bukharin and Rykov (Tomsky had taken his own life in the meantime) and 18 other 'Trotskyite-Rightists' were publicly arraigned on a variety of counts, including sabotage, spying and conspiracy to murder Stalin. The fact that Yagoda was one of the accused was a sign of the speed with which the terror was starting to consume its own kind. Fitzroy MacLean, a British diplomat, was one of the foreign contingent permitted to observe the trial. His description conveys the character of the proceedings:

> The prisoners were charged, collectively and individually, with every conceivable crime: high treason, murder, and sabotage. They had plotted to wreck industry and agriculture, to assassinate Stalin, to dismember the Soviet Union for the benefit of their capitalist allies. They were shown for the most part to have been traitors to the Soviet cause ever since the Revolution. One after another, using the same words, they admitted their guilt: Bukharin, Rykov, Yagoda. Each prisoner incriminated his fellows and was in turn incriminated by them.

At one point in the trial Bukharin embarrassed the court by attempting to defend himself, but he was eventually silenced by Vyshinsky's bullying and was sentenced to be shot along with the rest of the defendants. In his final speech in court, Bukharin showed the extraordinary character of the Bolshevik mentality. Despite the injustice of the proceedings to which he had been subjected, he accepted the infallibility of the Party and of Stalin:

When you ask yourself: 'If you must die, what are you dying for?' –
an absolutely black vacuity suddenly rises before you. There was
nothing to die for, if one wanted to die unrepented. And, on the
contrary, everything positive that glistens in the Soviet Union
acquires new dimensions in a man's mind. This in the end
disarmed me completely and led me to bend my knees before the
Party and the country … For in reality the whole country stands
behind Stalin; he is the hope of the world.

The Stalin Constitution 1936

A particular irony attached to Bukharin's execution. Only two
years previously he had been the principal draftsman of the new
constitution of the USSR. This 1936 Constitution, which Stalin
described as 'the most democratic in the world', was intended to
impress Western Communists and Soviet sympathisers. This was
the period in Soviet foreign policy when, in an effort to offset the
Nazi menace to the USSR, Stalin was urging the formation of
'popular fronts' between the Communist parties and the various
Left-wing groups in Europe (see page 116). Among the things
claimed in Constitution were that:

- Socialism had been established and there were no longer any
  'classes' in Soviet society.
- The basic civil rights of freedom of expression, assembly and
  worship were guaranteed.

However, the true character of Stalin's Constitution lay not in
what it said but in what it omitted. Hardly anywhere was the role
of the Party mentioned; its powers were not defined and,
therefore, were not restricted. It would remain the instrument
through which Stalin would exercise his total control of the USSR.
The contrast between the Constitution's democratic claims and

Lenin's General Staff of 1917

STALIN, THE EXECUTIONER, ALONE REMAINS

The Central Committee of The Bolshevik Party in 1917

This montage, composed by Trotsky's supporters, points to the remarkable fact that of the original 1917 Central Committee of the Bolshevik Party only Stalin was still alive in 1938. The majority of the other 23 members had, of course, been destroyed in the purges.

the reality of the situation in the Soviet Union could not have been greater.

b) The purge of the armed forces

Key question
Why did Stalin regard the leaders of the Soviet armed forces as a threat to his power?

A significant development occurred in 1937 when the Soviet military came under threat. Stalin's control of the Soviet Union would not have been complete if the armed services had continued as an independent force. It was essential that they be kept subservient. Knowing that military loyalties might make a purge of the army difficult to achieve, Stalin took the preliminary step of organising a large number of transfers within the higher ranks in order to lessen the possibility of centres of resistance being formed when the attack came.

With this accomplished, Vyshinksy announced, in May 1937, that 'a gigantic conspiracy' had been uncovered in the Red Army. Marshal Tukhachevsky, the popular and talented Chief of General Staff, was arrested along with seven other generals, all of whom had been 'heroes of the Civil War'. On the grounds that speed was essential to prevent a military *coup*, the trial was held immediately, this time in secret. The charge was treason; Tukhachevsky was accused of having spied for Germany and Japan. Documentary evidence, some of it supplied by German intelligence at the request of the NKVD, was produced in proof.

The outcome was predetermined and inevitable. In June 1937, after their ritual confession and condemnation, Tukhachevsky and his fellow generals were shot. There appears to have been a particularly personal element in all this. The president of the secret court that delivered the death sentences was Marshal Voroshilov, a devoted Stalinist, who had long been jealous of Tukhachevsky's talent and popularity.

Tukhachevsky's execution was the signal for an even greater blood-letting. To prevent any chance of a military reaction, a wholesale destruction of the Red Army establishment was undertaken. In the following 18 months:

- All 11 War Commissars were removed from office.
- Three of the five Marshals of the Soviet Union were dismissed.
- 75 of the 80-man Supreme Military Council were executed.
- 14 of the 16 army commanders, and nearly two-thirds of the 280 divisional commanders were removed.
- Half of the commissioned officer corps, 35,000 in total, were either imprisoned or shot.

It was reported that in some army camps at the height of the purge officers were taken away in lorry loads for execution. The Soviet Navy was also purged; all the serving admirals of the fleet were shot and thousands of naval officers were sent to labour camps. The Soviet Air Force was similarly decimated, only one of its senior commanders surviving the purge.

The devastation of the Soviet armed forces, wholly unrelated to any conceivable military purpose, was complete by 1939. It left all three services seriously undermanned and staffed by inexperienced or incompetent replacements. Given the defence needs of the

USSR, a theme constantly stressed by Stalin himself, the deliberate crippling of the Soviet military is the aspect of the purges that most defies logic. It is the strongest evidence suggesting that Stalin had lost touch with reality.

c) The purge of the people

Key question
Why did the purges continue?

Stalin's achievement of total dominance over Party, government and military did not mean the end of the purges. The apparatus of terror was retained and the search for enemies continued. Purges were used to achieve the goals of the FYPs; charges of industrial sabotage were made against managers and workers in the factories. The purge was also a way of forcing the regions and nationalities into total subordination to Stalin.

The show trials that had taken place in Moscow and Leningrad, with their catalogue of accusations, confessions and death sentences, were repeated in all the republics of the USSR. The terror they created was no less intense for being localised. For example, between 1937 and 1939 in Stalin's home state of Georgia, two state prime ministers were removed, and four-fifths of the regional Party secretaries and thousands of lesser officials lost their posts.

This was accompanied by a wide-ranging purge of the legal and academic professions. Foreign Communists living in the Soviet Union were not immune. Polish and German revolutionary exiles were rounded up in scores, and many of them were imprisoned or executed. The outstanding foreign victim was Bela Kun, the leader of the short-lived Communist revolution in Hungary in 1919 (see page 15). He died in a prison camp in 1941.

Mass repression

Understandably, historians have tended to concentrate on the central and dramatic features of the purges, such as the show trials and the attack upon the Party and the Red Army. Yet no area of Soviet life escaped being purged. Under Stalin, terror was elevated into a method of government. The constant fear that this created conditioned the way the Soviet people lived their lives. European scholars who have been working since the early 1990s in the newly opened archives in the former Soviet Union have discovered that in terms of numbers the greatest impact of the purges was on the middle and lower ranks of Soviet society. One in 18 of the population was arrested during Stalin's purges. Almost every family in the USSR suffered the loss of at least one of its members as a victim of the terror.

This was not an accidental outcome of the purges. The evidence now shows that in the years 1937–8 Yezhov deliberately followed a policy of mass repression. This **Yezhovschina** involved NKVD squads going into a range of selected localities, arresting and dragging off hundreds of inhabitants to be executed. The killings were carried out in specially prepared NKVD zones. One notorious example of this was Butovo, a village some 15 miles south of Moscow, which became one of the NKVD's killing grounds. Recent excavations by the Russian authorities have

Key term

Yezhovschina
The period of terror directed at ordinary Soviet citizens in the late 1930s and presided over by Yezhov, the head of the NKVD.

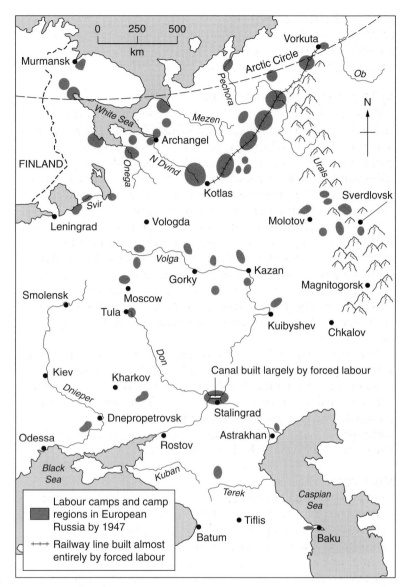

Figure 4.1: The Soviet labour camps, 1937–57. By 1941, as a result of the purges, there were an estimated eight million prisoners in the **gulag**. The average sentence was 10 years, which, given the terrible conditions in the camps, was equivalent to a death sentence. As an example of state-organised terror, Stalin's gulag stands alongside Hitler's concentration camps and Mao Zedong's *laogai* (Chinese prison camp system) in its attempt to suppress the human spirit.

Key term

Gulag
The term for the vast system of prison and labour camps that spread across the USSR during the purges.

revealed mass graves containing over 20,000 bodies, dating back to the late 1930s. Forensic analysis suggests that victims had been taken to Butovo nightly over many months and shot in batches of 100.

Quotas

Quotas of victims to be arrested were laid down like industrial production targets. People were no longer regarded as

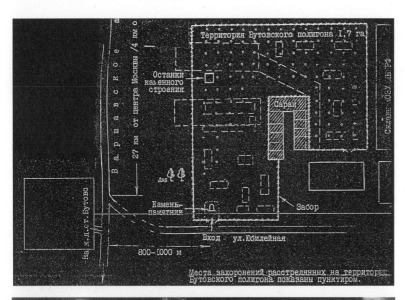

Part of an NKVD blueprint of the Butovo killing fields. The cross-hatched area shows the pit into which the victims were heaped after being shot.

Stalin signing an order for the execution of 6600 condemned prisoners. An interesting point of comparison is that this number exceeded that of all those executed for political offences in tsarist Russia in the 100 years up to 1917.

individuals. It was the numbers not the names that mattered. There was no appeal against sentence and the death warrant required that the execution 'be carried out immediately'.

One incident illustrates the mechanical, de-humanised process. A woman whose neighbour had been arrested called at a police station to ask permission to look after the child the neighbour had had to leave behind. After leaving her waiting for two hours, the police then decided that since they were one short of their daily quota of people to be arrested the caller would make up the number. She was grabbed and thrown into a cell.

Insofar as the terrorising of ordinary people had a specific purpose it was to frighten the USSR's national minorities into abandoning any lingering thoughts of challenging Moscow's control and to force waverers into a full acceptance of Stalin's enforced industrialisation programme.

In the headlong rush to uncover further conspiracies, interrogators themselves became victims and joined those they had condemned in execution cells and labour camps. Concepts such as innocence and guilt lost all meaning during the purges. Most of the population were frightened and bewildered. Fear had the effect of destroying moral values and traditional loyalties. The one aim was survival, even at the cost of betrayal. In a 1988 edition devoted to the Stalinist purges, the Moscow *Literary Gazette* referred to 'the special sadism whereby the nearest relatives were forced to incriminate each other – brother to slander brother, husband to blacken wife'. The chillingly systematic character of the purges was described in the minutes of a plenary session of the Central Committee, held in June 1957 during the de-Stalinisation period (see page 175):

> Between 27 February 1937 and 12 November 1938, the NKVD received approval from Stalin, Molotov and Kagonovich for the Supreme Court to sentence to death by shooting 38,697 people. On one day, 12 November 1938, Stalin and Molotov sanctioned the execution of 3167 people. On 21 November the NKVD received approval from Stalin and Molotov to shoot 229 people, including 23 members and candidate members of the Central Committee, 22 members of the Party Control Commission, 12 regional Party secretaries, 21 People's Commissars, 136 commissariat officials and 15 military personnel.

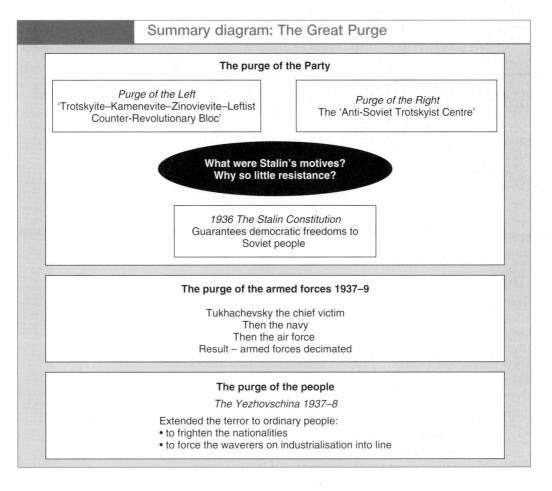

Summary diagram: The Great Purge

The purge of the Party

Purge of the Left
'Trotskyite–Kamenevite–Zinovievite–Leftist Counter-Revolutionary Bloc'

Purge of the Right
The 'Anti-Soviet Trotskyist Centre'

What were Stalin's motives? Why so little resistance?

1936 The Stalin Constitution
Guarantees democratic freedoms to Soviet people

The purge of the armed forces 1937–9

Tukhachevsky the chief victim
Then the navy
Then the air force
Result – armed forces decimated

The purge of the people

The Yezhovschina 1937–8

Extended the terror to ordinary people:
• to frighten the nationalities
• to force the waverers on industrialisation into line

4 | The Later Purges 1941–53

Key question
Why did the Stalinist purges continue into the war and the post-war period?

The purges did not end with the onset of war in 1941 or with the coming of peace in 1945. They had become an integral part of the Stalinist system of government. Stalin blamed military failures on internal sabotage and persecuted those held responsible. Nor did victory soften him. He emerged from the war harder in attitude towards the Soviet people, despite their heroic efforts, and more suspicious of the outside world, despite the alliances entered into by the USSR. It was undeniable that many Soviet troops had deserted to the enemy in the early phases of the war. When peace came, Stalin used this to justify a large-scale purge of the Soviet armed forces.

The tragedy was that he was helped in this by the Western Allies. At the Yalta and Potsdam Conferences in 1945 (see page 132), the victor nations had agreed in principle that all released prisoners of war (POWs) should be returned to their country of origin. In central and eastern Europe these included many Soviet citizens who had fought for Germany against the USSR in an attempt to break free of Stalin. They were terrified at the prospect of what awaited them and pleaded with their Allied captors not to be sent back. However, in the face of Stalin's insistence, the Allies gave in and forcibly repatriated the prisoners they held. There were heart-rending scenes as British troops forced Soviet prisoners at rifle and bayonet point to board the waiting trucks.

The consequences were as appalling as the prisoners had anticipated. Mass executions took place on Stalin's orders. What deepened the horror was that the victims were not only fighting men. On the grounds that whole communities had supported Hitler's forces, whole communities were made to suffer. It was at this time that the Cossacks as a people were virtually destroyed in retribution for their support of the German armies during the war.

Stalin was no gentler to the Soviet prisoners who returned from German captivity. Believing that their very survival indicated that they had collaborated with their captors, he treated them with contempt. It was not uncommon in 1945 for prisoners to be released from German prison camps, only to be transferred directly into Soviet labour camps.

'The Leningrad Affair'

As he grew older Stalin became still more suspicious of those around him. After 1947 he dispensed with the Central Committee and the Politburo, thus removing even the semblance of limitation upon his authority. In 1949 he initiated another Party purge, 'the Leningrad Affair', comparable in scale and style to those of the 1930s. Leading Party and city officials, including those who had previously been awarded the title 'Hero of the Soviet Union' in honour of their courageous defence of Leningrad during the war, were arrested, tried on charges of attempting to use Leningrad as an opposition base, and shot.

The 'doctors' plot'

Soviet Jews were the next section of the population to be selected for purging. Stalin ordered what amounted to a **pogrom** for no better reason than that his daughter, Alliluyeva, had had an affair with a Jew of whom he disapproved. Anti-Semitism was a long-established tradition in Russia and it was a factor in the last purge Stalin attempted. Early in 1953 it was officially announced from the Kremlin that a 'doctors' plot' had been uncovered in Moscow; it was asserted that the Jewish-dominated medical centre had planned to murder Stalin and the other Soviet leaders. Preparations began for a major assault on the Soviet medical profession, comparable to the pre-war devastation of the Red Army. What prevented those preparations being put into operation was the death of Stalin in March 1953.

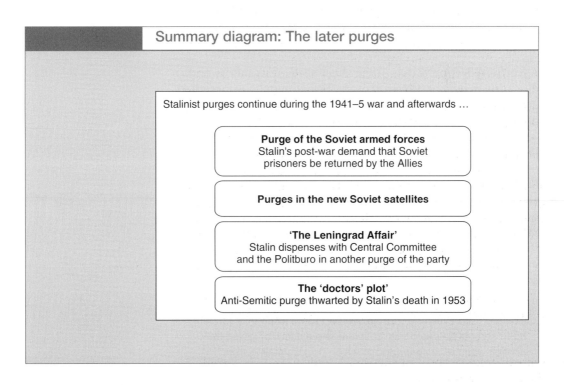

Summary diagram: The later purges

Stalinist purges continue during the 1941–5 war and afterwards …

Purge of the Soviet armed forces
Stalin's post-war demand that Soviet prisoners be returned by the Allies

Purges in the new Soviet satellites

'The Leningrad Affair'
Stalin dispenses with Central Committee and the Politburo in another purge of the party

The 'doctors' plot'
Anti-Semitic purge thwarted by Stalin's death in 1953

5 | The Purges as a Study in Stalin's Use of Power

Stalin's use of terror as a political and social weapon is a grim but fascinating theme. It is still not possible for historians to give a precise figure of those destroyed during the purges. However, in the 1990s access to the files of the KGB was granted to scholars. Major studies, such as Anne Applebaum's *The Gulag* (2003), which complements the earlier pioneering study by Robert Conquest, *The Great Terror* (1968), enable us to quote the following figures as the most reliable now available:

- In 1934, one million were arrested and executed in the first major purge, mainly in Moscow and Leningrad.

- By 1937, 17–18 million had been transported to labour camps; 10 million of these died.
- By 1939, another five to seven million had been 'repressed', one million of these being shot, another one to two million dying in the camps.
- In 1940, the occupation of the Baltic states (Lithuania, Estonia and Latvia), Bukovina and Bessarabia resulted in two million being deported, most of whom died.
- In 1941, the deportation to Siberia of various national groups, including Germans, Kalmyks, Ukrainians, Chechens and Crimean Tatars, led to the deaths of one-third of the four million involved.
- Between 1944 and 1946, the 'screening' of returned prisoners of war and those who had been under German occupation resulted in 10 million being transported to labour camps of the gulag; five to six million of these died in captivity.
- Between 1947 and 1953, one million died in the various purges and repressions during the last six years of Stalin's life.

A fearful reflection is that in the sheer scale of its misery and death the Stalinist repression of the Soviet peoples outweighed even the holocaust, the Nazi genocide of six million Jews in occupied Europe.

Only a partial answer can be offered as to why Stalin engaged for so long in such a brutal exercise. One motive was obviously the desire to impose his absolute authority by bringing all the organs of Party and State under his control. Yet, even after that aim had been achieved, the terror continued. The purges were so excessive and gratuitously vicious that they defy logical analysis. Stalin destroyed people not for what they had done but for what they might do. His suspicions and fears revealed a deep irrationality amounting to paranoia. That, indeed, was how his daughter, Svetlana Alliluyeva, saw it:

> As he'd got older my father had begun feeling lonely. He was so isolated from everyone that he seemed to be living in a vacuum. He hadn't a soul he could talk to. It was the system of which he himself was the prisoner and in which he was stifling from emptiness and lack of human companionship.

6 | The Key Debate

> How far beyond Stalin did the responsibility for the purges and the terror spread?

While fully accepting that Stalin was the architect of the terror, historians have begun to look beyond him in assessing the responsibility for the purges. Their approach has been prompted by their reading of Russian archival material that shows that Stalinism was not as monolithic a system of government as has been traditionally assumed. Attention has shifted to the disorganised state of much of Soviet bureaucracy, particularly at local level.

The purges were clearly initiated by Stalin himself, but he, after all, was only one man, no matter how powerful or feared. How the purges were actually carried out largely depended on the local Party organisation. Many welcomed the purges as an opportunity to settle old scores as well as a way of advancing themselves by filling the jobs vacated by the victims. It has to be acknowledged that the purges were popular with some Russians, those who believed their country could be prevented from slipping back into its historic weakness and backwardness only by being powerfully and ruthlessly led. To such people, Stalin was a genuine saviour whose unrelenting methods were precisely what the nation needed.

The character of Soviet society

It is also arguable that the disruption of Soviet society, caused by the massive upheavals of collectivisation and industrialisation, destroyed any semblance of social stability and so encouraged Party and government officials to resort to the most extreme measures. Civil society as it existed in Russia was not strong or advanced enough to offer an alternative to what was being done in the name of the Communist revolution.

Intrinsic violence of Russian society

Richard Overy, a distinguished modern scholar, draws attention to the violence that he regards as having been intrinsic in Soviet Communism. He quotes Stalin's assertion that 'violent proletarian revolution is an inevitable law of the revolutionary movement' and links it directly with Lenin's declaration that the task of Bolshevism was 'the ruthless destruction of the enemy'. The Stalinist purges, therefore, were a logical historical progression.

In this connection, other scholars have laid weight on how undeveloped the concepts of individual or civil rights were in Russia. Tsardom had been an autocracy in which the first duty of the people had been to obey. The Communists had not changed that. Indeed, they had re-emphasised the necessity of obedience to central authority. The purges were a deadly but logical extension of that principle.

An interesting interpretation relating to the idea that violence was an irremovable feature of Russian Communism has been advanced by a number of modern scholars, among whom J. Arch Getty is the most prominent. Their suggestion is that the purges came from below as much as from above. They mean by this that the purges started by Stalin were then sustained in their ferocity by the lower rank officials in government and party. These lower rank officials wanted to replace their superiors, whom they regarded as a conservative élite. This élite would never give up its power willingly, so it had to be smashed. Russian political tradition did not allow any other alternative.

Nomenklatura

It was certainly true Stalin had no difficulty in finding eager subordinates to organise the purges. The common characteristic of those who led Stalin's campaigns was their unswerving personal loyalty to him, a loyalty that overcame any doubts they might have had regarding the nature of their work. They formed what became known as the **nomenklatura**, the new class of officials whom Stalin created to replace the thousands of old Bolsheviks whom he decimated in the purges.

One prominent historian, M. Agursky, has stressed this development as a major explanation of why terror became so embedded in the Stalinist system. The *nomenklatura* had no loyalty to the old Bolshevik tradition. They were all totally Stalin's men:

> To replace the old élite there came a new stratum which had no continuity with its predecessors for the purges took place in different phases and in the end liquidated the entire body of activists who had taken part in the Revolution and the Civil War.

Dedicated to Stalin, on whom their positions depended, the *nomenklatura* enjoyed rights and privileges denied to the rest of the population. Including their families, they numbered around 600,000 (1.2 per cent of the population) by the late 1930s. It was what came with the job that mattered – plentiful food, luxury accommodation, motor cars with special Party lanes reserved for them to drive on, and top-quality education for their children (see pages 164–5). Once in post, those with such privileges were unlikely to risk them by questioning Stalin's orders. The more potential rivals they exterminated, the safer their jobs were.

In a major study, *Stalin: The Court of the Red Tsar* (2003), Simon Sebag Montefiore has illustrated the eagerness with which Stalin's top ministers carried out his campaigns of terror and persecution. Though they were terrified of him, they did not obey him simply out of fear. People like Yezhov, Beria and Molotov derived the same vindictive satisfaction from their work as their master. Like him, they appeared to have no moral scruples. Sebag Montefiore describes the extraordinary mixture of fear and callousness that made up the lives of the people Stalin surrounded himself with in the **Kremlin** under his tsar-like rule:

> Stalin was utterly unique but many of his views and features such as dependence on death as a political tool, and his paranoia, were shared by his comrades. They lived on ice, killing others to stay alive, sleeping with pistols under their pillows, their wives murdered on Stalin's whim, their children living by a code of lies. Yet they kept their **quasi-religious faith** in the Bolshevism that justified so much death.

An insight into the Soviet mind set that permitted all this to happen is offered by the Russian historian Dimitri Volkogonov, a biographer of Stalin:

> People like Stalin regard conscience as a **chimera**. One cannot speak of the conscience of a dictator; he simply did not have one.

Key terms

Nomenklatura
The Soviet 'establishment' – a privileged élite of officials who ran the Party machine.

Kremlin
The former tsarist fortress in Moscow that became the centre of Soviet government.

Quasi-religious faith
A conviction so powerful that it has the intensity of religious belief.

Chimera
A powerful but ultimately meaningless myth.

The people who did his dirty deeds for him, however, knew full well what they were doing. In such people conscience had 'gone cold'. In consequence, the people allowed their own consciences to be driven into a reservation, thus giving the grand inquisitor the authority to carry on with his dark deeds.

Role of idealism

Yet when seeking to explain the motives of those who implemented the vast terror that overtook the Soviet Union one should not leave out the role of idealism. It may have been a perverted idealism but it was compelling enough to those who shared it to convince them that the arrests, the shootings, the *gulag* were all justified since they were leading ultimately to the triumph of the revolution and the creation of a socialist paradise on earth.

Some key books in the debate
Svetlana Alliluyeva, *Twenty Letters to a Friend* (Penguin, 1968).
J. Arch Getty and Oleg V. Naumov, *The Road to Terror* (Cambridge, 1999).
Alec Nove, *Stalinism and After* (Unwin Hyman, 1975)
Richard Overy, *The Dictators: Hitler's Germany and Stalin's Russia* (Allen Lane, 2004).
Simon Sebag Montefiore, *Stalin: The Court of the Red Tsar* (Weidenfeld and Nicolson, 2003).
Robert Service, *Stalin: A Biography* (Macmillan, 2004).
Robert C. Tucker, *Stalinism – Essays in Historical Interpretation* (Transaction Publishers, 1999).
Dmitri Volkogonov, *Stalin Triumph and Tragedy* (Weidenfeld and Nicolson, 1991).

Study Guide: AS Questions

In the style of AQA

Read the following source then answer the questions that follow.

Adapted from: M. Lynch, Stalin and Khrushchev: The USSR, *1924–64, 1990.*

At the beginning, Party purges were by no means as violent and deadly as they later became. They did not necessarily involve dismissal from the Party, let alone imprisonment or execution.

(a) What is meant by 'Party purges' in the context of the USSR in the years 1929 to 1934? (3 marks)
(b) Explain why Stalin took action against possible opponents in the years 1929 to 1934. (7 marks)
(c) 'Stalin had fully consolidated his dictatorship by 1935'. With reference to the years 1929 to 1939, explain why you agree or disagree with this statement. (15 marks)

Source: AQA, June 2003

Exam tips

The cross-references are intended to take you straight to the material that will help you to answer the questions.

(a) Note that the quotation and question deal with the pre-Kirov purges (page 91). Keep your answer short and to the point. The key point to stress is the relative leniency of the purges of the quoted period.
(b) Here you need to draw on your own knowledge of the motives that led Stalin to take action against possible opponents (page 92). Do not merely describe his measures but *explain* why he took them. You might think it helpful to consider whether Stalin's actions were always entirely logical or rational.
(c) Be guided by the three dates you are given. Use them to contrast the period up to and after 1935. Had the pre-1935 purges put Stalin in complete authority by 1935 or did he need to continue the purges down to 1939 to enforce his absolute control? The relevant material is on pages 91–103. The verdict is yours and there is no finally correct answer. But, remember, whether you decide to agree or disagree with the statement you must *explain* the reasons for your judgement.

In the style of OCR

To what extent did Stalin's security in power rely on terror?

Exam tips

The cross-references are intended to take you straight to the material that will help you to answer the question.

Spend time making sure you fully grasp the question and its terms. The critical requirement is that you address the 'to what extent?' part of the question. You are not being asked simply to describe. You need, therefore, to balance factors against each other (pages 105–9 are particularly relevant). The following sub-questions may help you to structure an answer.

- What was the terror and how did it operate?
- Was Stalin entirely rational in his terror tactics?
- Stalin was only one man. Who carried out the terror in his name?
- Were there not party members who regarded the terror as necessary to fulfil the revolution in Russia?
- Could the USSR have been governed without terror? Remember it pre-dated Stalin. Lenin had believed terror to be necessary given the character of Russia (page 39).
- Terror was an extension of State control. In an unstable society, could State control have been maintained without it?
- Was Stalin's hold on power so insecure, in the Party and over the nation at large, that he needed to impose himself through violence?
- Stalin always stressed that his measures were to protect the USSR from its internal and external enemies. Was this simple hypocrisy or was there any truth in the claim?
- Were there any real challengers to Stalin within the Party to justify the scale of the terror?
- Was the terror imposed from above or welcomed by those below?

Study Guide: A2 Question

In the style of AQA

How effectively did Stalin employ terror to secure economic and political control in the years 1929–39?

Exam tips

The cross-references are intended to take you straight to the material that will help you to answer the question.

The key part of the question is 'how effectively?' Do not simply describe Stalin's economic and political policies and terror tactics, but offer an answer to the question, based on the evidence that you think is important. Key sub-questions to help order your thoughts include:

- How was terror used to enforce collectivisation and industrialisation (page 107 and Chapter 3, page 103)?
- How well did terror work in this context?
- How was terror used to enforce political control (pages 105–6)?
- How effective were the purges in this context?
- Had Stalin achieved full economic and political control in 1939?

Your response to such questions should help you to construct a reasoned, integrated answer.

5 Stalin's Foreign Policy 1929–45

POINTS TO CONSIDER

The foreign policy that Stalin followed between 1929 and 1941 helped to shape the international scene at a critical time in world history. His impact is studied in this chapter under the following themes:

- Stalin's approach to international affairs
- Soviet foreign policy in the 1930s
- The Nazi–Soviet Pact 1939–41
- The Great Patriotic War 1941–5

Key dates

1929	Britain formally recognised the USSR
1933–9	Nazi Germany a constant threat to Soviet security
1934	USSR admitted to the League of Nations
1935	Defensive agreement between USSR, France and Czechoslovakia
	Stalin encouraged European Communists to form 'popular fronts' with non-Marxist left-wing parties against fascism
1936	The Anti-Comintern Pact signed by Germany, Italy and Japan
1936–9	Soviet Union involved in the Spanish Civil War
1938	The Munich Agreement appeared to isolate the USSR
1939	The Nazi–Soviet Pact allowed Germany and USSR to carve up Poland
1941	Hitler unleashed Operation Barbarossa against the Soviet Union
1941–5	The Great Patriotic War

1 | Stalin's Approach to International Affairs

Fear of Western encroachment was a long-standing feature of Russian foreign policy, going back to the days of the tsars. That traditional anxiety had been intensified by the foreign interventions in Soviet Russia in the early 1920s (see page 13). Although the interventions had been overcome, they had revealed how internationally isolated Russia was. Lenin became determined

Key question
How committed was Stalin to international revolution?

that the nation must secure its own defence. In 1921 he had declared, 'Our foreign policy while we are alone and while the capitalist world is strong consists in our exploiting contradictions.' What he meant was that Soviet Russia would protect itself in a hostile world not by provoking the capitalist nations but by playing on the differences that separated them from each other. The conflicting self-interest of such countries as France, Britain and Germany would be exploited by the Soviet Union to prevent the build-up of an anti-Communist alliance.

So it was that compromise, rather than confrontation, was the guiding principle of the foreign policy that Stalin inherited from Lenin. He continued it by adopting an essentially defensive attitude towards the outside world. There is, therefore, an important distinction to be made between the theory and the practice of Soviet foreign policy under Stalin:

- Judged by its propaganda, the USSR was pledged to the active encouragement of worldwide revolution. The Comintern existed for this very purpose (see page 14).
- However, in practice the Bolsheviks did not regard Soviet Russia as being strong enough to sustain a genuinely revolutionary foreign policy. Their first task was to ensure the survival of the Revolution in Russia itself.

This meant that whatever its aggressive poses and claims may have been, the primary purpose of the Comintern was to safeguard the existence of Soviet Russia. The notion of international revolution was not abandoned, but it was no longer an immediate objective. One of Stalin's contemporaries, Dmitri Volkogonov, later reflected: 'From a frontal attack on the citadel of imperialism, with the aim of igniting world revolution, Stalin switched to the strategy of prolonged siege'.

The Comintern continued to have a role under Stalin but it was limited to protecting the USSR. It is significant that foreign Communist parties who wished to affiliate to the Comintern had to swear absolute obedience to the line dictated by the Soviet Union. Zinoviev coined the term **'Bolshevisation'** to describe this. Far from being the vanguard of international Communism, the Comintern became a branch of the Soviet foreign office.

Key term

Bolshevisation
The process of subjecting international Communist parties to the will of Moscow.

Summary diagram: Stalin's approach to international affairs

Lenin's legacy	Stalin
• Realism in foreign affairs • Soviet Union surrounded by hostile states • Soviet Union not strong enough to lead international revolution • Therefore, defensive approach based on 'exploiting contradictions in the capitalist world'	• Accepted Lenin's defensive policies • 'Socialism in one country' • Meant subordination of foreign affairs to domestic issues • Comintern's essential role to defend interests of Soviet Union

2 | Soviet Foreign Policy in the 1930s

Soviet foreign policy 1929–33

Although the Soviet Union was regarded with suspicion by most governments in western Europe, there were many people, usually on the **political Left**, who wanted to believe the best of Stalin's Russia and who considered that its poor image was a deliberate distortion by the capitalist-controlled Western press. For example, a large number of British trade unionists remained staunchly loyal to what they regarded as the Soviet experiment in workers' rule. Trade union influence was one of the factors prompting the second Labour government (1929–31) to develop contacts with the USSR. In 1929 Ramsay MacDonald's cabinet restored formal British recognition of the Soviet Union. This was followed by the signing of a commercial treaty between the two countries.

These appeared to be major diplomatic and commercial gains but they were lessened by political developments inside the Soviet Union. Stalin's victory over the Right (see page 62) coincided with his adopting a tougher approach towards other countries. This hard line was taken not so much towards their governments as towards the left-wing non-Communist parties. It was laid down that Communist parties in other countries were not allowed to form alliances with non-Marxist parties of whom Moscow disapproved. Movements, such as the Labour Party in Britain and the Social Democrats in Germany, and individual socialist leaders, such as Ramsay MacDonald and Leon Blum of France, were denounced as **'social-fascists'**. Oddly enough, real fascism, which had been in power in Italy since 1922 and was beginning to grow menacingly in its Nazi form in Germany, was largely ignored.

Part of the explanation for Stalin's blindness over this lies in the peculiar circumstances of the time. It was in the late 1920s and early 1930s that Stalin embarked on his massive collectivisation and industrialisation programme (see page 68). This happened to coincide with the onset of the **Great Depression** in North America and Europe. The contrast between the seeming success of Soviet economic planning and the capitalist crisis in the West could be interpreted as evidence of the superiority of the Soviet system. If this were indeed the case, then the Soviet Union had less to fear than it had hitherto thought. This reduced its need to cultivate links with the non-Marxist parties. It could continue its policy of direct contact with the capitalist governments, playing upon their weaknesses and exploiting the contradictions between them.

In the long term, the USSR was to pay dearly for Stalin's failure to grasp what was happening in Germany. Before 1933, the year Hitler come to power, Stalin considered that the Nazis were not strong enough to achieve their ends. He appears to have been misled by their title, National Socialist, into thinking that they might be useful in preparing the ground for an eventual workers' revolution in Germany. Accordingly, it made sense for the **KPD** to co-operate with the Nazis. He did not appreciate that the strength and appeal of Nazism derived from its nationalism,

Key question
Why was the Soviet Union initially reluctant to co-operate with the progressive parties in other countries?

Key terms

Political Left
Progressives who, without necessarily being Marxist, believed in state planning and radical social change, which made them sympathetic towards the USSR.

Social-fascists
Those who pretend to favour socialist progress but whose real aim is to prevent progress towards genuine revolution.

Great Depression
A period of economic stagnation in the USA and Europe that lasted for most of the 1930s.

KPD
The German Communist Party.

which made it fundamentally opposed to international Communism. His misjudgement prevented Stalin from seeing the need to organise an alliance of the German centre and Left against Nazism. Events were to show that the KPD's obedience to the Kremlin's command not to ally with the Social Democrats had destroyed the one real chance of creating a political barrier to Nazi power in Germany.

Soviet foreign policy 1933–9

Even after Hitler came to power in 1933, Stalin was still slow to read the signs. He tried to maintain the 11-year-old Soviet–German alliance which dated back to the **Treaty of Rapallo**. In the end it required such developments as the violent Nazi attacks upon the KPD, open discussion among German diplomats of their country's expansion into the USSR, and the signing in 1934 of a **German–Polish treaty**, to convince Stalin that Nazi Germany was a menace. The anti-Bolshevik propaganda that the Nazis began to produce in Germany was hardly less rabid than their anti-Semitism. The USSR's greatest fear – that of isolation – returned.

For the next six years Soviet foreign policy was primarily concerned with finding allies to nullify the German danger. This has sometimes been referred to as a 'turnabout' in Soviet policy, but the reality was that Stalin had no alternative. After 1933 it was no longer possible to pursue a pro-German policy. Far from being a means of security, Germany was now the chief danger. Tactics may have changed, but the central strategy, first introduced by Lenin, of avoiding Soviet Russia's international isolation, remained. Dominic Lieven, a modern analyst of Russian imperialism, sees Stalin's foreign policy as a direct continuation of that followed by the last of the tsars:

> In principle, Stalin, faced with the same threat, had the same options as Nicholas II. He could seek to deter and if necessary defeat this threat in alliance with the British and the French. Alternatively, he could seek to deflect German expansion westwards, hoping that the Germans, French and British would check, weaken and exhaust each other. Meanwhile Russia could increase her relative power by devoting herself to the development of her immense resources. In 1939, after failing to come to terms with the West European allies, Stalin opted for deflection.

One of the earliest opportunities for the USSR to lessen its isolation came with its admission into the **League of Nations** in 1934. The League provided a platform for the Soviet Union, led by its newly appointed Foreign Commissar, Maxim Litvinov, to call for the adoption of the principle of **collective security** in international affairs. One of the fruits of this was an agreement in 1935 between the USSR, France and Czechoslovakia, promising 'mutual assistance' if one of the partners suffered military attack. It was also in 1935 that preliminary Soviet diplomatic contact was made with the USA.

Key question
What was Stalin's foreign policy in these years intended to achieve?

Key terms

Treaty of Rapallo, April 1922
Provided German forces with training grounds in Soviet Russia in return for Russian trading rights in Germany.

German–Polish treaty, January 1934
A 10-year non-aggression pact between the two countries implied a strong security threat to the Soviet Union's western borders.

League of Nations
The body set up in 1919 with the aim of resolving all international disputes and so maintaining world peace.

Collective security
Nations acting together to protect individual states from attack.

Turnabout

Of more immediate significance than the diplomatic manoeuvrings in 1935 was the decision, taken in that same year, by the Comintern to reverse its former policy of non-alignment with the Left. The Comintern now appealed for a **'popular front'** in Europe to combat fascism. This was truly a turnabout in policy but it came too late. The damage had been done. European socialists, previously abused by the Soviet Union as 'social-fascists', were understandably reluctant to respond to what they regarded as mere Soviet expediency in the face of German aggression. Nonetheless, Stalin pressed on with his efforts to rally international support. The new Constitution, which he introduced in 1936 (see page 98), was basically a piece of propaganda aimed at convincing the outside world that the USSR was a free and democratic society.

Such gains as the new approach in Soviet foreign policy achieved proved largely superficial. Collective security was impressive as a principle, but was wholly unsuccessful in practice in the 1930s. The basic weakness was that Europe's two most powerful states, France and Britain, were not prepared to risk war in order to uphold the principle. Without their participation there was no possibility of collective security becoming a reality.

Indeed, the Soviet Union complained that as the 1930s wore on France and Britain lost their resolve to act as upholders of European security. This certainly seemed evident in the record of Anglo-French responses to fascist aggression in the mid-1930s:

- When Mussolini's Italy invaded Abyssinia in 1935, France and Britain responded not by condemning the invasion but by seeking ways to stop its becoming an international crisis. To this end, they agreed to a settlement with Mussolini that ceded two-thirds of Abyssinia to the Italians, leaving the native people with the remaining impoverished third.
- When Hitler, in direct breach of the Versailles Treaty, sent his forces to re-occupy the Rhineland in 1936, Britain and France offered formal protests but made no military moves to prevent the German takeover.

The year 1936 was to prove a very black one for the USSR's hopes of sheltering under collective security. In addition to the display of German aggression and Anglo-French weakness, the year saw the creation of an international alliance, the **Anti-Comintern Pact**, aimed directly against the Soviet Union. The danger that this represented threatened to destroy all the efforts made by the Soviet Union since 1933 to establish its security. It led Stalin to re-double his efforts to obtain reliable allies and guarantees. However, in his attempts to achieve this, Stalin was labouring under a handicap, largely of his own making. The plain fact was that Soviet Russia was not trusted. Enough was known of the Stalinist purges to make neutrals in other countries wary of making alliances with a nation where such treachery or such tyranny was possible.

Key terms

Popular front
An alliance of all Communist, socialist and progressive parties.

Anti-Comintern Pact
Formed by the fascist nations, Germany, Italy and Japan, it carried a clear threat of a two-front attack on the Soviet Union's European and Far-Eastern borders.

Key date

Formation of the Anti-Comintern Pact: November 1936

Key question
What were Stalin's intentions towards Spain?

Key terms

Spanish Civil War
Fought principally between General Franco's fascist forces and the republicans. Franco was the eventual winner.

Anschluss
Incorporation of Austria into the Third Reich in March 1938.

Key question
How did Stalin view the Munich settlement?

The Spanish Civil War

If Stalin made it difficult for neutrals and moderates to sympathise with the defence needs of the Soviet Union, he also put obstacles in the way of those on the political Left in other countries who should have been his natural supporters. His pursuit of defence agreements with the capitalist powers led to compromises that alienated many Soviet sympathisers. This was especially so with regard to Stalin's attitude towards the **Spanish Civil War** (1936–9). The struggle in Spain was a complex affair, but the rest of Europe tended to see it in simple terms as a conflict between the republican Left and the fascist Right, a reflection of the basic political divide in Europe. Stalin and the Comintern, in keeping with the new Soviet policy of encouraging anti-fascist 'popular fronts', sent agents into Spain to organise an alliance of pro-Republican forces.

Stalin's motives and policies were mixed. By focusing on Spain he hoped to divert foreign attention away from the current Soviet purges. The sending of Soviet military equipment to the Republican side was not simple generosity. In payment, the Spanish Republic had to transfer the greater part of its gold reserves to the USSR. Furthermore, the 'popular front' policy meant in practice that the Soviet Union required all the Republican contingents to put themselves under Soviet direction. The Spanish Left came to resent the Soviet Union's attempts at domination and to doubt whether Stalin really wanted the victory of the Spanish Republic.

They were correct; Stalin was anxious not to see a major victory for Marxism in Spain. The explanation for this paradox lay not in Spain, but in Europe at large. Stalin feared that, if Communism were installed in south-western Europe, this would so frighten France and Britain that they might well react by forming an anti-Soviet front with Germany and Italy, the very consequence that Soviet foreign policy was struggling to avoid.

The Munich settlement

Events in Spain had not run their full course when they were overtaken by dramatic developments in central Europe. In the autumn of 1938, France, Britain, Italy and Germany signed the Munich agreement, the climax to the Czechoslovak crisis. Hitler had demanded that the Sudetenland, an area that in 1919 had been incorporated into Czechoslovakia, be allowed to become part of Germany. He had threatened invasion if his requirements were not met. Although Hitler's demand was another breach of the Versailles settlement, neither Britain nor France was prepared to resist him militarily. The Munich agreement granted all his major demands.

This success came on top of Hitler's achievement, earlier in 1938, of the *Anschluss* in direct defiance of the Versailles settlement, which had forbidden the unification of Germany and Austria. Munich was thus a further example of Hitler's ability to get his way in Europe by exploiting French and British reluctance to contemplate armed resistance.

In the Western world the Munich settlement has customarily been seen as an act of 'appeasement', part of the Anglo-French policy of avoiding war by making concessions to the aggressor. That was not the interpretation put upon it by Stalin. For him,

'WHAT, NO CHAIR FOR ME?'

Low's cartoon of September 1938 accurately captured Stalin's response to the Munich settlement, which formally accepted Germany's demand for possession of the Sudeten region of Czechoslovakia. The Russian leader viewed the Munich conference, to which the USSR had pointedly not been invited despite its formal alliance of 1935 with Czechoslovakia, as a Western conspiracy. The other people represented are Hitler, Neville Chamberlain, Daladier of France, and Mussolini.

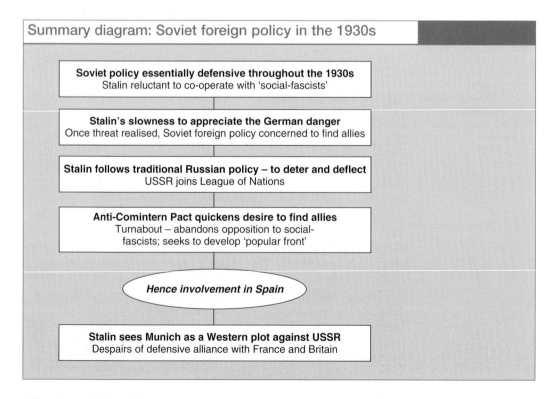

Summary diagram: Soviet foreign policy in the 1930s

Soviet policy essentially defensive throughout the 1930s
Stalin reluctant to co-operate with 'social-fascists'

Stalin's slowness to appreciate the German danger
Once threat realised, Soviet foreign policy concerned to find allies

Stalin follows traditional Russian policy – to deter and deflect
USSR joins League of Nations

Anti-Comintern Pact quickens desire to find allies
Turnabout – abandons opposition to social-fascists; seeks to develop 'popular front'

Hence involvement in Spain

Stalin sees Munich as a Western plot against USSR
Despairs of defensive alliance with France and Britain

Munich was a gathering of the anti-Soviet nations of Europe, intent on giving Germany a free hand to attack a diplomatically isolated USSR. To forestall this, Stalin intensified his efforts to reach agreement with France and Britain. In the year after Munich, Maxim Litvinov and his successor as foreign minister, Molotov, delivered a series of formal alliance proposals to the French and British governments. These went unanswered. France and Britain could not bring themselves to trust Stalin. Both countries also genuinely considered that an alliance with Poland rather than the USSR offered better protection against further German expansion.

Key question
Why was the Soviet Union willing to sign a non-aggression pact with Nazi Germany in 1939?

3 | The Nazi–Soviet Pact 1939–41

In August 1939 the impossible happened. Two deadly international enemies, Hitler's Germany and Stalin's Russia, came together in a formal agreement. Molotov, the Soviet foreign minister, and his German counterpart, Ribbentrop, signed the Nazi–Soviet Pact, in which both countries gave a solemn pledge to maintain peaceful relations with each other. The key articles read:

> Article I. The Government of the German Reich and the Government of the USSR obligate themselves to desist from any act of violence, any aggressive action, and any attack on each other, either individually or jointly with other powers.

> Article VI. The present treaty is concluded for a period of ten years.

Key dates
Signing of the Nazi–Soviet Pact: August 1939

Soviet–German agreement to divide Poland: 28 September 1939

In a 'Secret Additional Protocol', it was agreed that the USSR would take over the Baltic states of Estonia, Latvia and Lithuania, and that Poland would later be divided between Germany and the USSR. At the beginning of September 1939, German forces began to occupy Poland. Four weeks later, under the terms of the protocol, Germany and the Soviet Union signed a formal agreement that effectively carved up Poland between them.

The Nazi–Soviet Pact bewildered the USSR's friends and puzzled its foes. It seemed to defy history and logic. An official at the British Foreign Office dryly remarked that with the coming together of fascism and Communism, Nazism and Marxism 'all these -isms are now -wasms'. But there was a rationale to this remarkable change in Soviet foreign policy. Given the real threat that Germany presented and the indifference of Paris and London to his offers of a defensive alliance, Stalin felt he had been left no alternative. He had acted on the axiom 'if you can't beat them, join them', and had attempted to end the danger from Germany by the only move that international circumstances still allowed – an agreement with Germany.

Results of the Pact

The fruits of the Pact were gathered by both countries during the next two years. The USSR duly grabbed the eastern half of Poland. Germany was free to conduct its war against France and

Molotov signs the Nazi–Soviet Pact on 23 August 1939. A smiling Stalin looks on.

Britain in the west, while in the east the USSR added to its Polish prize by forcibly taking hold of the Baltic states, southern Finland and Bessarabia-Bukovina (see the map on page 136). By 1941 Soviet Russia had regained all the territories it had lost as a result of the First World War. All this, added to the 10-year guarantee of peace with Germany, seemed to justify the praise heaped on Stalin inside the Soviet Union for his diplomatic master-stroke.

The extravagant claim made for the Nazi–Soviet Pact was that it had safeguarded Soviet security by a guarantee of freedom from western attack, and had thus fulfilled the chief objective for which Soviet foreign policy had been struggling since the days of Lenin. Stalin appears to have believed his own propaganda. It is one of the inexplicable things about him that he remained oblivious to the fact that Hitler's ultimate aim in foreign affairs was the invasion and occupation of Russia. An outstanding and consistent feature of Nazism from its beginnings had been its conviction that Germany's destiny was to expand eastwards at the expense of the Slav lands, including Russia. That was the one clear strategy to be deduced from Hitler's *Mein Kampf*.

After August 1939, Stalin chose to ignore all this. It is remarkable that he failed to realise that the pact, which gave Germany a free hand in the war that broke out in Western Europe in September 1939, made the German invasion of Russia likely to come sooner rather than later. He was thus wholly unprepared for the German attack when it was launched in June 1941.

Summary diagram: The Nazi–Soviet Pact

Terms
- 10-year non-aggression agreement
- Secret clauses over Baltic states and Poland

Results
- Hailed as diplomatic triumph for Stalin
- Lulled him into false sense of security
- Gave Germany free rein in Western Europe
- Left Soviet exposed to German attack in June 1941

4 | The Great Patriotic War 1941–5

Operation Barbarossa 1941

Key question
Why did Stalin refuse initially to accept that a German invasion of the Soviet Union had taken place?

The fall of France in June 1940, and the inability of Britain to do more than survive, encouraged Hitler to launch his long-intended attack upon the USSR on 22 June 1941. Operation Barbarossa, Hitler's own code-name for the invasion, was on such a huge scale that preparations for it could not be concealed. For many months before it was unleashed the USSR had known of its likelihood. On 15 June, a week before the attack, the Kremlin received information from Richard Sorge, a Comintern agent in Japan, which provided hard evidence that Germany was about to launch a massive assault on western Russia. Stalin wrote dismissively on Sorge's message: 'This is German disinformation'.

On the following day Stalin received further news confirming Sorge's story, this time from Fitin, the head of Soviet Security. Fitin informed Stalin that a reliable source in the Luftwaffe had warned, 'Preparations for an armed invasion of the USSR are fully complete and the attack may be expected at any time'. Stalin's reaction was to write angrily to Fitin's boss, Merkulov, the Minister for State Security: 'You can tell your "source" in German air force headquarters to go fuck himself. He's not a "source", he's a disinformer'.

Key date

Operation Barbarossa launched: 22 June 1941.

Why Stalin refused to accept the truth defies reasonable explanation. Perhaps he could not bring himself to admit that the Nazi–Soviet Pact had failed. Perhaps he genuinely believed that Hitler could still be bought off. This might explain why in 1941 he had offered more and more Soviet military and economic concessions to Germany. Yet however baffling Stalin's reasoning, its consequences were abundantly clear. Because he was unwilling to admit the reality of the situation in June 1941 none of his underlings could take the initiative. For days after the German invasion had started, Stalin sat in his *dacha*, refusing to speak or give instructions. The result was that in the first week of the Second World War on the eastern front the German forces overran a Soviet Union that was without effective leadership or direction.

Key term

Dacha
Russian term for a country house.

Hitler declared that the world would hold its breath when it witnessed Barbarossa. He had every right to be dramatic. It was a huge enterprise, unprecedented in the history of warfare. Germany put into the field:

- three million troops
- half a million motorised vehicles
- 4000 tanks
- 3000 aircraft.

Yet it was not this great array that gave the invaders the initial advantage. Indeed, in terms of simple logistics, the Soviet Union had the larger forces. The USSR matched Germany in the number of troops, and had four times the number of tanks and three times the number of aircraft. What made the Soviet Union incapable of effective defence in the early days of the war was Stalin's mental paralysis.

Failure of Barbarossa

Three factors explain the German failure to defeat the USSR by the winter of 1941–2.

- Stalin pulled himself together and began to show the strength of leadership for which he became renowned for the rest of the war.
- The lateness of the launching of Barbarossa, which was delayed by some six weeks from its originally planned date, meant that, in spite of the rapid and crushing advance of German forces, the expected Russian capitulation had not come by the autumn of 1941. Neither Moscow nor Leningrad, though heavily besieged by then, had fallen.
- Fate intervened on Russia's side. The thick mud of a torrential autumn was followed by the snow and ice of one of the most severe winters in Russian memory. German movement slowed to a dead halt. Russian forces were able to regroup and begin counterattacks under Marshal Zhukov in December 1941. Germany was now involved in a struggle on its eastern front that would decide the outcome of the war itself.

> **Key question**
> Why was Germany unable to exploit Soviet anti-Stalinism to its own advantage?

A striking aspect of the Barbarossa campaign was that in many areas along the front the local Soviet population at first welcomed the invaders. Some were even willing to join the German forces. This was not from love of Germany but from hatred of Stalinism. Had the German high command grasped the significance of this, they might have enlisted the people of the occupied areas in a great anti-Stalin crusade. Otto Brautigam, the deputy leader of the German Ministry for the Occupied East, described how 'In the Soviet Union we found on our arrival a population weary of Bolshevism. The population greeted us with joy as liberators and placed themselves at our disposal.'

However, blinded by Nazi racial theory, the Germans treated the areas they overran with calculated savagery. The consequence, in Brautigam's words, was that 'our policy has forced both Bolsheviks and Russian nationalists into a common front against us. The Russian fights today with exceptional self-sacrifice for nothing more or less than recognition of his human dignity'.

Germany was eventually to pay a terrible price for this. The Soviet people responded to German brutality by committing themselves to a desperate struggle for survival that earned itself the title the Great Patriotic War, which climaxed in victory in 1945. In pushing into eastern Germany in the closing stages of the war, the Red Army subjected the civilian population to the same ferocity that the Soviet people had suffered.

The character of the war

The USSR's struggle against Germany was a simple one in its essentials. It was a **war of attrition**. From near defeat in 1941 the Soviet Union drew the German forces deeper and deeper into Russia until they were overstretched and vulnerable. The Soviet armies then counter-attacked, pushing the enemy back into Germany until Berlin itself fell in May 1945.

Two particular battles illustrate the character of the Soviet resistance and explain Germany's eventual defeat.

The Battle of Stalingrad 1942–3

As part of their push south-eastward to seize the oil fields of the Caucasus, the German forces besieged the city of Stalingrad. The city was not of major strategic value, but it bore Stalin's name. Defining it as a symbol of Russian resistance, Stalin demanded that his city be defended to the death. Hitler's response was perfectly matched. It was recorded in the official High Command report: 'The *Führer* orders that on entry into the city the entire male population be done away with'.

But having entered Stalingrad the Germans met such a ferocious resistance that they were forced onto the defensive. The besiegers became the besieged. Ignoring the appeals of his generals at the front, who urged a withdrawal, Hitler instructed his army to retreat not one millimetre. They were 'to fight to the last soldier and the last bullet'. The result was that the German forces, deprived of supplies and reinforcements, were battered and starved into submission. Their surrender on 31 January 1943 was a blow from which Germany never recovered:

- 200,000 German troops died in the battle.
- Another 91,000 became prisoners at its end; of these, only 6000 would survive their captivity.
- Hitler's Sixth Army, which had been the most successful of all Germany's forces since the start of the war, had been destroyed.

The Soviet forces themselves had suffered terribly. In the battle that occupied the winter months of 1942–3 over a million Soviet troops were killed. The life expectancy of a soldier at the front was 24 hours.

Stalingrad was singly the most important conflict of the war in Europe. It proved that Hitler's armies were not invincible and gave real promise of final victory to the Western allies. The Soviet newspaper *Red Star* summed up the significance of it all:

Key question
Why was the war on the eastern front so bitter and destructive?

Key term

War of attrition
A grinding conflict in which each side hopes to win by wearing the other down.

What was destroyed at Stalingrad was the flower of the German *Wehrmacht* [army]. Hitler was particularly proud of the 6th Army and its great striking power. It was the first to invade Belgium. It took Paris. It took part in the invasion of Yugoslavia and Greece. In 1942 it broke through from Karkov to Stalingrad. And now it does not exist.

The Battle of Kursk July 1943

It was in an effort to regain his army's prestige that Hitler backed a plan by his generals, who had noted that a large bulge had appeared where the Soviet forces had overextended their defensive line in the region of Kursk. If the Germans were to launch a full-scale panzer attack they could break through the Soviet line and so regain the initiative on the eastern front.

So it was that on 5 July 1943 **Operation Citadel** was begun. It produced the largest tank battle in history. The Soviet commanders with astonishing speed poured their forces into the Kursk salient. The number of troops and armaments deployed are shown in Table 5.1.

Operation Citadel
The German code name for the Battle of Kursk.

Key term

Table 5.1: Troops and armaments used in the Battle of Kursk

	Troops	Tanks	Aircraft
German	700,000	2400	1800
Soviet	1,300,000	3400	2100

It was superior numbers that mattered. After 12 days of savage attack and counter attack, the German forces still had not broken through. Mindful of Stalingrad, Hitler decided to save his armies from another devastating defeat by calling off the whole operation. The Soviet Union justifiably hailed it as another great victory. Kursk had confirmed what Stalingrad had first revealed – the Soviet forces were winning the war. And so it proved. Over the next two years they went over to the offensive, driving the German forces from Soviet territory and finally invading Germany itself. In the spring of 1945 a battered, occupied and devastated Germany surrendered.

The impact of the war on the USSR

The ferocity and scale of the four-year fight to the death meant that everything in the Soviet Union was subordinated to the sheer necessity of survival. After his initial paralysis of will, Stalin began to exercise his formidable powers of leadership. In his first radio broadcast of the war on 3 July 1941, he appealed to the people to defend 'Mother Russia' by adopting the scorched-earth methods of warfare that had always saved the nation in its glorious past:

Key question
How did the Soviet Union respond to the demands of war?

The issue is one of life and death for the peoples of the USSR. We must mobilise ourselves and reorganise all our work on a new wartime footing, where there can be no mercy to the enemy.

In areas occupied by the enemy, sabotage groups must be organised to combat enemy units, to foment guerrilla warfare everywhere, to blow up bridges and roads, damage telephone and telegraph lines, to set fire to forests, stores and transports. In occupied regions, conditions must be made unbearable for the enemy.

Stalin's insistence during the previous 13 years that the Soviet economy be put on a war footing began to show obvious benefits. Centralised authority was of great value when it came to organising the war effort. Furthermore, the harshness of the conditions under which the Soviet people had laboured in the 1930s had prepared them for the fearful hardships of war. The raw courage and resilience of the Russian people, seemingly inured to suffering, proved a priceless asset.

How much the Soviet people suffered can be expressed very simply. At the end of 1941, after only six months of war, the following losses had been suffered:

- Half the Soviet population was under German occupation.
- One-third of the nation's industrial plant was in German hands.
- Iron and steel production had dropped by 60 per cent.
- 40 per cent of the railway system was no longer usable.
- Livestock had been reduced by 60 per cent.
- Grain stocks had been reduced by 40 per cent.

Wartime reorganisation

The reason for this early catastrophe was that under the Five-Year Plans Soviet industrial expansion had been sited west of the Urals, the area most vulnerable to German attack. To offset the losses, extraordinary efforts were then made to transfer whole sectors of Soviet industry to the relative safety of the eastern USSR. All adults not involved in essential war work were conscripted into the armed forces. This, together with the huge number of casualties, amounting to four million in the first year of the war, meant that women and children had to fill the vacant places in the factories.

Work on the land became an almost totally female activity. Arms production received top priority. By 1942 over half of the national income was being devoted to military expenditure. This was the highest proportion by far of any of the countries involved in the Second World War. In such circumstances the pre-war levels of production could not be maintained. Figure 5.1 (page 126) suggests the degree of industrial disruption in the Soviet Union caused by the German occupation during the first two years of the war.

The year 1942 marked the lowest point in Soviet economic fortunes. But from then on, as things began to improve on the military front, there was a corresponding improvement in the economy. The new factories in the Urals began to come into production. The 17 million tons of war materials sent by the USA to the USSR under a **lend-lease programme** bolstered the Soviet's home-produced supply of weapons and motor transport. Of special significance was the recovery and expansion of the Soviet railway system, which enabled troops and supplies to be moved strategically. With the retreat of the German armies on a broad front, following their defeats in 1943 at Stalingrad and Kursk, the USSR began to regain its lost industrial sites. The scale of economic recovery that followed can be seen in Table 5.2 (page 126).

Key term

Lend-lease programme
The importing by the Soviet Union of war materials from the USA with no obligation to pay for them until after the war.

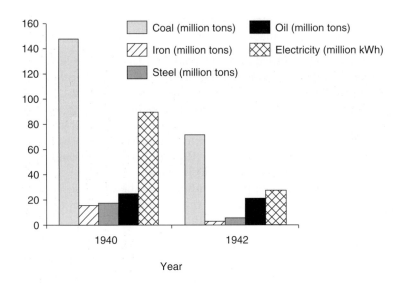

Figure 5.1: Industrial production in the USSR

Table 5.2: Wartime productivity in the USSR (calculated to a base unit of 100 in 1940)

	1941	1942	1943	1944
National income	92	66	74	88
Total industrial output	98	77	90	104
Armaments production	140	186	224	251
Fuel production	94	53	59	75
Agricultural output	42	38	37	54

The figures in Table 5.2 indicate the prodigious response of the Soviet Union to the demands of war. The ability to achieve a huge arms production at a time of acute shortages in plant, materials and manpower is the outstanding example of this response.

The suffering of the Soviet people

However, the recovery was achieved at the expense of even greater privation for the Soviet people than they had already borne during collectivisation and industrialisation. The long German occupation of the most fertile land, the shortage of agricultural labour, the re-imposition of State grain and livestock requisitions and the breakdown of the food distribution system – all these combined to transform the chronic Russian food shortage into famine. More than a quarter of the estimated 25 million fatalities suffered by Soviet Union during the war were the result of starvation.

Even so, Stalin had the last word. As the military struggle drew to its successful close in May 1945, he declared: 'We have survived the hardest of all wars ever experienced in the history of our Motherland. The point is that the Soviet social system has proved

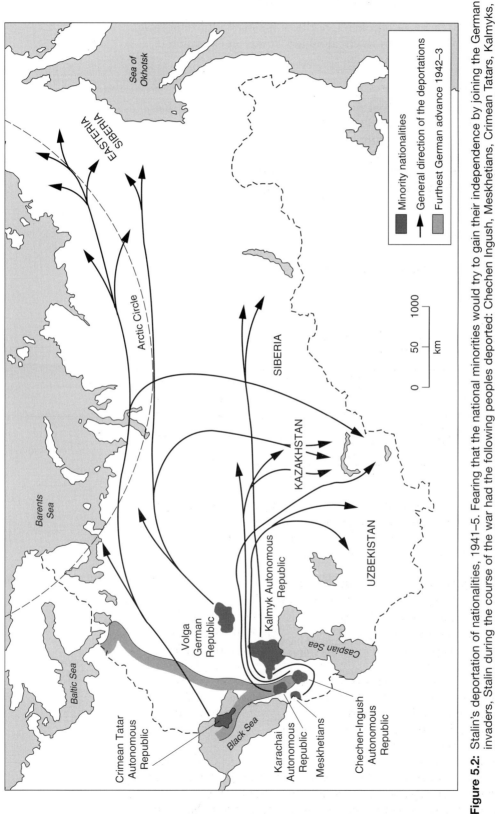

Figure 5.2: Stalin's deportation of nationalities, 1941–5. Fearing that the national minorities would try to gain their independence by joining the German invaders, Stalin during the course of the war had the following peoples deported: Chechen Ingush, Meskhetians, Crimean Tatars, Kalmyks, Karachai, and Volga Germans. The brutality with which the deportations were enforced caused great suffering and many thousands died. In all, it is reckoned that by 1945 some 20 million Soviet people had been uprooted.

to be more capable of life and more stable than a non-Soviet system'. He chose not to admit that much of the suffering had been caused by his own policies, not least his mania for deporting whole peoples whose loyalty he doubted. It was an extension of the purges on a massive scale.

The end of the war

In the USSR at the end of the war, Stalin gave instructions that his role in the nation's military triumph be given the highest place. Paintings, portraying him as the great wartime leader planning the victory of the Soviet Union, adorned all public buildings. But Stalin had been no Hitler. Although he had been brutally unforgiving of those in the military he regarded as failures, he had had the good sense to allow his generals, such as Georgi Zhukov, real freedom to direct the war. At the great victory parade held in Moscow's Red Square in 1945 it was Zhukov, mounted on a white charger, who reviewed the troops. He made an impressive figure.

Watching from the balcony above, Stalin became deeply jealous; he had originally intended to take the review himself but had changed his mind out of fear that he would not be able to control the horse.

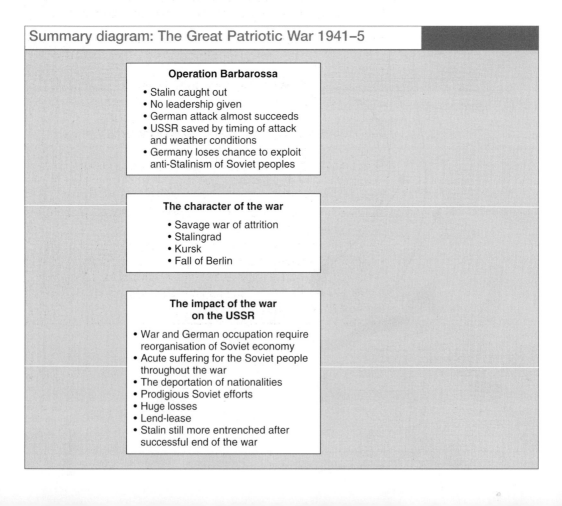

Summary diagram: The Great Patriotic War 1941–5

Operation Barbarossa

- Stalin caught out
- No leadership given
- German attack almost succeeds
- USSR saved by timing of attack and weather conditions
- Germany loses chance to exploit anti-Stalinism of Soviet peoples

The character of the war

- Savage war of attrition
- Stalingrad
- Kursk
- Fall of Berlin

The impact of the war on the USSR

- War and German occupation require reorganisation of Soviet economy
- Acute suffering for the Soviet people throughout the war
- The deportation of nationalities
- Prodigious Soviet efforts
- Huge losses
- Lend-lease
- Stalin still more entrenched after successful end of the war

Study Guide: AS Question

In the style of OCR

Assess the impact on the USSR of the Great Patriotic War (1941–5).

Source: OCR, May 2002

Exam tips

The cross-references are intended to take you straight to the material that will help you to answer the question.

Begin to order your thoughts by consulting pages 121–9. You might well consider that the question covers quite a wide range of effects and, so, in your preparation of the answer you might care to group your ideas under such heading as: military, economic, social, political. But do not simply provide a list of points. Your notes might well take this form, but in your answer you must integrate them into a reasoned evaluation. Remember, you are being asked not merely to describe but to 'assess' the impact. Clearly some themes will predominate over others. A major part of an assessment is the grading of individual points in terms of their relative importance, but it is your decision as to which points to emphasise.

The following points should help you in your consideration:

- How prepared for war was Stalin's Russia (pages 121–2)? This will help in your estimation of the impact of the war when it came.
- How well was the economy restructured in response to the war (pages 125–6)?
- How effectively did the Soviet armed forces respond?
- How helpful is it to quantify the suffering of the Soviet people, military and civilian (pages 126–9)?
- How much of the suffering was a result of Stalin's policies (e.g. deportation) rather than simply the German occupation (pages 126–7)?
- How were propaganda and Russia's cultural tradition used in the war effort (pages 167–9)?
- How did the eventual success in war encourage Soviet expansionism (pages 135–8)?
- What impact did the war have on Stalin's status as leader of the nation and the Soviet Union's international status (pages 172–4)?

Study Guide: A2 Question

In the style of AQA

How close to achieving his ideological and defensive aims in foreign policy did Stalin come in the period 1929 to 1941?

Exam tips

The cross-references are intended to take you straight to the material that will help you to answer the question.

Note precisely what the question asks you to do. The key term is 'how close?' To deal with this effectively you will need to compare what Stalin achieved by 1941 with what he actually set out to do. Among the points you might consider are:

- Stalin's basic approach to foreign affairs in 1929, how ideological was it? (pages 114–15).
- What role did defence needs play in his thinking (pages 112–13)?
- How committed was he to international revolution?
- What was the role of the Comintern (page 113)?
- His attitude to 'social fascists' (page 114).
- 'Turnabout' – search for allies after 1933 – idea of a 'popular front' (page 116).
- Impact of the anti-Comintern Pact on his attitudes (page 116).
- His aims in the Spanish Civil War (page 117).
- His interpretation of the Munich settlement in 1938 (pages 117–19).
- The Nazi–Soviet Pact – triumph of statesmanship or act of blindness (pages 119–20)?

This last point will doubtless have a major place in your answer, but do not concentrate solely on the Pact. You might see Barbarossa in June 1941 as clear proof of the failure of the defensive policy Stalin had followed since 1929. But were there not successes along the way after 1929? What place do these deserve in your estimation of Stalin's achievements? The 'how close' form of the question gives you a good opportunity to show some subtlety. It invites you to balance questions of bad luck, bad timing and bad judgement against each other.

6

Stalin and the Cold War

POINTS TO CONSIDER
During the last eight years of his life Stalin was the central figure in the development of the Cold War, the division of the world into two armed camps: East versus West. This chapter studies that development by following these major themes:

- Wartime tensions among the Allies
- The Eastern Bloc satellites
- Stalin, the Marshall Plan and the Truman Doctrine
- The German crisis
- East–West relations
- The blame for the Cold War

Key dates

1941–5	USSR allied with USA and Britain in the Grand Alliance
1944–8	Soviet formation of the Eastern Bloc
1945	The Yalta and Potsdam Conferences
1947	The Truman Doctrine and the Marshall Plan
1948	Soviet blockade of Berlin broken by Western airlift
1949	Soviet Union backed Red China's demand for a place in UN
	Soviet Union detonated its first atomic bomb
1950–3	Stalin backed Communist North in Korean War
1953	Stalin's death

1 | Wartime Tensions Among the Allies

Key question
Why were the Soviet Union's wartime relations with its Western allies so strained?

The victory of the USSR over Nazi Germany was portrayed in Soviet propaganda as the triumph of Stalin's great anti-fascist crusade. However, the truth was that Stalin had not entered the war against Germany willingly. As the Nazi–Soviet Pact had shown, the object of Stalin's policy before 1941 had been to reach a compromise with Nazism, not to fight against it.

The Grand Alliance
This had an important bearing on the nature of Stalin's relations with the USSR's principal wartime allies, Britain and the USA.

The three countries became allies not through choice but through circumstance. Before being attacked in June 1941 the Soviet Union had made no effort to assist Britain in its struggle with Germany that had begun in September 1939. Still less was the Soviet–American alliance a natural one. It came into being only after Germany, as an ally of Japan, declared war on the United States following the Japanese attack on Pearl Harbor in December 1941.

The coming together of the **'Big Three'** became known as 'the Grand Alliance'. However, a more accurate description might be 'the marriage of convenience'. What bound them together was their desire to defeat the common enemy. They had little else in common. In public, frequent tributes were made to the war efforts of their glorious allies, but behind the scenes there was constant bickering between the Soviet Union and its two Western partners.

A second front

A major contention was the question of a second front. From the beginning of the alliance Stalin pleaded with the other allies to create a second military front against Germany in occupied Europe in order to take the strain off the USSR. Britain's response was to promise that a second front would be started but only after sufficient military resources had been amassed to ensure its success. Stalin retorted that neither Britain nor the USA truly understood the intensity of the war on the eastern front, and that their caution was at the expense of the Russian dead. When Churchill referred to the opening of **allied fronts in North Africa**, Stalin taunted him by asking whether British troops were afraid to fight Germans. Churchill reacted by asking Stalin whether he had forgotten the sacrifice of the Royal and Merchant Navies in delivering vital war materials to the Soviet Union.

These taunts and recriminations did not prevent personal contact being maintained between the Allied leaders, but they did indicate the lack of true understanding between them. As the war drew towards its end and the defeat of Germany became increasingly probable, the ideological differences between the USSR and the other allies, which had been largely submerged because of the need for wartime co-operation, began to resurface. There was fear in the Soviet Union that Britain and the USA would show their true capitalist colours by attempting to enlist Germany in a war against Soviet Communism. On the Western side, there was anxiety that the Soviet advance into eastern Europe and Germany heralded the start of a new period of Communist expansion.

The Yalta Conference February 1945

The underlying hostility explains why, when Stalin, Churchill and Roosevelt, having first met at Teheran in 1943, met again at **Yalta** in February 1945 to plan the post-war settlement, there was mutual suspicion behind the official cordiality. As a result, the agreements they reached were temporary compromises that did not settle the larger issues.

Key dates

German invasion brings USSR into the war: June 1941

Japanese attack at Pearl Harbor brings USA into the war: December 1941

Key terms

Big Three
The Soviet Union, the USA and Britain.

Allied fronts in North Africa
Between 1940 and 1943 Anglo-American forces fought a series of campaigns against the Axis powers. In the early stages, these were largely a matter of British against Italian forces – hence Stalin's jeers.

Yalta
A Soviet resort in the Crimea, described by a British official as 'a sort of Russian Torquay'.

- On the question of the treatment of defeated Germany, it was agreed that the country would be divided into four zones, to be separately administered by the USA, the USSR, France and Britain, but there was no common understanding on what system of government should be introduced.
- Attempts to arrive at agreement on the scale of the German payment of war **reparations** proved equally fruitless. In the event, it was impossible to reconcile Stalin's demand that the harshest economic penalties be imposed on Germany with the Western allies' determination not to allow Russia to drain Germany dry while they were pouring in resources to prevent the country's collapse. Stalin was later to claim, in the face of Western denials, that Yalta had guaranteed the USSR 50 per cent of German reparations.
- The victors agreed that all prisoners of war be returned to their own countries. It soon became apparent from the news coming out of eastern Europe that this meant death or imprisonment for all those Soviet citizens who had fought for Germany. Stalin was massacring them in swathes (see page 104). Nonetheless, having made the original commitment, the Allies kept to it for fear of antagonising Stalin. It was an act of appeasement.

Reparations
Payments for the costs of the war.

United Nations Organisation
The international body agreed to at Yalta to replace the League of Nations.

The Polish issue

Among the most significant of the issues discussed at Yalta was the settlement of Poland. During the war Stalin had cynically allowed the German forces to crush Poland's capital, Warsaw, despite having every opportunity to come to the aid of the Polish resistance there. Then, towards the end of the war, the USSR had occupied Poland and had installed a pro-Soviet Provisional Government, with the promise of future democratic elections. Britain and the USA did not trust Stalin, and feared that Poland would simply become a Soviet puppet. However, the presence of the Red Army in Poland and the readiness of the Western allies to appease Stalin on some issues in order to gain concessions elsewhere led Churchill reluctantly to grant Stalin's wishes.

The differences that emerged between the powers over Poland and eastern Europe weakened such agreements as were reached at Yalta. There was deep suspicion between East and West. This was indicated by the Soviet Union's hesitation in joining the **United Nations Organisation**. It was fear of being out-numbered by the capitalist powers that led to Stalin's insistence, as a condition of the USSR's joining, on the right of the single-member veto in the proposed five-nation UN Security Council, made up of the four occupying powers of Europe plus Nationalist China.

Stalin and the Japanese war

At Yalta, the general expectation had been that the war against Japan would continue for a number of years. It was in the light of this that Stalin did a secret deal with Roosevelt. In return for the USSR's entering the war, large areas of Chinese territory would be ceded to it after Japan had been defeated. Stalin struck a hard

bargain. Later critics of Roosevelt suggested that his acceptance of Stalin's territorial demands in the Far East was an act of appeasement equivalent to Churchill's over Poland.

Ironically, the USA was to have no need of Soviet help in the war against Japan. The dropping of atomic bombs on Hiroshima on 6 August 1945 and Nagasaki three days later brought a swift and dramatic end to the Pacific war. This did not prevent Stalin's keeping to the letter of the original agreement. Immediately on receiving confirmation of the Hiroshima bombing, the USSR declared war on Japan. On 14 August, when Japan formally surrendered, Stalin duly proceeded to claim the Soviet Union's territorial rewards in the Far East.

The Potsdam Conference, July 1945

The Conference that began in July 1945 was essentially a continuation of Yalta. The issues under discussion – Germany, reparations, eastern Europe, Japan – were the same, and produced the same disagreements between the Soviet Union and the other allies. Indeed, in the short period between the two conferences relations had deteriorated further. The Reparations Commission, established at Yalta, had produced no acceptable settlement in regard to German war debts, and Soviet ruthlessness in Poland and eastern Europe suggested that Stalin was intent on imposing as rigid a system there as operated in the USSR itself.

Stalin's position at Potsdam

Stalin's attitude at Potsdam was even more uncompromising than it had been at Yalta. He was not prepared to concede on any of the major issues. He was strengthened in this by the fact that he was undoubtedly the dominant statesman at the Conference. Both the USA and Britain had new leaders, Truman and Attlee, respectively, whereas Stalin had attended both conferences. Such continuity worked to his advantage in negotiations. Even the news, which Truman gave him during the Potsdam Conference, of the USA's successful detonation of the world's first atom bomb did not shake Stalin from his strong diplomatic position. If anything, it made him still more determined to safeguard the USSR's recently acquired gains in Europe. The concessions over Poland and eastern Europe that he had extracted from Britain and the USA at the Yalta Conference remained substantially unaltered.

Soviet–American rivalry

The tension between the USSR and the USA during and after the war had an ideological base. Two deep fears conditioned East–West relations. On one side was the Western anticipation that the Soviets, through such organisations as the **Cominform**, were planning, in accordance with the message of the Communist Manifesto, 'the forcible overthrow' of all existing capitalist societies. On the other was Stalin's conviction that the West, led by the United States, was hell-bent on the crushing of Soviet

Key terms

Potsdam
A suburb of Berlin.

Cominform
As a gesture of goodwill towards its wartime allies, the Soviet Union had abolished the Comintern. However, in the strained post-war atmosphere the organisation was re-formed under the new title Cominform.

Communism. These mutual terrors were not ended by East–West co-operation in the war against Germany. Indeed, in many respects the profound disagreements over the strategy and purpose of the war increased the tensions.

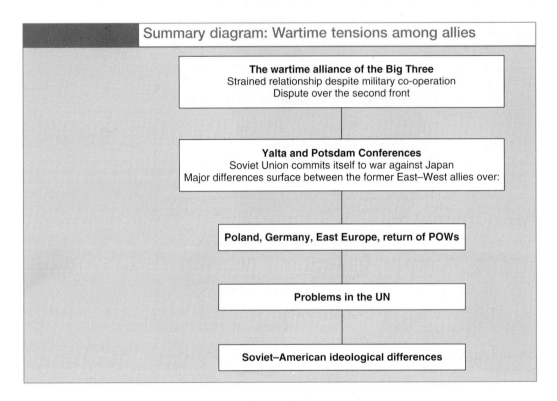

Summary diagram: Wartime tensions among allies

The wartime alliance of the Big Three
Strained relationship despite military co-operation
Dispute over the second front

Yalta and Potsdam Conferences
Soviet Union commits itself to war against Japan
Major differences surface between the former East–West allies over:

Poland, Germany, East Europe, return of POWs

Problems in the UN

Soviet–American ideological differences

Key question
What policy did Stalin follow towards eastern Europe?

Key term

Satellites
A Western metaphor denoting the various countries orbiting around the sun (the USSR) and held unbreakably in its magnetic grip.

2 | The Eastern Bloc Satellites

During the later stages of the war as the Red Army pushed westwards, it liberated the nations of central and eastern Europe from German control. The USSR then imposed its own authority over them, as **satellites**. As in the case of Poland, Stalin refused to withdraw the Red Army from these areas until they had set up pro-Soviet governments. Force and threats were used to achieve this. On the few occasions when elections were permitted they were rigged so as to return large Communist majorities. The methods by which Stalin ruled in Russia were then enforced on the satellites. The national Communist parties were kept loyal to the USSR by frequent purges.

The one exception to this was Yugoslavia, whose leader, Marshal Tito, refused to toe Stalin's line. Although a committed Communist, and in spite of continuous threats from Moscow, Tito never allowed his country to fall under the Soviet Union's domination.

Stalin's treatment of the satellites was in direct defiance of a joint 'Allied Declaration on Liberated Europe', which all the victorious powers had signed, formally committing them to pursue a policy of democracy in the areas they occupied. But

Figure 6.1: Soviet expansion 1939–49. The term 'iron curtain' was used by Winston Churchill to describe the frontier lines dividing the Eastern Bloc from the West.

Stalin's interpretation of democracy was very different from that of the other allies. The position that he took was a simple one. He was determined to create a large buffer against any future German aggression, which he now equated with Western anti-Communism. He was not prepared to withdraw Soviet forces from the countries of eastern Europe unless Communist regimes subservient to Moscow had been installed. The **Eastern Bloc** would have to pay the price for Soviet security.

Eastern Bloc
The USSR and its satellites.

Key term

Key question
Why did
Czechoslovakia
become a Soviet
satellite in 1948?

Czechoslovakia

How determined Stalin was over the establishment of Communist regimes subservient to Moscow was illustrated by the fate of Czechoslovakia. Of all the satellite peoples, the Czechs were the nearest to having a tradition of democracy. They also had a very recent and bitter history of partition and occupation by Germany. This gave them strong motives not to be enslaved again. However, their strong anti-Nazism had encouraged the growth of a sizeable Communist party.

It was the Czech Communists who now plotted to hand over their country to their Soviet masters. In earlier elections, the Communists had gained 114 of the parliamentary 300 seats. This had resulted in their leader, Clement Gottwald, forming a coalition government. But the Communists wanted full power; they were particularly restless because Jan Masaryk, a popular opposition leader, seemed likely to win seats away from them should another election be held. Rather than wait for this to happen, the Czech Communists, prompted by Stalin, used physical force to crush their opponents. Masaryk was thrown to his death from a window. His murder marked the end of the short-lived democratic experiment. A pro-Soviet Communist government was now in control.

Protests were voiced by the West at the United Nations, but the USSR used its veto to prevent a formal condemnation being passed. The fact was that Czechoslovakia was regarded as lying within the Soviet sphere of influence. The notion of spheres of influence was an unofficial Cold War understanding that each bloc had certain regions that fell under their control and protection. That is why the Soviet Union gave up in Greece (see page 138) and why the West made no move to help the Czechs.

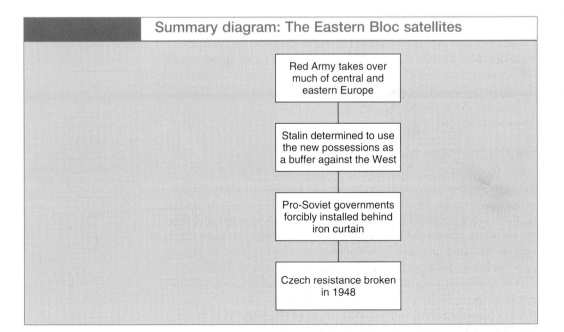

Summary diagram: The Eastern Bloc satellites

Red Army takes over much of central and eastern Europe

Stalin determined to use the new possessions as a buffer against the West

Pro-Soviet governments forcibly installed behind iron curtain

Czech resistance broken in 1948

3 | The Truman Doctrine and the Marshall Plan

Turkish and Persian crises

The USA's readiness to resist the Soviet Union was evident in its reaction to crises over Turkey and Persia. Beginning in 1946, the USSR had massed troops on Turkey's borders with the aim of intimidating the Turks into allowing Soviet naval bases to be set up along the Dardanelles. Britain feared that this was a move towards Soviet expansion into the Middle East with Persia (present day Iran) as a prime target. Ernest Bevin, the British foreign secretary, admitted to the Americans that Britain was not strong enough to protect either Turkey or Persia. The USA responded by drawing up military plans to repel any Soviet incursion into either country. When Stalin learned of the American determination, he backed down and ordered the withdrawal of Soviet forces.

Stalin may have simply been checking to see how far the Americans were prepared to go in defending key areas. Britain, however, was convinced that Stalin had designs on the British Empire itself, hence his attempt to push into the Middle East as a step towards India. A Foreign Office report questioned whether there was 'any limit to Soviet aggression'.

The Greek crisis

Greece was another area where the resolution of the two Cold War sides was put to the test. In the post-war period, a civil war had broken out in Greece. Here the monarchy was supported, as election results showed, by nearly 70 per cent of the people, but was challenged by Communist guerrillas. Stalin, eager to extend the Soviet bloc as far into the Balkans as possible, backed the Communists. British forces countered this by fighting on the government's side. But, as over Turkey and Persia, Britain had to confess that its resources were stretched to the limit. Fortunately for the British, the Americans were again prepared to become involved. Indeed, the Americans made a test case of it, seeing in Greece an example of Stalin's expansionist aims that ultimately threatened the Middle East, an area vital to the security of the United States. It was the Greek question that led to the Truman Doctrine.

The Truman Doctrine

It was in promising to undertake the defence of Greece and Turkey that President Truman made the famous statement that became known as the Truman Doctrine. He publicly announced that the USA regarded it as its duty 'to support free peoples who are resisting attempted subjugation by armed minorities or by outside pressures'. The USSR was not expressly named as an aggressor, but Truman pointedly referred to a world divided between democracy and totalitarianism. The implication could not have been clearer.

The Truman Doctrine gave definition to the Cold War. It committed the USA and its allies to continuous confrontation

Key question
What factors led to the introductions of the Truman Doctrine and the Marshall Plan in 1947?

Key dates

The Truman Doctrine declared: March 1947

The Marshall Plan announced: June 1947

with the USSR. To the Soviets, the Doctrine was an act of bad faith, finally destroying what remained of the Grand Alliance, and representing the renewal of American imperialism.

The Marshall Plan 1947

Key question
Why did Stalin reject the Marshall Plan?

Stalin's worries regarding the Truman Doctrine were deepened by his anxieties about American moves on the economic front. The abiding concern of the USA after 1945 was that Europe, enfeebled by war, would easily fall prey to an expansionist Soviet Union. Already many countries were experiencing severe economic problems. To prevent these becoming worse, the United States in 1947 introduced the Marshall Aid Plan, which offered large amounts of American capital to Europe to enable it to undertake post-war reconstruction. The Western European nations accepted the Plan, and their recovery began. Altogether Europe received some $15 billion from the USA.

The USA's intention was expressed by General Marshall when he introduced his plan in June 1947:

> Our policy is directed not against any country or doctrine but against hunger, poverty, desperation, and chaos. Its purpose should be the revival of a working economy in the world, so as to permit the emergence of political and social conditions in which free institutions can exist.

That was not how the Soviet Union saw it. It condemned the Plan as an extension of the Truman Doctrine. Both were a cover for American imperialism. Stalin's reaction was angrily voiced at the UN by Vyshinsky, the Soviet representative.

> As is now clear, the Marshall Plan constitutes in essence merely a variant of the Truman Doctrine, adapted to the conditions of post-war Europe. It is becoming more and more evident that the implementation of the Marshall Plan will mean placing European countries under the economic and political control of the United States.

If the announcement of the Marshall Plan had preceded rather than followed the issuing of the Truman Doctrine, there might have been a chance of the Soviet Union's accepting it. This in turn might have prevented the hardening of the Cold War. The Eastern Bloc's economic plight made Marshall Aid a tempting offer, particularly to the poverty-stricken satellites. Stalin for a brief period considered accepting it. But in the end, as Vyshinsky's speech illustrated, he felt that he could not risk allowing the Eastern Bloc to become financially dependent upon the United States. The political dangers were too great. To accept Marshall aid from the USA would be an admission of Soviet weakness.

Instead, in 1949, under Soviet direction, the Eastern Bloc formed **COMECON**. This was meant as a counterweight to the Marshall Plan and to the various economic organisations, such as **OEEC**, formed by the Western European nations. Since it lacked Marshall Aid funding, COMECON was always a pale shadow of its Western counterparts. It became in practice a mechanism by which the Soviet Union controlled its satellites.

Key terms

COMECON
The Council for Mutual Economic Assistance.

OEEC
The Organisation for European Economic Co-operation.

NATO and the Warsaw Pact

It is arguable that Cold War suspicions rendered an economic arrangement between East and West impossible. Distrust of the intentions of the USA was further justified in Soviet eyes by the formation of **NATO** in 1949. In the West this was represented as a defensive alliance, freely entered into by the nations of Western Europe and North America for their mutual protection. To the Soviet Union, it was a further stage in the spread of American imperialism, begun by the Truman Doctrine. It responded in kind by building a military alliance in the Eastern Bloc.

The eventual outcome was the **Warsaw Pact** of 1955, whose member states agreed to consult collectively in the event of a major crisis in Europe and to come to the aid of any member state should it be involved in conflict. As with NATO, the Pact declared that each state was sovereign and independent, but from the beginning it was dominated by the USSR. The high command was permanently based in Moscow and the Commander-in-Chief was always to be a Soviet marshal.

Key question
How did Stalin react to the formation of NATO?

Key terms

NATO
The North Atlantic Treaty Organisation, made up of 12 west European countries plus the USA and Canada.

Warsaw Pact
The member countries were Albania, Bulgaria, Czechoslovakia, East Germany, Hungary, Poland, Romania and the USSR.

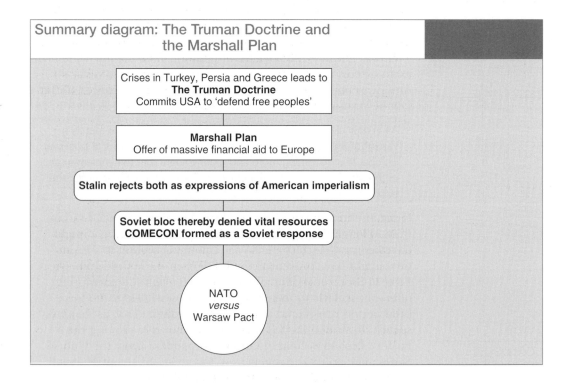

Summary diagram: The Truman Doctrine and the Marshall Plan

Crises in Turkey, Persia and Greece leads to
The Truman Doctrine
Commits USA to 'defend free peoples'

Marshall Plan
Offer of massive financial aid to Europe

Stalin rejects both as expressions of American imperialism

Soviet bloc thereby denied vital resources
COMECON formed as a Soviet response

NATO
versus
Warsaw Pact

4 | Crisis over Germany

In 1914 and again in 1941, Russia had been invaded and occupied by Germany. The suffering of the Russian people in the two wars that followed was immense. Over 20 million deaths were recorded in the Soviet Union between 1941 and 1945. This

Key question
Why was Stalin determined not to give ground on the question of Germany?

collective experience conditioned Russian attitudes towards Germany after 1945. Russia under Stalin was determined that never again should Germany be in a position to threaten her existence. His refusal to contemplate the reunification of Germany has to be set against that background.

In its push westwards in the closing stages of the war, the USSR had occupied one-third of Germany. Within that area was the capital, Berlin, lying 100 miles inside what became the Russian zone at the end of the war. In accordance with the Yalta agreements, Berlin, as with greater Germany, was divided into four **occupation zones**.

Within a short time the three areas of the city occupied by the Western Allies had amalgamated as West Berlin, which thus became a Western island in a Communist sea. This was why Stalin became so sensitive and uncooperative over the German question, always regarding Western suggestions for a settlement as the thin end of a wedge being driven into Soviet security. All future German questions had Berlin at their centre. It became a potent symbol of the Cold War divide.

At the Yalta and Potsdam Conferences it had been accepted that the four occupying powers would administer their zones only for as long as was necessary to establish stable conditions. Stalin, however, soon let it be known that the Soviet Union would not withdraw so long as Germany was regarded as a potential menace to Russia; in effect, this meant indefinitely. This stubbornness undermined the attempts of the **Allied Control Commission** to reach agreement on free elections and economic recovery. Clearly what Stalin wanted was to see the Russian zone develop as a buffer between Soviet-controlled eastern Europe and the West.

The Berlin blockade 1948–9

The result of Stalin's tough line was clear in the contrast between the Western Allies' pouring aid into their zones and the USSR's draining its zone of resources to meet Soviet needs. This difference in approach produced the first major Berlin crisis in 1948. The glaring gap between the rapidly recovering Western Germany and the bleak Eastern region was becoming a serious propaganda weakness to the USSR. When the Western powers in June 1948 introduced the new German currency, already operative in West Germany, into West Berlin, the Soviet Union claimed that this was a breach of the Potsdam agreements, and retaliated by imposing a blockade. All electricity and fuel supplies to West Berlin were cut off and all road links from the city to West Germany were closed.

The object of the blockade was four-fold:

- To restore damaged Soviet prestige by obliging America and her allies to abandon their plans for a separate German state.
- To end the affront to Soviet security of a Western outpost 100 miles inside Soviet-controlled East Germany.
- To break West Berlin economically.

Key terms

Occupation zones
Administered separately by Britain, the USA, France and the USSR. Berlin was similarly divided into four sectors administered by the same four powers.

Allied Control Commission
The body set up to co-ordinate ways of administering Germany.

Key question
Why did Stalin order a blockade of West Berlin?

- To test how far the Western powers were prepared to go in support of Berlin.

The Western response was typified by the warning of General Clay, the American commander in Berlin: 'When Berlin falls, Western Germany will be next. If we withdraw our position in Berlin, Communism will run rampant'. The Western powers decided to relieve the siege by a massive airlift of essential supplies, using the narrow air corridors; if the Soviet Union chose to intercept the planes, it would be an act of war. Over a period of 318 days the Western allies, principally the United States and Britain, mounted an airlift of supplies to the two and a half million West Berliners. The figures of the operation are striking: an average of over 600 individual flights per day successfully supplied West Berlin with one and a quarter million tons of food and fuel. Accepting that his bluff had been called, Stalin ordered the blockade to be abandoned in May 1949.

Results of the airlift
- West Berlin had been preserved.
- The commitment of the Western powers was put beyond doubt.
- Western co-operation over Berlin helped lead to the formation of NATO in 1949.

Some historians also interpret the successful Berlin airlift as marking the end of the first stage of the Cold War. The formal separation of Germany into the Western **FDR** and the Eastern **DDR** that followed represented the onset of 'bipolarity', the division of the world between East and West.

For the Soviet Union, Berlin remained a major irritant. The death of Stalin in 1953 did something to ease the international tension over it. But the relative prosperity of West Berlin continued to embarrass the Communist authorities. Between 1949 and 1958 over two million refugees fled from East Germany to the West by way of West Berlin.

FDR
West German Federal Republic.

DDR
East German People's Republic.

Key terms

Summary diagram: Crisis over Germany

Division of Germany and Berlin creates a permanent problem

Stalin determined to keep East Germany as a buffer against West

Growth of West Berlin and stagnation of East lead Stalin to impose Berlin blockade 1948–9

This broken by Allied Berlin airlift

Germany and Berlin remain unresolved problems

Key question
What impact did the development of nuclear weapons have on the Cold war?

5 | East–West Relations to 1956

The nuclear arms race

It was during the Potsdam Conference in July 1945 that the news of the first successful American detonation of a nuclear device was passed by Truman to Stalin. The Soviet leader already knew; Russian spies had passed the information to him. His reaction was to become even more determined to keep hold of the USSR's wartime territorial gains. The first diplomatic response, therefore, to the United States' nuclear break-through was to strengthen, not weaken, the Soviet Union's resolve.

Two major motives had prompted the USA towards the rapid development of an atomic bomb:

- The obvious need to shorten the war against Japan.
- The unstated, but equally powerful desire, to establish an unassailable advantage over the USSR.

It has often been suggested that the atomic bombing of Hiroshima and Nagasaki in August of that year was undertaken as much to impress the USSR as to defeat Japan.

The American achievements in July 1945 increased East–West tension. In view of this, it was surprising that the USA should have offered, in 1946, to pass control of nuclear weaponry and research over to the new UN organisation. However, the generosity was more apparent than real since in its early formation the United Nations was heavily American dominated. Stalin, in any case, was determined that Russia should have its own bomb; Soviet scientists had been working on it since 1942. Their efforts were accelerated in 1945 when the United States' **Manhattan project** made the critical breakthrough.

Defence experts in the USA knew that the Soviet Union would respond by building its own nuclear weapon, but they calculated that this would probably take decades. In the event the USSR required only four years. In September 1949 Soviet scientists produced and detonated an atomic bomb. They had been considerably aided by the information sent to them by spies in the West. But such detail was a mere incidental beside the astounding realisation that in just four years since Hiroshima, the USSR had caught up with the United States. It was now a nuclear power. As the Stalinist propaganda machine was swift to point out, the USSR under its great leader had elevated itself as a nation to the highest rank.

American anti-Communism intensifies

By chance, the Soviet acquisition of nuclear power in 1949 coincided with another equally remarkable development in world affairs. Only a week after the Soviet nuclear achievement, the news came through of the establishment of the People's Republic of China under the peasant leader, Mao Zedong. China was now a Communist state. The sense of shock among the Western nations was profound. Not only was the United States' great adversary now a nuclear power, but it now formed the western part of a

Key term

Manhattan project
The code name for the US nuclear development programme.

great Communist monolith that stretched unbroken across two continents from the iron curtain in Europe to the China seas of Asia.

That was how the Americans saw it and it terrified them. From 1949 onwards the anti-Communism of the American people deepened. This was a mixture of fear and recrimination; fear of the new Sino-Soviet colossus and recrimination against those pro-Communist spies and sympathisers in America who had betrayed their country. New restrictive laws were rushed through against un-American activities and a witch-hunt began.

McCarthyism in the USA

The most notorious examples of US anti-Communism were the McCarthy hearings. With passionate zeal, Joe McCarthy, Senator for Wisconsin, used Congress's Un-American Activities Committee, which he chaired, to mount a campaign against suspected Communist sympathisers in public life. In a series of Committee hearings held between 1950 and 1954, McCarthy and his team of officials used the law to force named individuals to appear publicly before them. There they were aggressively questioned about their possible Communist or Soviet affiliations. The good name and the careers of many were destroyed.

Eventually McCarthy over-reached himself; it was revealed that he had used false evidence to concoct his charges. There was a disturbing parallel between all this and the Stalinist purges. Nevertheless, despite McCarthy's fall from grace and the end of the hearings, the affair had indicated the depth of anti-Communism in the United States. It was a factor that meant the Cold War would continue so long as the Soviet Union was seen as the implacable enemy of American values.

The impact of the arms race

The success of the Russian atomic programme gave the United States added incentive to expand its own weapons programme, with the result that the world moved into the thermonuclear age. An arms race had begun that would last throughout the Cold War. By 1953 the Soviet Union had again caught up with its adversary. Both powers could now manufacture **hydrogen bombs**; both embarked on a proliferating policy, stock-piling weapons of ever-increasing destructiveness. Very much of a side-show were France and Britain who became independent nuclear powers by the late 1950s.

At various times before 1956, the nuclear powers discussed the possibilities of arms and research limitation but little of substance was achieved. Suspicions were too powerful. But it should be said that though the growth of nuclear weapons certainly intensified Cold War hostility, it did not necessarily create it. It is arguable, though controversial, that the reason why the Cold War did not become the long-feared hot one was that the nuclear-arms race created a balance of terror between East and West that kept the peace. The mutually destructive capabilities of the superpowers led to a stalemate, which provided a form of international stability.

Hydrogen bombs Weapons of awesome explosive power, which used the atomic bomb simply as a detonator.

Key term

Stalin, the UN and the Korean War 1950–3

Relations between the USA and the USSR were not eased by their contacts in the United Nations. If anything, their membership of the UN sharpened their hostility. Both the **General Assembly**, in which all member-states were represented, and the **Security Council**, the permanent five-member body responsible for settling international disputes, provided platforms for propaganda and point-scoring. In the Security Council, discussion of the major international problems of the post-war world became a constant battleground between the USSR, regularly using its **veto**, and the non-Communist members. Outnumbered as it was, Soviet Russia did not view the veto as a last resort but as the instrument for redressing the anti-Soviet imbalance of the Security Council.

The Korean War

Soviet–American rivalry in the UN was particularly pronounced over China. The Chinese Communist Party under Mao had come to power there in 1949 and had created the People's Republic of China (PRC). In gaining victory, the Communists had driven their main enemy, Chiang Kai-shek's Nationalists, from the Chinese mainland, forcing them to take refuge on the offshore island of Taiwan (Formosa). Nonetheless, the USA chose to continue recognising the defeated Nationalists as the real China and committed itself to the economic assistance and military defence of Taiwan.

The USSR's response was to demand that Mao's new China replace Nationalist China at the UN and on the Security Council. It was the China issue that lay at the base of the Cold War's first military confrontation, the war in Korea between 1950 and 1953. After Japan's defeat in 1945 Korea had been partitioned between an American-dominated south and a Soviet-dominated north. In 1950, the North Koreans crossed the dividing line of the 38th parallel with the intention of establishing Communist control over the whole country.

It was once believed that the whole Korean affair had been initiated by Mao in collusion with Stalin. However, what commentators now suggest is that Stalin had colluded with Kim Il Sung, the North Korean leader, in organising the venture and that he called upon the Chinese to give support only after the fighting had started. Having been convinced by Kim that the North Koreans were capable of sustaining a major war effort against the Americans, Stalin calculated that:

- The USA would be humiliated by being sucked into a conflict in Asia that it could not win.
- In contrast, the Soviet Union would gain a very powerful position in the Far East at very little cost to itself since Soviet forces would not be directly involved.

In outcome, the war did not fulfil Stalin's hopes. The Soviet Union always denied that it was involved militarily in Korea.

Key question
Why were Soviet–American relations strained in the UN?

Key question
What was Stalin's involvement in the Korean War and what did he hope to achieve?

Key terms

General Assembly
The UN body in which all member-states were represented.

Security Council
The permanent five-member body (originally made up of the USSR, the USA, Britain, France and Chiang Kai-shek's China) responsible for settling international disputes.

Veto
At Stalin's insistence, each single member of the Security Council had the right to block the collective decisions of the other members.

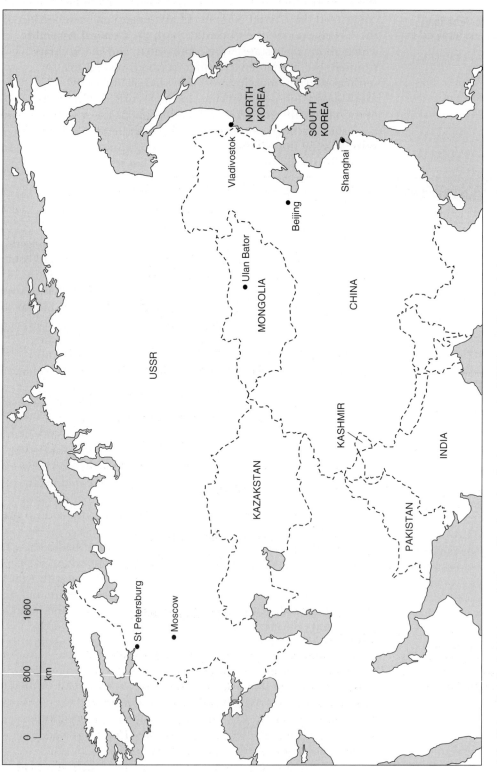

Figure 6.2: China, the Soviet Union and Korea. The long border between the USSR and China meant that there was constant friction in their relations.

Certainly Soviet forces did not take part. Nonetheless, masses of
Soviet weapons were used, and there was a large number of Soviet
advisers on the North Korean side throughout the three-year
conflict.

Yet the effort did not repay itself. The war ended in stalemate
in 1953. Korea was still divided and with no prospect of a
Communist takeover in the south. A further consequence was that
the USA pledged itself to the defence of Taiwan and to the
continued support of Nationalist China's membership of the UN,
a position that was maintained until 1972. This was hardly an
advantage to the USSR.

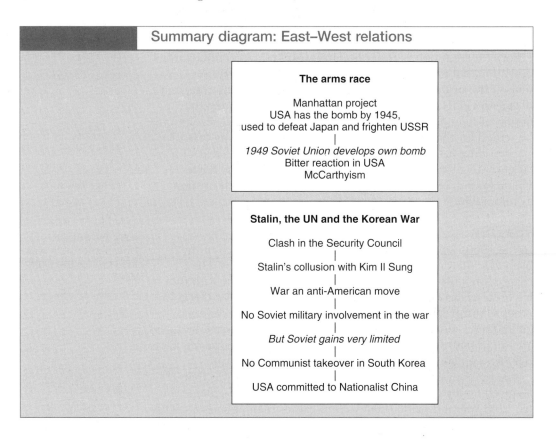

Summary diagram: East–West relations

The arms race

Manhattan project
USA has the bomb by 1945,
used to defeat Japan and frighten USSR
|
1949 Soviet Union develops own bomb
Bitter reaction in USA
McCarthyism

Stalin, the UN and the Korean War

Clash in the Security Council
|
Stalin's collusion with Kim Il Sung
|
War an anti-American move
|
No Soviet military involvement in the war
|
But Soviet gains very limited
|
No Communist takeover in South Korea
|
USA committed to Nationalist China

6 | The Blame for the Cold War

The USSR

Key question
How responsible was
Stalin for the onset of
the Cold War after
1945?

Many commentators have emphasised Stalin's refusal to consider
German reunification or to give up the USSR's wartime gains in
eastern Europe as major factors in creating the Cold War. It has
also frequently been suggested that Stalin never fully understood
the Western position. Yet, while this is true, it is not the whole
story. The misunderstanding was two way. There was a Soviet
perspective that the West never fully appreciated. Despite the
Soviet victory over Germany and the emergence of Stalin as an
outstanding world statesman, the USSR in 1945 felt more
vulnerable than at any time since the Bolshevik Revolution in 1917.

Economics lay at the heart of Soviet anxieties. While the Five-Year Plans had advanced Soviet industry so successfully that it was able to sustain itself through four years of total war, the strain involved had exhausted the Russian economy by 1945. This was one reason why Stalin had been so insistent at Yalta on the issue of German reparations. His constant fear that the West intended to crush the USSR had been intensified by the war's revelation of America's formidable economic and military power.

Since the USSR could not hope to compete on equal economic terms with the USA, Stalin calculated that the only policy available to him after 1945 was to withdraw the Soviet Union behind its new defensive barrier, provided by the wartime acquisition of eastern Europe. Germany became the new frontline in this defensive system.

Soviet foreign policy under Stalin was sometimes complex in its operation, but it was essentially simple in its design. He set himself the primary task of defending his country's interests in a hostile world. Having, in any practical sense, abandoned the notion of the USSR's leading an international Marxist revolution, he settled for the less ambitious but equally demanding task of safeguarding national security. He never lost his deep fear of a Western invasion. No matter how powerful he and the Soviet Union became, Stalin never ceased to regard the Soviet Union as vulnerable.

The USA

In the 1960s American revisionist historians laid much of the blame for the Cold War's origins on their own country. They charged that the United States' government, in league with the big industrial corporations, had exaggerated the Soviet threat in order to justify large defence budgets with profitable contracts going to the American arms manufacturers. It was a stimulating argument but its weakness was lack of hard evidence proving a link between government actions and corporate pressure.

The point of greatest interest about the argument was that it absolved Stalin and the USSR from being primarily to blame for the Cold War and made them victims rather than aggressors. This it must be said is hard to sustain. Whatever fault may be attached to the USA, the Soviet Union under Stalin was hardly blameless. Stalin deliberately chose to maintain the notion that the USSR was a threatened nation whose best means of defence was to keep the territories and peoples it had taken as a result of the war as a barrier against Western aggression. He further chose to speak in the threatening language of international revolution and to regard all diplomatic overtures and all offers of international co-operation as covers for anti-Soviet manoeuvres. The paranoia that characterised his domestic policies also shaped his approach to foreign affairs.

Ideology

There was, it must be added, an ideological purpose to all this. Officially, it was still the policy of the USSR to present itself as the

Key question
How responsible was the USA for the Cold War?

Key question
What role did ideology play in the Soviet–Western divide?

voice of Communism. Its declared aim was to use its own example to inspire the world to international proletarian revolution. This was why the Cominform was set up in 1947.

It is now known that this was largely bluff. The USSR had neither the military strength nor the economic resources to engage in such a policy. Nonetheless, in all its propaganda it insisted that it was the wave of the future and that the capitalist nations would be right to tremble at the thought of the revolution to come.

Such an attitude made it very difficult for other nations and statesmen to engage easily with the Soviet Union and Stalin. There was a constant air of aggression about Soviet diplomacy. Paradoxically, it was an aggression born of defensiveness, part of Stalin's paranoia that led to the belief that he as a person and the USSR as a nation were surrounded by enemies who had to be resisted or destroyed. Ernest Bevin, the post-war British foreign secretary, when attacked by the Left in Britain for not following a pro-Soviet line replied that, try as he might, he found Stalin and his Soviet officials so single-minded in defending their own interests and so stubborn in following their revolutionary line that it was impossible to come to terms with them.

It is odd that the only foreign statesman Stalin ever trusted was Hitler. When that trust was abused in 1941 in the form of the German invasion of Russia, Stalin resolved to trust no-one in international affairs ever again. All his policies from 1941 onwards were an illustration of that.

Stalin's legacy

Key question
What was Stalin's
Cold War legacy?

Defenders of Stalin suggest that whatever the criticisms about his character and methods, it cannot be denied that he fulfilled the basic duty of any national leader – he preserved the security and independence of the nation he led. Far more than that, in a hostile capitalist world he turned the Soviet Union into a superpower, capable of matching the USA. Those unimpressed by such claims point to the problems he left behind. These included:

- the intensity of Cold War divisions
- the iron curtain with its suppression of democracy in the satellites
- the unresolved problem of Germany and Berlin
- Soviet ambitions and threats in the Middle East
- the economic poverty of the Eastern Bloc
- the nuclear arms race
- a record of unyielding refusal to trust the West
- the use of meddling and subterfuge in Asia
- a form of crude, uncompromising personal diplomacy that embittered international relations.

It is also worth stressing that Stalin was the only statesman on either side to have led his country continuously from 1941 when the Grand Alliance was formed through to his death in 1953. He was involved in some way in every crisis that occurred in those

12 years. If any one individual can be said to have shaped, indeed to have personified, the Cold War it was Joseph Stalin.

With his death the opportunity for an easing of East–West relations appeared to have arrived and in some respects this did occur. His eventual successor in 1956, Nikita Khrushchev, began a process of de-Stalinisation (see page 175), which appeared to hold out the prospects of a lessening of international tensions. But it proved a false dawn. No matter how affable and human he often appeared, in contrast with his grim predecessor, Khrushchev was a hard-line Communist who had learned his politics under Stalin. He retained a deeply Stalinist conviction that the Communist Soviet Union represented a superior social and political system that would eventually triumph over its international enemies. In that sense Stalinism long outlived Stalin. It was why the Cold War lasted for almost 40 years after Stalin's death.

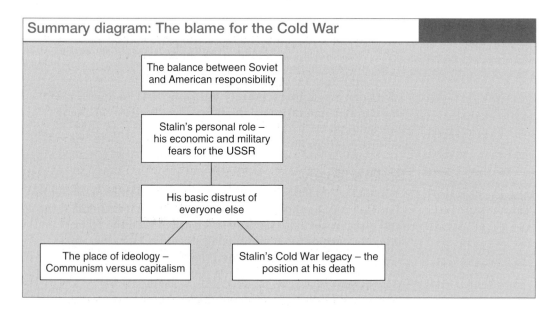

Summary diagram: The blame for the Cold War

The balance between Soviet and American responsibility

Stalin's personal role – his economic and military fears for the USSR

His basic distrust of everyone else

The place of ideology – Communism versus capitalism

Stalin's Cold War legacy – the position at his death

Study Guide: A2 Question

In the style of OCR

Study the following four passages, A, B, C and D, about the wartime relationship between the USA, the USSR and Great Britain, and answer the questions that follow.

A

From: Winston Churchill, Triumph and Tragedy, *published in 1954. This passage is about the conclusion of the 'Balkan Bargain' or 'Percentages Agreement' on post-war spheres of influence that he made with Stalin in October 1944. It suggests that Churchill was anxious to secure British interests in eastern Europe at the end of the Second World War.*

We reached Moscow on October 9, and were received very heartily. That night we held our first important meeting in the Kremlin. The moment was apt for business, so I said, 'let us settle our affairs in the Balkans. Your armies are in Rumania and Bulgaria. We have interests there. Don't let us get at cross-purposes in small ways. So far as Britain and Russia are concerned, how would it do for you to have 90% predominance in Rumania, for us to have 90% of the say in Greece, and go fifty–fifty about Yugoslavia?' I wrote it out on a sheet of paper, I pushed this across to Stalin. There was a slight pause. Then he took his blue pencil and made a large tick upon it. It was all settled in no more time that it takes to set down. After this there was a long silence. At length I said, 'Might it not be thought rather cynical if it had seemed we had disposed of these issues, so fateful to millions of people, in such an offhand manner? Let us burn the paper.' 'No, you keep it', said Stalin.

B

From: James Fitzgerald, The Cold War and Beyond, *published in 1989. This historian argues that the independence of post-war Poland was undermined by decisions taken at the Teheran Conference in November 1943.*

The first occasion on which Stalin, Churchill and Roosevelt all met was at the Teheran Conference. Roosevelt supported Stalin in his insistence that invading France should be given highest priority. It was then inevitable that discussion would focus on questions related to the post-war settlement. There was discussion over the boundaries of post-war Poland. In effect, Poland was moved westward. Churchill suggested that the Russians should be allowed to keep the areas of eastern Poland they had seized in 1939, with Poland being compensated by receiving territory on her western border from Germany. By agreeing to the Polish boundary in the east set in 1939 by the Nazi–Soviet Pact, the Western Allies created a situation which no independent Polish government could accept and ensured that a puppet government would have to be installed.

C

From: Martin McCauley, The Origins of the Cold War 1941–1949, *published in 1995. This historian discusses Roosevelt's relationships with Stalin and Churchill, and argues that Roosevelt hoped to create a post-war partnership with Stalin and the Russians.*

The Allies had been forced into a shotgun marriage during the war but Roosevelt hoped that out of this would come a real and lasting partnership. Europeans would simply have to endure Russian domination, in the hope that in ten or twenty years they would be capable of living well with the Russians. He set out to reach an agreement with Stalin personally, even if aspects of it ran counter to the interests of his British allies. At Yalta he made plain to Stalin his mistrust of Churchill, whom he suspected of seeking to keep the British Empire intact after the war. Roosevelt saw Stalin as an anti-colonial ally and therefore tried to win the cooperation of the Soviet dictator in planning the new post-war world.

D

From: Jeremy Isaacs and Taylor Downing, Cold War, *published in 1996. These historians describe the actions of the Red Army in Poland in 1944 and argue that hopes for post-war independence for Poland were crushed by Stalin.*

As the Red Army pushed westwards it paused only once, near Warsaw. When the Russians approached, the free Polish resistance rose up and took control of the Polish capital, ready to proclaim an independent Poland. The Soviet troops unexpectedly waited at the Vistula River, and allowed the Nazis to return and crush the Poles. Churchill pleaded with Stalin to intervene; the Soviet leader said his armies needed time to regroup. For 63 days the Poles held out. Finally, the Nazis, in an orgy of slaughter, put down the rising. 200,000 Poles were killed, nine out of ten of them civilians. Stalin had permitted the flower of the free Polish resistance to be massacred, so that he could hand Poland over to his puppets. Hopes for genuine democracy in Eastern Europe after the war were destroyed in the ruins of Warsaw.

(i) Compare Passages A and D on the policies of Great Britain and Russia towards Eastern Europe in 1944. (15 marks)
(ii) Using these four passages and your own knowledge, assess the claim that Stalin's actions in Eastern Europe during 1944 and 1945 were the most important reason for disputes between the wartime allies at that time. (30 marks)

Source: OCR, January 2003

Exam tips

(i) You are being asked to make a straight comparison. Restrict yourself, therefore, to the passages. Do not bring in your own knowledge. The introduction to each passage contains useful information. Be guided by this. The following sub-questions should help your response:

- How does Passage A illustrate Churchill's anxieties to secure British interests in eastern Europe at the end of the war?
- How does Passage B illustrate Stalin's intention to prevent Poland's achieving post-war independence?
- What are the main differences between the two passages in terms of the time they were written and the aim and standpoint of the writers?

Do not write an over-long answer. One exam script side should be sufficient. Remember that you must express your points in your own words. To put in long extracts from the passages would be a sad waste of time.

(ii)
- Note that you have to use all four passages *and* your own knowledge.
- Notice how much information you are given about the passages in the introduction to each. Do be prepared to use this.
- The question is essentially about Stalin's actions but the wording requires you to give thought to other possible factors. What do you judge these to have been? Here you will have to draw considerably on your own knowledge. The nuclear question and underlying ideological hostility might figure (pages 143–8).
- You may care to note that Passage A is a first-hand description by one of the major participants in the events. The other three passages are all later descriptions by non-participants.
- Notice that in Passage A Churchill is described as aiming at compromise with Stalin. Would this have increased or lessened the disputes between the East–West allies?
- Passage B similarly shows the Western allies' readiness to compromise, this time by restricting Poland to its 1939 borders.
- Passage C shows Roosevelt playing a double game playing off his western European allies against the Soviet Union.
- Passage D is the most revealing of the passages since it explains why there was such resentment towards Stalin among the Western allies. His ruthless treatment of Poland during the war made them deeply suspicious of him.
- Yet from the passages and your own knowledge, you will know that at Yalta and Potsdam the Allies largely granted him what he wanted. Why then did East–West hostility remain? Is it arguable perhaps that their underlying ideological distrust meant that details, such as Stalin's actions in eastern Europe, were symptoms, not causes of their disputes?

In your answer try to avoid treating the passages one by one in sequence. Instead, group them according to their view of the debate. Do not be tempted into writing an essay to show off how much you know. The role of your own knowledge here is to help you evaluate the views in the four extracts.

7 Life in Stalin's Russia

POINTS TO CONSIDER
The impact of Stalinism was not restricted to politics and economics. The whole of Soviet life was influenced by it. This chapter examines some of the main ways in which this occurred by exploring the following themes:

- Soviet culture
- The cult of personality
- Education
- Religion
- Women and the family
- Stalin's legacy
- De-Stalinisation

1 | Soviet Culture

Key question
What was the place of culture in the USSR under Stalin?

Lenin had declared that 'the purpose of art and literature is to serve the people'. Stalin was equally determined that culture should perform a social and political role. In the Russia that he was building, the arts had to have the same driving purpose that his economic policies had. Culture was not simply a matter of refined tastes. It was an expression of society's values and had to be shaped and directed in the same way that agriculture and industry had been. In creating the first truly socialist state there had to be a cultural revolution to accompany the political and economic one. It followed that the test to be applied to any aspect of culture was whether it promoted socialist values.

In practice what this came to mean was that, given the despotic power that Stalin wielded, cultural works in all their various forms, from buildings to paintings to novels to operas, had to conform to the standards set by Joseph Stalin. He became the great cultural judge and arbiter. Stalinist terror pervaded the realm of the arts, just as it did the political and industrial worlds. Artists who did not conform were as likely to be purged as politicians who were deemed to be a danger to Stalin or industrial managers who did not meet their quotas.

Socialist realism

In 1932, Stalin famously declared to a gathering of Soviet writers that they were 'engineers of the human soul'. This was a highly revealing remark. What he was telling his audience was that their task was essentially a social not an artistic one. They were not to regard themselves as individuals concerned with self-expression, but as contributors to the great collective effort of reshaping the thinking and behaviour of the Soviet people. This was a radical departure from the European tradition, which had always valued the right of the artist to express himself as he wished; that was the way genuine art was created. Stalin rejected such notions. Artists were to be treated as if they were part of the industrial system; their task was to create a useful product. Self-expression had to be subordinated to the political and social needs of the new nation. It was not the individual but the people who mattered. The artist's first task was to make his work appropriate and relevant to the society he was serving. If he failed to do this he was engaging in bourgeois self-indulgence, making himself more important than the people he was meant to serve.

Key question
How did 'socialist realism' affect the work and lives of writers?

Key terms

Soviet Union of Writers
The body that had authority over all published writers. Under Stalin's direction it had the right to ban or censor any work of which it disapproved.

Socialist realism
A form of art that is directly accessible to the people who can recognise it and relate it to their own lives.

Writers

It is not surprising, therefore, that when the **Soviet Union of Writers** was formed in 1934 it should have declared that its first objective was to convince all writers that they must struggle for '**socialist realism**' in their works. This could be best achieved by conforming to a set of guidelines. Writers were to make sure that their work:

- was acceptable to the Party in theme and presentation
- was written in a style and vocabulary that would be immediately understandable to the workers who would read it
- contained characters whom the readers could either identify with as socialist role models or directly recognise as examples of class enemies
- was optimistic and uplifting in its message and thus advanced the cause of socialism.

These rules applied to creative writing in all its forms: novels, plays, poems and film scripts. It was not easy for genuine writers to continue working within these restrictions, but conformity was the price of acceptance, even of survival. Before his death in 1934 Maxim Gorky was the leading voice among Russian writers. He used his undoubted skills to praise Stalin's first Five-Year Plan not merely as a great industrial achievement but as something of 'the highest spiritual value'. Other writers found it less easy to sell their soul. One author, Boris Pasternak, later celebrated in the West for his *Dr Zhivago*, a novel that was forbidden in the USSR during his lifetime, found some way out of his dilemma by restricting himself to translating historical works into Russian.

Many others who were not prepared to compromise their integrity lost their position, their liberty and sometimes their lives. Surveillance, scrutiny and denunciations intensified throughout the 1930s. The author Alexander Solzhenitsyn spent many years in the *gulag* for falling foul of Stalin's censors. His documentary novels, such as *The Gulag Archipelago*, which was published after Stalin's death, described the horrific conditions in the labour camps.

In such an intimidating atmosphere, suicides became common. Robert Service notes in his biography of Stalin that 'More great intellectuals perished in the 1930s than survived'. In 1934, Osip Mandelstam, a leading poet, was informed on following a private gathering of writers at which he had recited a mocking poem about Stalin, containing the lines 'Around him, fawning half-men for him to play with, as he prates and points a finger'. Mandelstam died two years later in the *gulag*.

Stalin took a close personal interest in new works. One word of criticism from him was enough for a writer to be thrown out of the Union, often followed by arrest and imprisonment. Part of the tragedy was the readiness of so many second- and third-rate writers to expose and bring down their betters as a means of advancing their own careers. This was a common characteristic of totalitarian regimes in the twentieth century. The atmosphere of repression and the demand for conformity elevated the mediocre to positions of influence and power. Fortunately, the coming of the war in 1941 brought some respite to the beleaguered writers since they were now able to throw themselves wholeheartedly into the task of writing heroic tales of the Russian people working for glorious victory under their beloved Stalin.

It should be noted that historians have on occasion queried whether the term totalitarian should be used to describe Stalinism, their argument being that the limited technology of the time simply did not permit total control to be imposed. Yet, after allowing for that point, the fact remains that Stalin's aim in culture as in politics and economics was total conformity. And it was this aim that created the atmosphere and conditioned the way in which artists worked.

Other art forms

The Union of Writers set the tone for all other organisations in the arts. Painting and sculpture, film-making, opera and ballet all had to respond to the Stalinist demand for socialist realism. Abstract and experimental forms were frowned upon because they broke the rules that works should be immediately accessible and meaningful to the public. Jazz was condemned as decadent.

Key question
What was the impact of Stalinism on other art forms?

Theatre and film

An idea of the repression that operated can be gained from the following figures:

- In 1936–7, 68 films had to be withdrawn in mid-production and another 30 taken out of circulation.
- In the same period, 10 out of 19 plays and ballets were ordered to be withdrawn.

- In the 1937–8 theatre season, 60 plays were banned from performance, 10 theatres closed in Moscow and another 10 in Leningrad.

Key term

'Total theatre'
An approach which endeavours to break down the barriers between players and audience by revolutionary use of lighting, sound and stage-settings.

A prominent victim was the director, Vsevolod Meyerhold, whose concept of **'total theatre'** had a major influence on European theatre. It might be thought that Meyerhold's techniques for bringing theatre closer to the people would have perfectly fitted the notion of socialist realism. But his appeal for artistic liberty, 'The theatre is a living creative thing. We must have freedom – yes, freedom', led to a campaign being mounted against him by the toadies who served Stalin. He was arrested in 1938. After a two-year imprisonment, during which he was regularly flogged with rubber straps until he fainted, he was shot. His name was one on a list of 346 death sentences that Stalin signed on 16 January 1940.

Even the internationally acclaimed director, Sergei Eisenstein, whose films *Battleship Potemkin* and *October* had done so much to advance the Communist cause, was heavily censured when his work *Ivan the Terrible* was judged to be an unflattering portrait of a great Russian leader and, therefore, by implication disrespectful of Stalin.

Painting and sculpture

Painters and sculptors were left in no doubt as to what was required of them. Their duty to conform to socialist realism in their style, and at the same time honour their mighty leader, was captured in an article in the art magazine *Iskusstvo* commenting on a painting that had won a Stalin prize in 1948.

> On a bright morning Comrade Stalin is seen walking in the vast collective farm fields with high-voltage power transmission lines in the distance. His exalted face and his whole figure are lit with the golden rays of springtime sun. The image of Comrade Stalin is the triumphant march of communism, the symbol of courage, the symbol of the Soviet people's glory, calling for new heroic exploits for the benefit of our great motherland.

Music

Since music is an essentially abstract form of art, it was more difficult to make composers respond to Stalin's notions of socialist realism. Nevertheless, it was the art form that most interested Stalin, who regarded himself as something of an expert in the field. He claimed to be able to recognise socialist music when he heard it and to know what type of song would inspire the people. He had many a battle with the Soviet Union's leading composer, Dmitri Shostakovich, who had a chequered career under Stalinism. In 1936, his opera *Lady Macbeth of Mzensk* was banned on the grounds that it was 'bourgeois and formalistic'. In the same year, his fourth symphony was withdrawn from the repertoire for similar reasons.

However, as with a number of writers, the war gave Shostakovich the opportunity to express his deep patriotism. His powerful orchestral works, particularly the seventh symphony composed during the siege of Leningrad in 1941, was a highly dramatic and stirring piece, depicting in sound the courageous struggle and final victory of the people of the city. At the end of the war in return for being reinstated he promised to bring his music closer to 'the folk art of the people'. This left him artistically freer than he had been before, though Stalin was still apt to criticise some of his new works. Shostakovich's growing international reputation helped protect him.

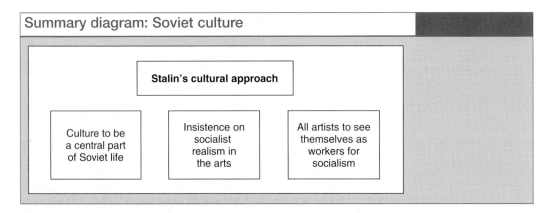

Summary diagram: Soviet culture

Stalin's cultural approach

- Culture to be a central part of Soviet life
- Insistence on socialist realism in the arts
- All artists to see themselves as workers for socialism

2 | The Cult of Personality

Key question
How did Stalin build up a cult of personality?

Adolf Hitler once wrote that 'the personality cult is the best form of government'. It is not certain whether Stalin ever read this but it would be a fitting commentary on his leadership of the Soviet Union. One of the strongest charges made by Nikita Khrushchev in his attack on Stalin's record was that he had indulged in the cult of personality (see page 175). He was referring to the way Stalin dominated every aspect of Soviet life, so that he became not simply a leader but the embodiment of the nation itself. Similarly, the Communist Party became indistinguishable from Stalin himself as a person. Communism was no longer a set of theories; it was no longer Leninism. It was whatever Stalin said and did. Soviet Communism was Stalinism.

From the 1930s onwards Stalin's picture began to appear everywhere. Each newspaper, book and film, no matter what its theme, carried a reference to Stalin's greatness. Every achievement of the USSR was credited to Stalin. Such was Stalin's all-pervasive presence that Soviet Communism became personalised around him. On occasion in private Stalin protested that he did not seek the glorification he received but, significantly, he made no effort to prevent it.

Biographies poured off the press, each one trying to outbid the other in its veneration of the leader. Typical of the tone and contents was a study by G.F. Alexandrov in 1947:

Stalin guides the destinies of a multi-national Socialist state. His advice is taken as a guide to action in all fields of Socialist construction. His work is extraordinary for its variety; his energy is truly amazing. The range of questions which engage his attention is immense. Stalin is wise and deliberate in solving complex political questions where a thorough weighing of pros and cons is required. At the same time, he is a supreme master of bold revolutionary decisions and of swift adaptations to changed conditions. Stalin is the Lenin of today.

'Under the leadership of the Great Stalin, Forward to Communism!'

'Thank you, dear Stalin, for our happy childhood'

Posters from the 1930s, typical of the propaganda of the time, showing Stalin as the leader of his adoring people. Poster art was a very effective way for the Stalinist authorities to put their message across.
In what ways do the posters illustrate the artistic notion of socialist realism?

It is one of the many paradoxes of Soviet history that the Communist movement, which in theory drew its authority from the will of the masses, became so dependent on the idea of the great leader. Such was Stalin's standing and authority that he transcended politics. Since he represented not simply the Party but the nation itself, he became the personification of all that was best in Russia. This was an extraordinary achievement for a Georgian and it produced a further remarkable development. It became common to assert that many of the great achievements in world history were the work of Russians. The claims reached ridiculous proportions: that Shakespeare was really a Russian, that Russian navigators had been the first Europeans to discover America and that Russian mathematicians had discovered the secrets of the atom long before Einstein. Eventually Stalin over-reached himself. Given a bottle of Coca Cola at the Potsdam Conference in 1945 by President Truman, Stalin ordered his scientists to come up with a Russian drink to match it. They tried but finally had to admit that, while Soviet science could achieve the impossible, miracles were beyond it.

Propaganda

The cult of personality was not a spontaneous response of the people. It did not come from below; it was imposed from above. The image of Stalin as hero and saviour of the Soviet people was manufactured. It was a product of the Communist Party machine, which controlled all the main forms of information – newspapers, cinema and radio. Roy Medvedev, a Soviet historian, who lived through Stalinism, later explained:

Key question
How was state propaganda used to promote Stalin's image?

> Stalin did not rely on terror alone, but also on the support of the majority of the people; effectively deceived by cunning propaganda, they gave Stalin credit for the successes of others and even in fact for 'achievements' that were in fact totally fictitious.

A fascinating example of building on the fictitious was the Stakhanovite movement (see page 81). It is now generally accepted that the official claim made in August 1935 that the miner, Alexei Stakhanov, had individually hewn 14 times his required quota of coal in one shift was a fabrication. Nevertheless, so well was the story presented and developed by the authorities at the time that his achievement became a contemporary legend, illustrating what heights of endeavour could be reached by selfless workers responding to the appeals and the example of their great leader.

Worship of Stalin

Despite the Soviet attack on the Church, the powerful religious sense of the Russian people remained, and it was cleverly exploited by the authorities. Traditional worship with its veneration of the saints, its **icons**, prayers and incantations translated easily into the new regime. Stalin became an icon. This was literally true. His picture was carried on giant flags in

Icons
Two-dimensional representations of Jesus Christ and the saints. The beauty of its icons is one of the great glories of the Orthodox Church.

Key term

May Day
Or 'Labour Day' –
usually reckoned as
1 May, became
traditionally
regarded as a
special day for
honouring the
workers and the
achievements of
socialism.

**Ivan the Terrible
(reigned 1547–84)**
A powerful tsar who
considerably
extended Russian
territory through
conquest.

**Peter the Great
(reigned
1689–1725)**
A reforming tsar
who attempted to
modernise his
nation by
incorporating
Western European
ways.

Komsomol
The Communist
Union of Youth.

processions. A French visitor watching at one of the **May Day** celebrations in Moscow's Red Square was staggered by the sight of a flypast of planes all trailing huge portraits of Stalin. 'My God!', he exclaimed. 'Exactly, Monsieur', said his Russian guide.

Even May Day came to take second place to the celebration of Stalin's birthday each December. Beginning in 1929 on his 50th birthday, the occasion was turned each year into the greatest celebration in the Soviet calendar. Day-long parades in Red Square of marching troops, rolling tanks, dancing children and applauding workers, all presided over by an occasionally smiling Stalin on a rostrum overlooking Lenin's tomb, became the high moment of the year. It was a new form of tsar worship.

Stalin's wisdom and brilliance was extolled daily in *Pravda* and *Isvestiya*, the official Soviet newspapers. Hardly an article appeared in any journal that did not include the obligatory reference to his greatness. Children learned from their earliest moments to venerate Stalin as the provider of all good things. At school they were taught continually and in all subjects that Stalin was their guide and protector. It was an interesting aspect of the prescribed school curriculum that history was to be taught not as 'an abstract sociological scheme' but as a chronological story full of stirring tales of the great Russian heroes of the past such as **Ivan the Terrible** and **Peter the Great**, leading up to the triumph of Lenin and the Bolsheviks in 1917.

The climax of this story was Stalin, who, building on the work of Lenin, was securing and extending the Soviet Union. This adulation of Stalin was not confined to history books. There were no textbooks in any subject that did not extol the virtues of Stalin, the master builder of the Soviet nation, inspiration to his people and glorious model for struggling peoples everywhere.

Komsomol

A particularly useful instrument for the spread of Stalinist propaganda was **Komsomol**, a youth movement that had begun in Lenin's time but was created as a formal body in 1926 under the direct control of the CPSU. Among its main features were:

- It was open to those ages between 14 and 28 (a Young Pioneer movement existed for those under 14).
- It pledged itself totally to Stalin and the Party (in this regard it was a parallel of the Hitler Youth in Nazi Germany).
- Membership was not compulsory but its attraction to young people was that it offered them the chance of eventual full membership of the CPSU.
- It grew from two million members in 1927 to 10 million in 1940.

The idealism of the young was very effectively exploited by Stalin's regime. *Komsomol* members were among the most enthusiastic supporters of the Five-Year Plans as they proved by going off in their thousands to help build the new industrial cities such as Magnitogorsk. It was *Komsomol* who provided the flag wavers and the cheer-leaders and who organised the huge gymnastic displays that were the centre pieces of the massive parades on May Day and Stalin's birthday.

Every political gathering was a study in the advancement of the Stalin cult. The exaggeration and the sycophantic character of it all is clear in the following extract from a speech given by a delegate to the Seventh Congress of Soviets in 1935:

> Thank you, Stalin. Thank you because I am joyful. Thank you because I am well. Centuries will pass, and the generations still to come will regard us as the happiest of mortals, because we lived in the century of centuries, because we were privileged to see Stalin, our inspired leader. Yes and we regard ourselves as the happiest of mortals because we are the contemporaries of a man who never had an equal in world history.
>
> The men of all ages will call on thy name, which is strong, beautiful, wise and marvellous. Thy name is engraven on every factory, every machine, every place on the earth and in the hearts of all men.

Stalin's popularity

Key question
How popular was Stalin in the Soviet Union?

Stalin's popularity in real terms is impossible to gauge. The applause that greeted his appearance in public or in cinema newsreels was more likely to have been more a matter of prudence than of real affection. The same is true of the tears shed by thousands at his passing in 1953. There was no way in which criticism or opposition could be voiced. The *gulag* was full of comrades who had spoken out of turn.

The intense political correctness of the day required that Stalin be publicly referred to as the faultless leader and inspirer of the nation. He made occasional broadcasts, but he was no orator. Stalin could never match Hitler's gift for arousing an audience or Churchill's for inspiring one. In wartime it was the gravity of the situation that gave Stalin's broadcasts their power. Perhaps it was Stalin's own recognition of his limitations in this regard that explains why after 1945 he made only three public speeches and they were only a few minutes long. Yet, in an odd way, Stalin's remoteness helped. Seen as a distant figure on a high rostrum or in the selected views of him in the official newsreels, he retained a mystique.

The Great Fatherland War was critical here. Whatever doubts might have been whispered about Stalin before the war became scarcely possible to consider, let alone utter, after 1945. The Soviet Union's victory over Germany in 1945 was a supreme moment in Russian history. Under Stalin, the nation had survived perhaps the most savage conflict in European history. This gave him a prestige as the nation's saviour that mattered far more than whether he was simply liked. The important point was that the Soviet people held him in even greater awe and fear than before. And, as the tsars had always known, it does not matter whether a regime is loved as long as it is feared.

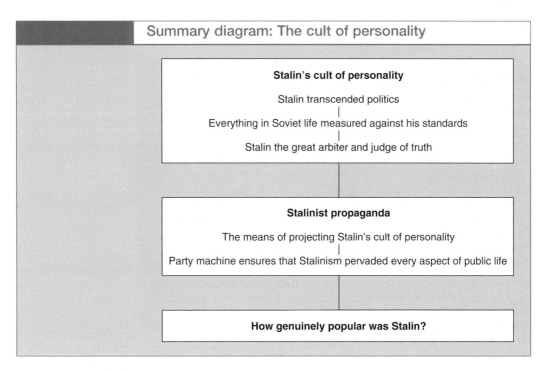

Summary diagram: The cult of personality

Stalin's cult of personality

Stalin transcended politics

Everything in Soviet life measured against his standards

Stalin the great arbiter and judge of truth

Stalinist propaganda

The means of projecting Stalin's cult of personality

Party machine ensures that Stalinism pervaded every aspect of public life

How genuinely popular was Stalin?

Key question
Why was Stalin so
determined to reform
the Soviet education
system?

3 | Education

The initial attitudes of Lenin and the Bolsheviks when they came
to power were shaped by their desire to reject bourgeois
standards. In the field of education this led to an attack on book
learning and traditional academic subjects. For a brief period,
textbooks were thrown away, exams abolished, and schools either
shut or opened only for a limited number of days. Young people
were encouraged to learn trades and engage in activities that were
of practical value.

But by the time Stalin came to power it was generally accepted
that the dismissal of the old ways had gone too far. As in so many
areas of Russian life, Stalin reversed the trends initiated by the
Bolsheviks after 1917. His driving aim was to modernise the
Soviet Union and he believed that to achieve this the population,
especially the young, must be made literate. He was aware of the
complaints of parents and employers that young people were
entering the workplace without having mastered the basic skills in
reading and writing. To meet this crippling problem, formal
education was to be made a priority. The need for discipline and
order was stressed. It made little sense to insist on strict rules of
conduct for workers in the factories, if schools were to allow
pupils to behave in a free and easy manner. The education system
must develop the same serious, committed attitude that prevailed
in the workplace.

Key features of the education system developed under Stalin:

- 10 years of compulsory schooling for all children
- core curriculum laid down: reading, writing, mathematics, science, history, geography, Russian (and for the national minorities their native language), Marxist theory
- state-prescribed textbooks to be used
- homework to be a regular requirement
- state-organised tests and examinations
- school uniforms made compulsory (girls were obliged to have their hair in pigtails)
- fees to be charged for the last three years (15–18) of non-compulsory secondary schooling.

The emphasis on regulation was not accidental. The intention behind these requirements, which were introduced during the 1930s, was to create a disciplined, trained generation of young people fully ready to join the workforce that was engaged through the Five-Year Plans in constructing the new Communist society.

An egalitarian system?

Key question
Was the educational system genuinely egalitarian?

The last feature regarding the payment of fees may appear to challenge the notion of an egalitarian education system. But the official justification for it was that all societies, including socialist ones, need a trained section of the community to serve the people in expert ways. Doctors, managers, scientists, administrators and so on, clearly required particular training in order to be able to fill that social role. Those who stayed on at school after 15 were obviously young people of marked ability who would eventually go on to university to become the specialists of the future. This was undeniably a selection process, but the argument was that it was selection by ability, not, as in the corrupt tsarist days or in the decadent capitalist world, by class. Moreover, the requirement to pay fees would not prove an obstacle since there were many grants and scholarships in the gift of the government, the Party and the trade unions.

The role of the élite

The official line emphasised equal opportunity. But behind the undoubted rise in educational standards and the marked increase in **literacy rates**, the system was creating a privileged élite. This was one of the paradoxes of revolutionary Russia. Before 1917 the Bolsheviks had poured scorn on the bourgeois governing élites that monopolised power in all capitalist societies. But the equivalent very quickly developed in Soviet Russia. The intelligentsia that formed the *nomenklatura* appreciated that education was the key to opportunity; that is why they took great pains to ensure that their children received the best form of it. Private tuition and private education became normal for the élite of Soviet society.

The unfair and unsocialist nature of all this was covered up by claims that the schools were 'specialist' institutions for children with particular aptitudes, rather than a matter of privilege. The

Key term

Literacy rates
By the beginning of the 1940s, 88 per cent of adults in the USSR could read and write.

party had the right to nominate those who were to receive the higher grade training that would give them access to university. As university education expanded, it was Party members or their children who had the first claim on the best places. In the period 1928–32, for example, a third of all undergraduates were Party nominees. After graduating they were then invited into one or other of the three key areas of Soviet administration – industry, the civil service or the armed forces. This educational and promotional process had an important political aspect. It enhanced Stalin's power by creating a class of privileged administrators who had every motive for supporting him since they were his creatures. Osip Mandelstam, the disgraced poet (see page 156), described this precisely:

> At the end of the twenties and in the thirties our authorities, making no concession to 'egalitarianism', started to raise the living standards of those who had proved their usefulness ... everybody was concerned to keep the material benefits he had worked so hard to earn ... a thin layer of privileged people gradually came into being with 'packets' [special benefits], country villas and cars ... those who had been granted a share of the cake eagerly did everything asked of them.

Universities

Key question
How did Soviet scholars respond to the demands of Stalinism?

In intellectual terms, the Soviet Union's most prestigious institution was the Academy of Sciences. Based on the famed tsarist Imperial Academy, it became in the new Russia an umbrella body incorporating all the major research organisations, some 250 in number with over 50,000 individual members. The term 'sciences' translates broadly to cover all the main intellectual and scientific streams: the arts, agriculture, medicine, management. All the major scholars in their fields were academicians. In 1935, the Academy was brought under direct government control. In return for increased academic and social privileges, it pledged itself to total loyalty to Stalin in his building of the new Communist society. What this meant in practice was that all the academicians would henceforth produce work wholly in keeping with Stalinist values.

One particularly distressing aspect of this was that Soviet historians no longer engaged in genuine historical research and analysis. Their reputation and acceptance as scholars depended on their presenting history shaped and interpreted as Stalin wanted. They ceased to be historians in any meaningful sense and became intellectual lackeys of the regime.

The Lysenko affair

Key question
What was the importance of the Lysenko affair?

Where such academic subservience could lead was evident in an infamous case that damaged Soviet science and agriculture for decades. In the 1930s, Trofim Lysenko, a quack geneticist, claimed to have discovered ways of developing 'super-crops', which would grow in any season and produce a yield anything up to 16 times greater than the harvests produced by traditional methods. Stalin, who had convinced himself that there was such a thing as 'socialist science', which was superior to that practised in the bourgeois West, was excited by Lysenko's claims and gave him his full support. This meant that, although the claims were in fact wholly false, based on rigged experiments and doctored figures, Lysenko was unchallengeable by his colleagues. Those who dared protest that his methods were faulty were removed from their posts and dumped in the *gulag*.

It was not until many years after Stalin's death that Lysenko's ideas were finally exposed in the Soviet Union for the nonsense they were. The tragedy was that by then they had played a part in creating the famines that so frequently ravaged Stalin's USSR.

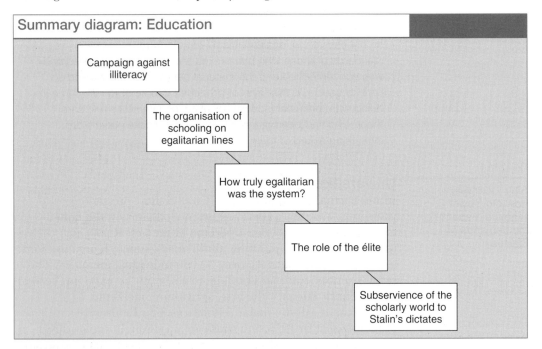

Summary diagram: Education

- Campaign against illiteracy
- The organisation of schooling on egalitarian lines
- How truly egalitarian was the system?
- The role of the élite
- Subservience of the scholarly world to Stalin's dictates

4 | Religion

An organised attack on religion had been launched in Lenin's time (see page 36). This was renewed under Stalin who, despite his own training as a priest and his mother's profound religious devotion, shared his predecessor's view that religion had no place in a socialist society.

Coinciding with the beginning of the first Five-Year Plan in 1928, a new campaign against the churches began. The Orthodox Church was again the main target but all religions and denominations were at risk. Along with the prohibition on Orthodox churches and monasteries went the closure of synagogues and mosques. Clerics who refused to co-operate were arrested; thousands in Moscow and Leningrad were sent into exile. The timing was not accidental. Stalin's drive for industrialisation was on such an epic scale that it required the whole nation to be committed to it. That was why the purges

Key question
What was the role of religion and the Orthodox Church in Stalin's Russia?

became an accompaniment of it (see page 100). Conformity was essential and had to be imposed. Religion, with its other-worldly values, was seen as an affront to the collective needs of the nation.

The suppression of religion in the urban areas proved a fairly straightforward affair. It was a different story in the countryside. The destruction of the rural churches and the confiscation of the relics and icons that most peasants had in their homes led to revolts in many areas. The carrying away of the church bells particularly incensed local people. The authorities had failed to understand that what to their secular mind were merely superstitious practices were to the peasants a precious part of the traditions by which they lived. The result was widespread resistance across the rural provinces of the USSR. The authorities responded by declaring that those who opposed the restrictions on religion were really doing so in order to resist collectivisation. This allowed the requisition squads to brand the religious protesters as 'Kulaks' and to seize their property. Priests were publicly humiliated by being forced to perform demeaning tasks in public, such as clearing out pigsties and latrines.

Such was the misery the suppression created that Stalin instructed his officials to call a halt. This was not through compassion. The severity of the anti-religious programme had attracted worldwide attention. In March 1930, in protest against the persecutions, Pope Pius XI announced a special day of prayer throughout the Catholic Church. For diplomatic reasons, Stalin judged it prudent to take a softer line. But this was only temporary. In the late 1930s, as part of the Great Terror, the assault on religion was renewed. Some 800 higher clergy and 4000 ordinary priests were imprisoned, along with many thousands of the **laity**. By 1940 only 500 churches were open for worship in the Soviet Union – one per cent of the figure for 1917.

Key term

Laity
The congregation who attend church services.

Key question
How did the war of 1941–5 alter Stalin's attitude towards the Church?

The impact of the Great Patriotic War

The war that began for the USSR in June 1941 brought a respite in the persecution of the churches. Stalin was aware of how deep the religious instinct was in the great majority of Russians. While official policy was to denigrate and ridicule religion at every opportunity and the leading Communists were always anxious to display their distaste for it, there were occasions when it proved highly useful to the authorities. Wartime provided such an occasion. Stalin was shrewd enough to enlist religion in fighting the Great Patriotic War. The churches were re-opened, the clergy released and the people encouraged to celebrate the great church ceremonies.

The majestic grandeur of the Orthodox liturgy provided a huge emotional and spiritual uplift. There are few things more nerve-tinglingly exciting than a Russian church congregation in full voice. Those besieged in Leningrad recorded that while worship did not lessen their hunger or soften the German bombardment, it lifted their morale and strengthened their resolve to endure the unendurable.

What is particularly fascinating and revealing is that for the period of the war the Soviet authorities under Stalin played down politics and emphasised nationalism. Talk of the proletarian struggle gave way to an appeal to defend holy Russia against the godless invaders.

The Church leaders responded as Stalin had intended. Bishops and priests turned their services into patriotic gatherings. Sermons and prayers expressed passionate defiance towards the Germans and the people were urged to rally behind their great leader, Stalin, in a supreme war effort. The reward for the Church's co-operation was a lifting of the anti-religious persecution. The improved Church–State relations continued after the war. By the time of Stalin's death in 1953 25,000 churches had re-opened along with a number of monasteries and **seminaries**.

This improved relationship with the State did not, however, represent any real freedom for the Orthodox church. The price for being allowed to exist openly was its total subservience to the regime. In 1946 Stalin required that all the Christian denominations in the Soviet Union come under the authority of the Orthodox Church, which was made responsible for ensuring that organised religion did not become a source of political opposition. It was an inglorious period for the Church. Lacking the will to resist, it became, in effect, an arm of government. Its leaders, obsequiously carrying out Stalin's orders, were barely distinguishable from the *nomenklatura*.

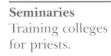

Seminaries
Training colleges for priests.

Key term

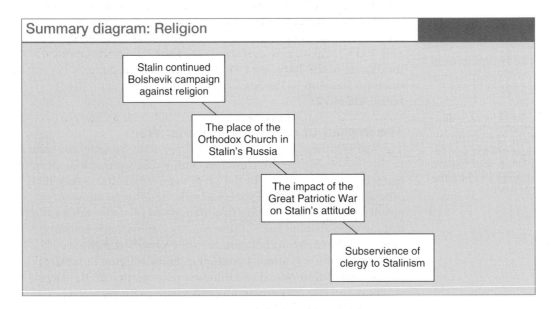

Summary diagram: Religion

Stalin continued Bolshevik campaign against religion

The place of the Orthodox Church in Stalin's Russia

The impact of the Great Patriotic War on Stalin's attitude

Subservience of clergy to Stalinism

5 | Women and the Family

In keeping with their Marxist rejection of marriage as a bourgeois institution, Lenin's Bolsheviks had made divorce easier and had attempted to liberate women from the bondage of children and family. However, after only a brief experiment along these lines, Lenin's government had come to doubt its earlier enthusiasm for

Key question
Why did Stalin reverse the earlier Bolshevik policies regarding women and the family?

sweeping change in this area (see page 38). Stalin shared their doubts. Indeed, by the time he was fully installed in power in the 1930s, he was convinced the earlier Bolshevik social experiment had failed.

By the end of the 1930s the Soviet divorce rate was the highest in Europe, one divorce for every two marriages. This led him to embark on what Sheila Fitzpatrick, the modern social historian, has called 'the great retreat'. Stalin began to stress the value of the family as a stabilising influence in society. He let it be known that he did not approve of the sexual freedoms that had followed the 1917 Revolution, claiming with some justification that Lenin himself had not approved of the free love movement that had developed around such figures as Alexandra Kollontai (see page 37). Stalin argued that a good Communist was a socially responsible one, who took the duties of parenthood and family life seriously: 'a poor husband and father, a poor wife and mother, cannot be good citizens'.

It was as if Stalin, aware of the social upheavals his modernisation programme was causing, was trying to create some form of balance by emphasising the traditional social values attaching to the role of women as home-makers and child raisers. He was also greatly exercised by the number of orphaned children living on the streets of the urban areas. They were the victims of the disruption caused by the Civil War, collectivisation, and the growth in illegitimacy that resulted from the greater amount of casual sex. The orphanages set up to care for them had been overwhelmed by sheer numbers. Left to fend for themselves, the children had formed themselves into gangs of scavengers attacking and robbing passers-by. Disorder of this kind further convinced Stalin of the need to re-establish family values.

Main policies

Stalin's first major move came in June 1936 with a decree that reversed much of earlier Bolshevik social policy:

- Unregistered marriages were no longer recognised.
- Divorce was made more difficult.
- The right to abortion was severely restricted.
- The family was declared to be the basis of Soviet society.
- Homosexuality was outlawed.

Conscious both of the falling birthrate and of how many Russians were dying in the Great Patriotic War, the authorities introduced measures in July 1944 re-affirming the importance of the family in Communist Russia and giving incentives to women to have large numbers of children:

- Restrictions on divorce were tightened still further.
- Abortion was totally outlawed.
- Mothers with more than two children were to be made 'heroines of the Soviet Union'.
- Taxes increased on parents with fewer than two children.
- The right to inherit family property was re-established.

Key dates

Decree outlawing abortion: 27 June 1936

New family laws introduced: 9 July 1944

Status of Soviet women

One group that certainly felt they had lost out were the female members of the Party and the intelligentsia, who, like Kollontai, had welcomed the Revolution as the beginning of female liberation. However, the strictures on sexual freedom under Stalin, and the emphasis on family and motherhood allowed little room for the notion of the independent, self-sufficient female. Such gains as the feminists had made were undermined by Stalin's appeal for the nation to act selflessly in its hour of need.

It is true that Soviet propaganda spoke of the true equality of women but there was a patronising air about much that went on. *Zhenotdel*, set up under Lenin as an organisation to represent the views of the party's female members, was allowed to lapse in 1930 on the grounds that its work was done. A 'Housewives' Movement' was created in 1936 under Stalin's patronage. Composed largely of the wives of high-ranking industrialists and managers, it set itself the task of 'civilising' the tastes and improving the conditions of the workers.

In a less-fevered age these women's organisations might have made some impact, but, as with all the movements of Stalin's time, it has to be set against the desperate struggle in which the USSR was engaged. Stalin continually spoke of the nation being under siege and of the need to build a war economy. This made any movement not directly concerned with industrial production or defence seem largely irrelevant. Most of the women's organisations fell into this category.

Female exploitation

There were individual cases of women gaining in status and income in Stalin's time. But these were very much a minority and were invariably unmarried women or those without children. Married women with children carried a double burden. The great demand for labour that followed from Stalin's massive industrialisation drive required that women became essential members of the workforce. Therefore, whatever the theory about women being granted equality under Communism, in practice their burdens increased. They now had to fulfil two roles, as mothers raising the young to take their place in the new society, and as workers contributing to the modernisation of the Soviet Union. This imposed great strains upon them. This was especially the case in the war of 1941–5. The terrible death toll of men at the front and the desperate need to keep the armaments factories running meant that women became indispensable (see Figure 7.1).

Equally striking figures show that during the war over half a million women fought in the Soviet armed forces and that by 1945 half of all Soviet workers were female. Without their effort the USSR could not have survived. Yet women received no comparable reward. Despite their contribution to the Five-Year Plans and to the war effort, women's pay rates in real terms dropped between 1930 and 1945.

The clear conclusion is that, for all the Soviet talk of the liberation of women under Stalinism, the evidence suggests that

Key question
Did women become more emancipated under Stalinism?

Key term

Zhenotdel
The Women's Bureau of the Communist Party.

they were increasingly exploited. It is hard to dispute the conclusion of the distinguished scholar Geoffrey Hosking, that 'the fruits of female emancipation became building blocks of the Stalinist **neopatriarchal** social system.'

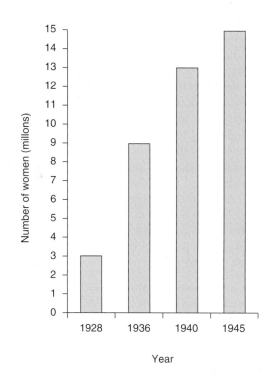

Figure 7.1: Number of women in the Soviet industrial workforce

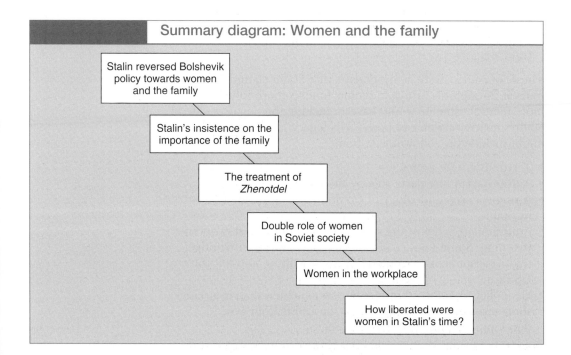

Summary diagram: Women and the family

Stalin reversed Bolshevik policy towards women and the family

Stalin's insistence on the importance of the family

The treatment of *Zhenotdel*

Double role of women in Soviet society

Women in the workplace

How liberated were women in Stalin's time?

6 | Stalin's Legacy

Key question
What was Stalin's legacy?

Joseph Stalin's death was a bizarre affair. At four o'clock on the morning of 1 March 1953, after a night of drinking with comrades, he retired alone to his study. Soon after he collapsed. He lay unattended for over 12 hours on his divan-bed, soaked in his own urine and unable to speak coherently. Even in his last hours he continued to terrify. His security guards knew something was wrong since he was not keeping to his regular routine. But they were afraid to act on their own initiative. They contacted the Kremlin, where the officials were equally scared to do anything without authority. Eventually a number of doctors went in to see him. They reported that Stalin appeared to have had a stroke but they were too frightened to recommend any particular treatment. Bizarrely, the leading medical experts who had been imprisoned in the first stages of the doctors' purge (see page 105) had to be consulted. They delivered their diagnosis from their cells. On the evidence they were given they suggested that Stalin's condition was very serious. And so it proved. He never recovered consciousness. Four days after first collapsing, Stalin was dead.

At his death Stalin's reputation in the Soviet Union could not have been higher. He was the great leader who had:

- Made himself an outstanding world statesman.
- Fulfilled the socialist revolution begun by Lenin.
- Purged the USSR of its internal traitors and enemies.
- Turned the USSR into a great modern economy through collectivisation and industrialisation.
- Led the nation to victory over fascism in the Great Patriotic War.
- Elevated the USSR to the status of superpower with its own nuclear weapons.
- Extended Soviet borders deep into central and eastern Europe.
- Created a Communist bloc that rivalled the West in the Cold War.

These, of course, were achievements that Stalin claimed for himself through his propaganda machine. A more sober and more neutral estimate would have to include the negative side of Stalin's quarter century of power. His legacy judged in this way might include the following. At home:

- Terror as a state policy.
- Authoritarian one-party rule by the CPSU.
- A single 'correct' ideology of Communism as dictated by Stalin.
- A misguided belief in the supremacy of Communist economic planning. Stalin's policy of collectivisation was so disruptive that it permanently crippled Soviet agriculture and left the USSR incapable of feeding itself.
- His policy of enforced industrialisation achieved a remarkable short-term success but prevented the USSR from ever developing a truly modern economy.

- The abuse and deportations suffered by the national minorities of the Soviet empire left them with a burning hatred that would eventually help to bring down the USSR.

Abroad:
- A deep hostility towards the non-Communist world.
- The Cold War.
- International economic rivalry.
- Conflict with China for the leadership of world Communism.

Key question
What was Stalin's role as Party leader and leader of the nation?

Stalin's role

It was the memory of Lenin's dominance of the Bolshevik Party that endured as the most powerful legacy of the 1917 Revolution. After 1917, reverence for the achievements of Lenin became a vital part of Communist tradition. It was Stalin's ability to suggest that he was continuing the work of Lenin that eased his own path to supremacy after 1924. Circumstances had made loyalty to the Party and loyalty to Lenin inseparable. Similarly, by the late 1920s, Stalin had succeeded in identifying his own authority with that of the rule of the Party. This made it extremely difficult for his fellow Communists to oppose him. To criticise Stalin was equivalent to doubting Lenin, the Party and the Revolution.

Stalin's intimate knowledge of the workings of the Secretariat aided him in his rise to power. By 1924 he had come to hold a number of important administrative positions, chief of which was the office of General Secretary of the CPSU. This left him ideally placed to control the appointment of members to the various posts within the Party's gift. Stalin became the indispensable link-man in the expanding system of Soviet government. Large numbers of Communist officials, the *nomenklatura* (see pages 107–8), owed their positions to Stalin's influence. They could not afford to be disloyal to him. This gave him a power-base that his rivals could not match. In the 1920s he was able to defeat all other contenders in the power struggle that followed Lenin's death.

The clear proof of how powerful Stalin had become was evident in the 1930s when he launched a series of purges of his real or imagined enemies in the government, the armed services and the Party. From then until his death in 1953, he exercised absolute authority over the Soviet Union.

From time to time, analysts have suggested that Stalin was not all powerful – no one individual in a nation can be – and that his authority depended on the willingness of thousands of underlings to carry out his orders and policies. In one obvious sense this must be true; no one person can do it all. Yet the truth remains that whatever the motives of those who carried out Stalin's policies, he was the great motivator. Little of importance took place in the USSR of which he did not approve. As Robert Service observes in regard to the purges: 'Nowadays, virtually all writers accept that he initiated the Great Terror'.

The key debate

For decades scholars have debated the following issue:

Was the totalitarianism of Stalin a logical progression from the authoritarianism of Lenin?

Isaac Deutscher and Roy Medvedev, both of whom suffered personally under Stalin, followed Trotsky in suggesting that Stalin had perverted the basically democratic nature of Leninism into a personal dictatorship. However, Alexander Solzhenitsyn, a leading dissident Soviet writer who underwent long years of imprisonment in the *gulag*, regarded Stalin as a 'blind, mechanical executor of Lenin's will' and stressed that the apparatus of the police state was already in place when Stalin took over. One-party rule, the secret police, the use of terror tactics, show trials; these were already in existence by 1924. Sozhenitsyn's analysis was backed by Western commentators such as Edward Crankshaw and Robert Conquest, who described Stalin's tyranny as simply a fully developed form of Lenin's essentially repressive creed of revolution.

Dmitri Volkogonov, the Russian biographer of the great trio who made the Russian Revolution, Lenin, Stalin and Trotsky, went further. He suggested that not only was there a direct line of continuity between Lenin and Stalin but the methods they used to impose Communism on Russia meant that the Soviet Union could never become a truly modern state:

The one-dimensional approach laid down by Lenin doomed Stalinism historically. By welding the Party organisation to that of the state, Stalinism gradually reshaped the legions of 'revolutionaries' into an army of bureaucrats. By adopting revolutionary methods to speed up the natural course of events, Stalinism ultimately brought the country to real backwardness.

Such interpretations were given powerful support by the opening up of the Soviet state archives in the 1990s following the fall of Communism and the break-up of the USSR. Building on the work of such analysts as Richard Pipes and Walter Laqueur, Robert Service, in his authoritative biography of Lenin, published in 2004, pointed to an essential link between Lenin and Stalin. He produced compelling evidence to establish his claim that Stalin, far from corrupting Lenin's policies, had fulfilled them. He confirmed that all the main features of the tyranny that Stalin exerted over the Soviet State had been inherited directly from Lenin.

Some key books in the debate

Robert Conquest, *The Great Terror: Stalin's Purge of the Thirties* (Penguin, 1971).

Robert Conquest, *Harvest of Sorrow* (Macmillan, 1988).

Walter Laqueur, *Stalin: The Glasnost Revelations* (Macmillan, 1990).

Roy Medvedev, *Let History Judge: The Origins and Consequences of Stalinism* (OUP, 1989).

Robert Service, *Lenin: A Biography* (Macmillan, 2000).

Robert Service, *Stalin: A Biography* (Macmillan, 2004).

Alexander Solzhenitsyn, *The Gulag Archipelago* (Collins, 1974–8).

Richard Pipes (ed.), *The Unknown Lenin: From the Soviet Archives* (Yale, 1996).

Dmitri Volkogonov, *Lenin: Life and Legacy* (HarperCollins, 1994).

Dmitri Volkogonov, *Stalin: Triumph and Tragedy* (Weidenfeld and Nicholson, 1991).

7 | De-Stalinisation

Key question
What were the motives behind Khrushchev's policy of de-Stalinisation?

Key date
Khrushchev's secret report denounces Stalin's record: February 1956

The power vacuum that Stalin left was eventually filled by Nikita Khrushchev. In 1956, after a three-year power struggle, Khrushchev had outmanoeuvred his rivals to become the most prominent figure in Soviet politics. Yet he knew that Stalin's impact over nearly a quarter of a century as Soviet leader had been so great that no change or progress could be achieved in the USSR unless some way could be found to undermine Stalin's reputation. That was what lay behind Khrushchev's introduction of de-Stalinisation.

Khrushchev's 'secret report'

The process of destroying Stalin's reputation began dramatically with Khrushchev's 'secret report' to the 20th Congress of the CPSU in February 1956. Some mild criticisms of Stalin's record had already appeared between 1953 and 1956 and the customary references in the press to his greatness had become less frequent. However, what was totally unexpected was the range and venom of Khrushchev's attack. In his report, which took a whole weekend to deliver, Khrushchev surveyed Stalin's career since the 1930s, exposing in detail the errors and crimes that Stalin had committed against the Party. Stalin had been guilty of 'flagrant abuses of power'. He had been personally responsible for the purges, 'those mass arrests that brought tremendous harm to our country and to the cause of socialist progress'.

Khrushchev quoted a host of names of innocent Party members who had suffered at Stalin's hands. Individual cases of gross injustice were cited and examples given of the brutality and torture used to extract confessions. Khrushchev's address was frequently interrupted by outbursts of amazement and disbelief from the assembled members as he gave the details of the Stalinist terror.

In denouncing Stalin, Khrushchev did not limit himself to the purges. He attacked him for his failures in foreign policy, particularly with regard to the Eastern Bloc countries. He also ridiculed the idea of Stalin as a war hero, pointing out his incompetence as an organiser and strategist; one of Khrushchev's jibes was that Stalin had used a globe rather than a detailed map to plan the defence of the Soviet Union. The special term that Khrushchev used to describe the Stalinism that he was condemning was 'the cult of personality'. He meant by this that all the mistakes perpetrated in the Soviet Union since the 1930s had been a consequence of Stalin's lust for personal power, his 'mania for greatness'.

Khrushchev's aims

It is significant that although Khrushchev read out a long series of Stalin's victims, who were now to be officially pardoned, the list did not go back before 1934 and did not include such names as Trotsky or Bukharin. Khrushchev's list was a selective one. His purpose was to blacken Stalin's name, not to criticise the Communist Party. It was important that the illegality and terror he was exposing should be seen as the crimes of one individual. In theory and in practice the Party was the essential source of power in the Soviet system, and Khrushchev was anxious not to challenge the justification for his own authority.

By any measure Khrushchev's 'secret' speech was a remarkable event in Soviet and Communist history. For a quarter of a century before 1953, Stalin had exercised astonishing power. Having destroyed his opponents, he had assumed an unchallengeable leadership. Revered as Lenin's heir, Stalin had come to personify Communism itself. To attack such a legend so soon after Stalin's death created a real danger of disruption within the Soviet Union and in the ranks of international Communism.

Why, then, did Khrushchev do it? De-Stalinisation had three basic aims:

- To justify the introduction of more progressive economic measures within the USSR.
- To make co-existence with the West easier.
- To absolve Khrushchev and the other Soviet leaders from their complicity in Stalin's errors.

This last aim was of particular importance. Criticism of Stalin personally was the only way to explain the otherwise inexplicable failures of the Soviet system during the post-Lenin era. Khrushchev was taking a risk in undermining Stalin's reputation. He knew that he was laying himself open to the charge of having been an accessory to the offences that he was now condemning. After all, he had helped carry out the purges in Moscow and the Ukraine. But Khrushchev calculated that, since all the Soviet leaders had climbed to their present positions by carrying out Stalin's orders, none of them had a clean record. Their shared guilt would prevent any serious challenge being offered to his denunciation of Stalin. As Geoffrey Hosking memorably puts it,

'It was unequivocally the speech of the *nomenklatura* élite defending itself against Stalin's ghost'.

At the time, the peoples of the Soviet satellites and many observers in the West interpreted these developments as signs that the USSR was moving towards tolerance and freedom. They were mistaken. De-Stalinisation was never intended to be a genuine liberalising of Soviet society. It is true that large numbers of political prisoners were released from the *gulag*, the labour camps which had proliferated under Stalin. There was also some lifting of State censorship. However, these were gestures rather than a wholesale abandonment of Soviet totalitarianism. At no time did Khrushchev denounce Stalin for having terrorised the Soviet people. The charge against him was always expressed in terms of crimes against the Party. By concentrating his attack on Stalin's 'cult of personality' Khrushchev was placing the responsibility for the errors of the past on one man. The reputation and authority of the Party were thereby undiminished. This left the new leaders of the Party free to introduce changes of policy and strategy. Khrushchev considered that without de-Stalinisation it would be impossible to begin the attempt to reform the Soviet Union.

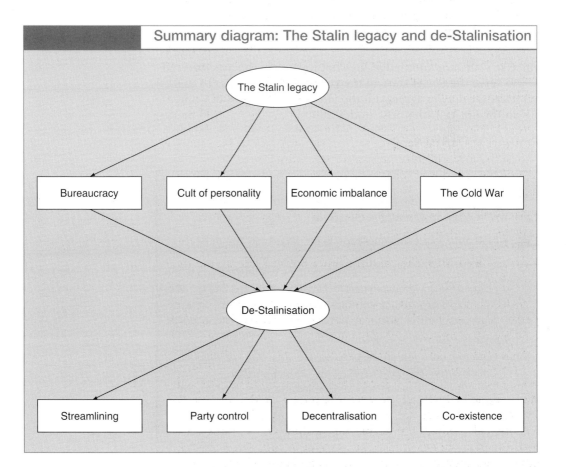

Summary diagram: The Stalin legacy and de-Stalinisation

Study Guide: AS Question

In the style of Edexcel

Study the source below and then answer the questions that follow.

Source 1

From: a confidential letter sent from Kalinin, the President of the Soviet Union, to Sergo Ordzhonikidze, a member of the Politburo in 1930.

All the efforts of local authorities are directed towards 'dekulakising' ministers of religion along with the Kulaks. This illegal 'dekulakisation' is conducted under the guise of taxation. They try to tax ministers of religion in every possible way and in such amounts that the clergy cannot fulfil the demands made on them. Then all their property is confiscated, even necessities for the family, and the family is evicted. Clergymen and members of their family have been drafted to hard work at tree felling, regardless of sex, age or health. Sometimes this harassment of the clergy literally becomes a mockery. For example, there have been cases in one district where ministers of religion were conscripted to clean pigsties, stables, toilets etc.

(a) Study Source 1
    What does this source reveal about the policy of the Soviet government towards ministers of religion in Soviet Russia?
    (10 marks)
(b) Use your own knowledge. In what ways were the arts directed to serve the Soviet state in the years 1928–41? (14 marks)
(c) How far do you agree with the view that the status of women in the Soviet Union rose under Stalin? (36 marks)

Source: Edexcel, May 2003

Exam tips

The cross-references are intended to take you straight to the material that will help you to answer the questions.

(a) • Note that your own knowledge is not called for. You must restrict your answer to what is in the document.
   • Read the text carefully and draw from it the material relating to the policy of the Soviet government towards the clergy and their families.
   • Key points that might be noted: taxation, seizure of property, enforced physical labour, humiliation and mockery of the clergy.
   • Collate your points to illustrate the government's policy.

(b) • Note that here you are required to use your own knowledge. Check pages 166–8 to refresh your understanding.
   • The question is asking you to examine the ways in which the State controlled the arts.
   • Note the dates. These indicate that you should deal with Stalin's policies towards the arts in the 1930s.
   • You may care to identify how two of the following were controlled: writing, film, theatre, architecture, painting and music.

- What place would you give to the importance of the demand for 'socialist realism' in the arts?

(c) Note the 'How far' formula in the question that invites you to weigh the evidence and make your own decision. Be careful not simply to describe the changes in the role of women that occurred under Stalin. Integrate your points in such a way that your conclusion genuinely flows from the body of your answer. You need throughout the answer to link the experience of women with its implications for their changed status. The following sub-questions may help to shape your approach.

- Did Stalin genuinely seek the emancipation of women (page 169)?
- Were the feminist gains of the early 1920s lost under Stalin (page 170)?
- How successfully did women reconcile their double role as mothers and workers (page 170)?
- Did the various social measures relating to women and the family actually improve the condition of women (page 170)?
- Did the contribution of women to the Great Patriotic War effort advance or retard their interests (page 167)?
- Were such advances as women gained restricted to only certain groups of them (page 170)?
- Did the fate of such female organisations as *Zhenotdel* indicate that women were not regarded as politically important (page 170)?
- Did Stalin's Russia become increasingly neopatriarchal under Stalin (page 172)?

It is worth suggesting that at this stage, having worked through the various chapters in this book, you should aim to bring together your skills in source analysis, integration of own knowledge and cross-referencing. Always try to see the relationship between these, so that you get a full return on your understanding of text and sources and your ability to relate them to your wider reading and expanding knowledge.

Study Guide: A2 Questions

In the style of AQA

How did 'socialist realism' in the arts help Stalin to consolidate his power in the Soviet Union? You should refer in your answer to at least two different art forms.

Exam tips

The cross-references are intended to take you straight to the material that will help you to answer the question.

Note that a key term dominates the question. Clearly, this suggests that you incorporate a definition of 'socialist realism' into your answer. However, bear in mind that it would not be enough simply to describe how 'socialist realism' acted as a cultural guide and artistic restraint. The question requires you to explain how Stalin used all this to strengthen his grip on the Soviet Union. The following sub-questions should help you to prepare your response. Check pages 154–8:

- What was meant by the notion of socialist realism?
- How pervasive was it?
- How was it used to impose cultural and artistic conformity?
- What were its political implications?
- How did it relate to Stalin's cult of personality?

In the style of Edexcel

Study Sources 1–5 below and then answer questions (a) and (b) that follow.

Source 1

From: L. Feuchtwanger, Moscow 1937, *published in Amsterdam 1937.*

The worship and boundless cult with which the population surrounds Stalin is the first thing that strikes the foreigner visiting the Soviet Union. On every corner, at every crossroads, in appropriate and inappropriate places alike, one sees gigantic busts and portraits of Stalin. The speeches one hears, not only the political ones, but even on any scientific and artistic subject, are peppered with glorification of Stalin, and at times this deification takes on tasteless forms.

It had grown naturally with the success of economic construction. The people were grateful to Stalin for their bread and meat, for the order in their lives, for their education and for creating their army which secured this new well-being. The people have to have someone to whom to express their gratitude for the undoubted improvement in their living conditions, and for this purpose they do not select an abstract concept, such as 'communism', but a real man, Stalin. Their unbounded reverence is consequently not for Stalin, but for him as a symbol of the patently successful economic construction.

Source 2

From: Evgenia Ginsburg, Into the Whirlwind, *published in 1967. Ginsburg was a victim of the Purges. Here she is writing about 1934.*

I don't want to sound pretentious but quite honestly, had I been ordered to die for the party, not once but three times, that same night, in that snowy winter dawn, I would have obeyed without a moment's hesitation. I had not the slightest doubt that the party line was right. My only, I suppose instinctive, reservation was that I could not bring myself to make a god out of Stalin, in spite of the growing fashion. But if I had this guarded feeling about him, I carefully concealed it from myself.

Source 3

From: Testimony: the Memoirs of Dimitri Shostakovich, published in 1979.

The great leader of all peoples needed inspired singers from all the peoples, and it was the state's function to seek out these singers. If they couldn't find them, they created them. They needed a native Kazakh poet to praise Stalin. Someone remembered that they had seen an appropriately colourful old man, who sang and played the dombra and who would photograph well. The old man didn't know a word of Russian, but there would be no problems. They would just have to find a good 'translator'. So they found Dzhambul Dzhabayev and a hurried song in his name praising Stalin which was sent off to Moscow. Stalin liked the song, that was the most important thing, and so Dzhambul Dzhabayev's new life began.

Source 4

From: S. Fitzpatrick, Everyday Stalinism, *published in 1999.*

Despite its promises of future abundance and the massive propaganda that surrounded its current achievements, the Stalinist regime did little to improve the life of its people in the 1930s. Judging by the NKVD's soundings of public opinion, a problematic source but the only one available to us, the Stalinist regime was relatively, though not desperately, unpopular in Russian towns. (In Russian villages, especially in the first half of the 1930s, its unpopularity was much greater.) Overall, as the NKVD regularly reported, and official statements repeated, the ordinary 'little man' in Soviet towns, who thought only of his own and his family's welfare, was 'dissatisfied with Soviet Power', though in a somewhat fatalistic and passive manner. The post NEP situation was compared unfavourably with NEP, and Stalin – despite the officially fostered Stalin cult – was compared unfavourably with Lenin, sometimes because he was more repressive but often because he let people go hungry.

Source 5

From: R.W. Davies, Soviet Economic Development from Lenin to Khrushchev, *published in 1998.*

While personal consumption deteriorated, state expenditure on health and education increased rapidly. Substantial growth of the social infrastructure often distinguishes industrialisation in the twentieth century from its classic predecessors; the increase in the Soviet case was particularly rapid. Employment increased even more rapidly in education than industry. The number of children at school rose from 12 million in the school year 1928–9 to 35 million in the school year 1940–1. Four-year education became almost universal during the first five-year plan (1928–32), and by 1939 seven-year education (from 8+ to 14+) was almost universal in the towns. According to the population censuses, the percentage of literate persons in the population (from nine years of age) increased from 51 per cent in 1926 to 81 per cent in 1939. This was due partly to the higher proportion of children attending school, partly to the literacy campaign.

(a) Using the evidence of Sources 1, 2 and 3 and your own knowledge, explain why the cult of Stalin's personality grew so extensively in the years 1929–41. (20 marks)

(b) 'Despite its promises of future abundance and the massive propaganda surrounding its achievements at the time, Stalin's modernisation programme did little to improve the life of the Soviet people.' Using all five sources and your own knowledge, how far do you agree with this opinion?

(40 marks)

Source: Edexcel, June 2003

Exam tips

The cross-references are intended to take you straight to the material that will help you in the exam.

(a) Note that your analysis has to be based on three specific sources and your own knowledge (pages 158–62).

- Search for the key evidence in each of three sources relating to the growth of the Stalin cult. Suggested points:
  - Source 1 – pervasive nature of propaganda, people's gratitude for Stalin's economic achievements, respect for him as national symbol
  - Source 2 – members' devotion to the party that overcame reservations about Stalin
  - Source 3 – deliberate creation of cultural myths to elevate Stalin.
- How does all this relate to what you already know?

Remember you are not being asked simply to describe what is in the sources; you have to use the evidence to explain why the cult grew so extensively in the given period. Similarly, your own knowledge must be used to the same effect. Do not merely list the evidence from the sources and then add your own knowledge. Try to integrate the points you make so that your answer is a genuine combination of source evidence and your own knowledge.

(b) Here you are given a quotation that you have to examine in the light of the evidence in the sources and you own knowledge (pages 172–5 and Chapter 3, pages 70–84) and then offer a judgement.

- Weigh the value of the sources in relation to the assertion in the quotation that Stalin did little to improve the life of the Soviet people. Are they all of equal relevance and importance? You may decide that Sources 4 and 5 are the most valuable in building your argument. But do not neglect the first three sources; the question requires that 'all five sources' be considered.
- Do the sources all tell the same story? What contradictions are there between them?
- Are Sources 4 and 5 making separate claims or is their apparent difference of interpretation a result of their concentrating on different aspects of Stalin's policies?
- Notice that you are being asked 'how far' you agree or disagree. This gives you a good opportunity to examine and interpret the sources in the light of your own knowledge. You do not have to give a straight acceptance or rejection. You can point out how the range of evidence can be used both to accept and to challenge the quoted assertion. But whatever verdict you give, it must genuinely be based on the evidence in the sources as filtered through your own knowledge.

Glossary

All-Russian Constituent Assembly
A parliament representing the whole of
Russia.

Allied Control Commission   The body
set up in 1945 to co-ordinate ways of
administering Germany.

American Relief Association   Formed by
Herbert Hoover (a future President of the
USA, 1928–32) to provide food and
medical supplies for post-war Europe.

Anschluss Incorporation of Austria into the
Third Reich in March 1938.

Anti-Comintern Pact   Formed by the
fascist nations, Germany, Italy and Japan.

Anti-Semitism   Hatred of the Jewish race.

Big Three   The Soviet Union, the USA
and Britain.

Bolshevisation   The process of subjecting
international Communist parties to the
will of Moscow.

Bourgeoisie   The owners of capital, the
boss class, who exploited the workers.

Brest-Litovsk Treaty 1918   Ended the
war with Germany. Russia had to give up a
third of its European territory, including
the Ukraine, and pay three million roubles
to Germany for the cost of the war.

Cadres   Party members who were sent
into factories and onto construction sites
to spy and report back on managers and
workers.

Centralisation   The concentration of
political and economic power at the
centre.

Cheka   'The All-Russian Extraordinary
Commission for Fighting Counter-
Revolution, Sabotage and Speculation'.

Chimera   A powerful but ultimately
meaningless myth.

Collective farms   Run as co-operatives in
which the peasants pooled their resources
and shared the labour and the wages.

Collective security   Nations acting
together to protect individual states from
attack.

Collectivisation   The taking over by the
Soviet State of the land and property
previously owned by the peasants
accompanied by the requirement that the
peasants now live and work communally.

COMECON   The Council for Mutual
Economic Assistance.

Cominform   As a gesture of goodwill
towards its wartime allies, the Soviet Union
had abolished the Comintern. However, in
the strained post-war atmosphere the
organisation was re-formed under the new
title Cominform in 1947.

Comintern   The Communist
International, a body set up in Moscow in
March 1919 to organise global revolution.

Commissar for Foreign Affairs
Equivalent to the Foreign Secretary in
Britain.

Commissar for Nationalities   Minister
responsible for liaising with the non-
Russian national minorities.

Commissar of Enlightenment   Equivalent
to an arts minister.

Conscription   The forcing of large
numbers of peasants to join the armed
services.

Co-operatives   Groups of workers or
farmers working together on their own
enterprise.

Council of Peoples' Commissars
A cabinet of ministers, responsible for
creating government policies.

Counter-revolution A term used by the Bolsheviks to cover any action of which they disapproved by branding it as reactionary.

CPSU The Communist Party of the Soviet Union.

Dacha Russian term for country house.

DDR East German People's Republic.

Decree against terrorist acts Gave the NKVD limitless powers in pursuing the enemies of the State and the Party.

Decree on Nationalisation Announced the take-over by the State of the larger industrial concerns in Russia.

Democratic centralism The notion that true democracy in the Bolshevik party lay in the obedience of the members to the instructions of the leaders.

Eastern Bloc The USSR and its satellites.

Economism Putting the improvement of the workers' conditions before the need for revolution.

Factionalism The forming within the party of groups with a particular complaint or grievance.

FDR West German Federal Republic.

February Revolution The collapse of the tsarist system in February 1917.

General Assembly The UN body in which all member-states were represented.

German–Polish treaty, January 1934 A 10-year non-aggression pact between the two countries.

Gosplan The government body responsible for national economic planning, which replaced *Vesenkha*.

Great Depression A period of economic stagnation in the USA and Europe that lasted for most of the 1930s. It affected the whole of the industrial world and was interpreted by Marxists as the beginning of the final collapse of capitalism.

Gulag The term for the vast system of prison and labour camps that spread across the USSR during the purges.

Hydrogen bombs Weapons of awesome explosive power, which used the atomic bomb simply as a detonator.

Icons Two-dimensional representations of Jesus Christ and the saints.

Industrialisation The introduction of a vast scheme for the building of factories which would produce heavy goods such as iron and steel.

Intelligentsia The group in society distinguished by their intellectual or creative abilities, e.g. writers, artists, composers, academics.

International revolutionary A Marxist willing to sacrifice national interests for the worldwide rising of the workers.

Ivan the Terrible (reigned 1547–84) A powerful tsar who considerably extended Russian territory through conquest.

Kadets (The Constitutional Democrats) The major liberal reforming party in Russia.

Komsomol The Communist Union of Youth.

KPD The German Communist Party.

Kremlin The former tsarist fortress in Moscow that became the centre of Soviet government.

Kulaks The Bolshevik term for the class of rich exploiting peasants. The notion was largely a myth.

Labour Code Severe regulations imposed on the workers.

Labour commissar Equivalent to a minister of labour, responsible for industry and its workers.

Laity The congregation who attend church services.

League of Nations The body set up in 1919 with the aim of resolving all international disputes and so maintaining world peace.

Left Communists   Those members of the CPSU who opposed the continuation of NEP.

Lend-lease programme   The importing by the Soviet Union of war materials from the USA with no obligation to pay for them until after the war.

Leningrad   Petrograd was renamed in Lenin's honour.

Manhattan project   The code name for the US nuclear development programme.

Martial law   The whole of the population being placed under military discipline.

Marxism–Leninism   The notion that Marx's theory of class war as interpreted by Lenin was a supremely accurate and unchallengeable piece of scientific analysis.

Marxist   Relates to the ideas of Karl Marx (1818–83), a German revolutionary, who believed that the whole of history was a story of class struggle between those who possessed economic and political power and those who did not.

May Day   Or 'Labour Day' – usually reckoned as 1 May, became traditionally regarded as a special day for honouring the workers and the achievements of socialism.

Mein Kampf   'My Struggle', the title of Hitler's autobiographical book, written in the 1920s and regarded as the Nazi bible.

Mensheviks   A Marxist party that had broken with the Bolsheviks in 1903.

Moscow   In 1918, for security reasons, Moscow replaced Petrograd as the capital of Soviet Russia.

NATO   The North Atlantic Treaty Organisation, made up of 12 West European countries plus the USA and Canada.

Neopatriarchy   A new form of male domination.

Nepmen   Those who stood to gain from the free trading permitted under NEP, e.g. rich peasants, retailers, traders.

Sukhanov, Nicolai   An anti-Bolshevik who wrote one of the most influential accounts of the Revolution.

NKVD   The State secret police, a successor of the *Cheka* and a forerunner of the KGB.

Nomenklatura   The Soviet 'establishment' – a privileged élite of officials who ran the Party machine.

October deserters   Those Bolsheviks who in October 1917, believing that the Party was not yet strong enough, had advised against a Bolshevik rising.

OEEC   The Organisation for European Economic Co-operation.

OGPU   Succeeded the GPU as the State security force. In turn it became the NKVD and then the KGB.

Orgburo   Short for Organisation Bureau.

Paranoia   A persecution complex, a conviction in the sufferer that he is surrounded by enemies intent on harming him.

Party card   An official CPSU document granting membership and guaranteeing privileges to the holder. It was a prized possession in Soviet Russia.

Patronage   The right to appoint individuals to official posts in the Party and government.

Peter the Great (reigned 1689–1725)   A reforming tsar who attempted to modernise his nation by incorporating western European ways.

Pogrom   State-organised persecution that involved physical attacks upon Jews and the destruction of their property.

Politburo   Short for the Political Bureau, responsible for major policy decisions.

Political commissars   Party workers who permanently accompanied the army officers and reported on their political correctness.

Political Left   Progressives who, without necessarily being Marxist, believed in state planning and radical social change, which made them sympathetic towards the USSR.

Popular front   An alliance of all Communist, socialist and progressive parties.

Potsdam   A suburb of Berlin.

Pravda **(the truth)**   The Bolshevik newspaper dating from 1912 that, after October 1917, became a principal means of spreading government propaganda.

Proletkult   Proletarian culture.

Proletariat   The exploited industrial working class.

Purge   In theory a means of purifying the Communist Party. In practice, it was a terror tactic by which Stalin removed anyone regarded as a threat to his authority.

Quasi-religious faith   A conviction so powerful that it has the intensity of religious belief.

Reactionary   Resistant to any form of progressive change.

Reparations   Payments for the costs of the war.

Right Communists   Those members of the CPSU who favoured the continuation of NEP.

Ryutin group   The followers of M.N. Ryutin, a Right Communist, who had published an attack on Stalin, describing him as 'the evil genius who had brought the Revolution to the verge of destruction'.

Satellites   A Western metaphor denoting the various countries orbiting around the sun (the USSR) and held unbreakably in its magnetic grip.

Secretariat   A form of civil service that carried out the administration of policies.

Security Council   The permanent five-member body (originally made up of the USSR, the USA, Britain, France and Chiang Kai-shek's China) responsible for settling international disputes.

Seminaries   Training colleges for priests.

Show trial   A special public court hearing, meant as a propaganda exercise in which the accused, whose guilt is assumed, are paraded as enemies of the people.

Social-fascists   Those who pretend to favour socialist progress but whose real aim is to prevent progress towards genuine revolution.

Social Revolutionaries   Before 1918 the largest of the revolutionary parties in Russia, particularly popular among the peasants.

Socialist realism   A form of art that is directly accessible to the people, who can recognise it and relate it to their own lives.

Soviet Union of Writers   The body that had authority over all published writers. Under Stalin's direction it had the right to ban or censor any work of which it disapproved.

Soviets   The soviets began as organisations to represent the workers and soldiers. However, by October 1917 they had been infiltrated by the Bolsheviks who then made them a cover for their actions.

Sovnarkom   The government that Lenin set up after coming to power. It was composed of commissars (ministers) under his direction.

Spanish Civil War 1936–9   Fought principally between General Franco's fascist forces and the republicans. Franco was the eventual winner.

Spartacists   German Communist movement (named after Spartacus, the leader of the slave rebellion in ancient Rome).

State capitalism The pre-revolutionary economic system, which the Bolsheviks left in place during their first year of rule, 1917–18.

State farms Peasants worked directly for the State, which paid them a wage.

State grain procurements Enforced collections of fixed quotas of grain from the peasants.

Tax in kind The surrendering by the peasant of a certain amount of his produce, equivalent to a fixed sum of money.

'To deliver the votes' To use one's control of the party machine to gain majority support in key votes.

Total theatre An approach which endeavours to break down the barriers between players and audience by revolutionary use of lighting, sound and stage-settings.

Treaty of Rapallo, April 1922 Provided German forces with training grounds in Soviet Russia in return for Russian trading rights in Germany.

Triumvirate A ruling or influential bloc of three persons.

United Nations Organisation The international body agreed to at Yalta to replace the League of Nations.

United Opposition The group led by Kamenev and Zinoviev, sometimes known as the New Opposition, who called for an end to NEP and the adoption of an industrialisation programme.

Vesenkha The Supreme Council of the National Economy, forerunner of *Gosplan*.

Warsaw Pact, May 1955 The member countries were Albania, Bulgaria, Czechoslovakia, East Germany, Hungary, Poland, Romania and the USSR.

Yezhovschina The period of terror directed at ordinary Soviet citizens in the late 1930s and presided over by Yezhov, the head of the NKVD.

Zhenotdel The Women's Bureau of the Communist Party.

Index